W9-CJO-174

Nuclear Forces in Europe

LEON V. SIGAL

Nuclear Forces in Europe

Enduring Dilemmas, Present Prospects

THE BROOKINGS INSTITUTION
Washington, D.C.

CARNEGIE LIBRARY
LIVINGSTONE COLLEGE
SALISBURY, N. C. 28144

Copyright © 1984 by
THE BROOKINGS INSTITUTION
1775 Massachusetts Ave. N.W., Washington, D.C. 20036

Library of Congress Cataloging in Publication data:

Sigal, Leon V.
  Nuclear forces in Europe.
  Includes bibliographical references and index.
  1. North Atlantic Treaty Organization—
Armed Forces. 2. Atomic weapons. 3. Cruise missiles.
4. Intermediate-range ballistic missiles. 5. Warsaw
Treaty Organization—Armed Forces. I. Brookings
Institution. II. Title.
UA646.3.S536 1984   358'.17'094   83-45960
ISBN 0-8157-7904-6
ISBN 0-8157-7903-8 (pbk.)

9 8 7 6 5 4 3 2 1

358.17
Si574

Board of Trustees
Robert V. Roosa
Chairman
Andrew Heiskell
Vice Chairman;
Chairman, Executive Committee
Louis W. Cabot
Vice Chairman;
Chairman, Development Committee
Samuel H. Armacost
J. David Barnes
Vincent M. Barnett, Jr.
Barton M. Biggs
Frank T. Cary
A. W. Clausen
William T. Coleman, Jr.
Lloyd N. Cutler
Thomas Donahue
Charles W. Duncan, Jr.
Robert F. Erburu
Hanna H. Gray
Robert D. Haas
Philip M. Hawley
Roy M. Huffington
B. R. Inman
James T. Lynn
Donald F. McHenry
Bruce K. MacLaury
Robert S. McNamara
Arjay Miller
Donald S. Perkins
J. Woodward Redmond
Charles W. Robinson
James D. Robinson III
Ralph S. Saul
Henry B. Schacht
Roger D. Semerad
Gerard C. Smith
Howard R. Swearer
Morris Tanenbaum
Phyllis A. Wallace
James D. Wolfensohn
Charles J. Zwick

Honorary Trustees
Eugene R. Black
Robert D. Calkins
Edward W. Carter
Bruce B. Dayton
Douglas Dillon
George M. Elsey
Huntington Harris
Roger W. Heyns
John E. Lockwood
William McC. Martin, Jr.
Herbert P. Patterson
H. Chapman Rose
Robert Brookings Smith
Sydney Stein, Jr.

THE BROOKINGS INSTITUTION is an independent organization devoted to nonpartisan research, education, and publication in economics, government, foreign policy, and the social sciences generally. Its principal purposes are to aid in the development of sound public policies and to promote public understanding of issues of national importance.

The Institution was founded on December 8, 1927, to merge the activities of the Institute for Government Research, founded in 1916, the Institute of Economics, founded in 1922, and the Robert Brookings Graduate School of Economics and Government, founded in 1924.

The Board of Trustees is responsible for the general administration of the Institution, while the immediate direction of the policies, program, and staff is vested in the President, assisted by an advisory committee of the officers and staff. The by-laws of the Institution state: "It is the function of the Trustees to make possible the conduct of scientific research, and publication, under the most favorable conditions, and to safeguard the independence of the research staff in the pursuit of their studies and in the publication of the results of such studies. It is not a part of their function to determine, control, or influence the conduct of particular investigations or the conclusions reached."

The President bears final responsibility for the decision to publish a manuscript as a Brookings book. In reaching his judgment on the competence, accuracy, and objectivity of each study, the President is advised by the director of the appropriate research program and weighs the views of a panel of expert outside readers who report to him in confidence on the quality of the work. Publication of a work signifies that it is deemed a competent treatment worthy of public consideration but does not imply endorsement of conclusions or recommendations.

The Institution maintains its position of neutrality on issues of public policy in order to safeguard the intellectual freedom of the staff. Hence interpretations or conclusions in Brookings publications should be understood to be solely those of the authors and should not be attributed to the Institution, to its trustees, officers, or other staff members, or to the organizations that support its research.

116682

Foreword

IN DECEMBER 1979, after the Soviet Union had begun to deploy new theater nuclear missiles within range of Europe, NATO ministers decided to deploy new American nuclear-armed cruise and ballistic missiles capable of striking deep into the USSR from bases in Great Britain, West Germany, Italy, Belgium, and the Netherlands. At the same time, NATO announced its intent to pursue arms control negotiations with the USSR. No decision in recent years has so divided public opinion in Europe or so strained relations with the Warsaw Pact. What began as an attempt to reassure Western European leaders that the United States was committed to deterring war on the Continent had the effect of engendering deep fears among European publics that new deployments might instead increase the chances of nuclear war.

In this study, Leon V. Sigal examines the dilemmas created by NATO's nuclear doctrines and the ambivalence of Western Europeans about the role of nuclear weapons. He discusses the paradoxes and inconsistencies inherent in the logic on which NATO's nuclear doctrine is based and the consequent contradictions in the military rationale developed for deploying cruise and Pershing II missiles. He analyzes the European political parties and movements that influenced the alliance's 1979 decision and the ensuing public protests. Sigal also takes a hard look at recent arms control negotiations and assesses prospects for the stalled INF and START talks.

Leon V. Sigal is a visiting scholar at Brookings and professor of government at Wesleyan University. As an International Affairs Fellow at the State Department and later as the special assistant to the director of the Bureau of Politico-Military Affairs in 1979–80, he was involved in the issue of deploying the Euromissiles. His work at Brookings was supported by the Ford Foundation.

The author thanks Jan R. Liss and Patricia O'Brien for administrative aid, Susan E. Nichols and Ann M. Ziegler for secretarial help, James R. Schneider for editing the manuscript and Alan G. Hoden for verifying its factual content, Nancy Snyder for proofreading, and Florence Robinson for preparing the index. He is especially grateful to Raymond L. Garthoff, Michael K. MccGwire, John Newhouse, Robert Nurick, John D. Steinbruner, and Richard Ullman, who were helpful in their comments on the manuscript, and to Meg Fidler Sigal.

The views expressed are those of the author and should not be ascribed to the Ford Foundation, to those who commented on the manuscript, or to the trustees, officers, or staff members of the Brookings Institution.

BRUCE K. MACLAURY
President

March 1984
Washington, D.C.

Contents

CHAPTER ONE

A Faustian Bargain

MEPHISTOPHELES. Here *to your service I will bind me;*
Beck when you will, I will not pause or rest;
But in return when yonder *you will find me,*
Then likewise shall you be at my behest.
FAUST. *The* yonder *is to me a trifling matter.*
Should you this world to ruins shatter,
The other then may rise, its place to fill.

Goethe, *Faust*

IN DECEMBER 1979 NATO foreign and defense ministers meeting in Brussels decided to deploy new American nuclear-armed cruise and ballistic missiles in Europe, missiles capable of striking deep into the USSR from bases in Great Britain, West Germany, Italy, Belgium, and the Netherlands. At the same time they decided to have the United States seek an arms control agreement with the Soviet Union on these and other nuclear weapons of less than intercontinental range.

The decision to tie nuclear deployments to arms control seemed a Faustian bargain to many observers. Those who saw peace in Europe threatened by growing Soviet military strength considered arms control an impediment to NATO's efforts to redress any perceived imbalance of forces. Others, who saw no basic shift in the military balance, regarded peace in Europe as jeopardized by political differences between East and West that deployment of the new missiles would exacerbate. They wanted to ameliorate if not resolve these differences through mutual accommodation, including negotiations of limits on the nuclear arsenals of both sides at the lowest possible levels. The December 1979 decision satisfied few in either group. Buffeted from both right and left, it seemed politically unstable from its inception.

Yet for NATO to have sought either nuclear buildup or arms control alone would have made little sense politically or militarily. Politically, either decision would have been unsustainable. Negotiations to limit

1

Soviet theater nuclear forces would have had little chance of success without the leverage created by the prospect of at least some new NATO deployment, unless the United States were willing to reduce some of its strategic forces in return for reductions in Soviet theater nuclear forces. And deployment without a good-faith attempt at arms control would not have mustered even the tepid public and parliamentary support it now has.

Militarily, the proposed deployment of a modest number of U.S. missiles in Europe seemed to many to promise little improvement in the nuclear component of NATO's strategy of flexible response. For most Europeans the means at America's disposal were not in doubt, but some did question the willingness to use those means, especially strategic nuclear weapons based in the United States and at sea, in Europe's behalf. For the United States to threaten nuclear escalation in order to deter hostilities in Europe, as called for in NATO's strategy, no longer seemed wholly credible after the early 1960s when the United States became vulnerable to Soviet nuclear retaliation. Just how the deployment of new American missiles would restore that credibility—or what NATO experts call "coupling" American nuclear might to European security— was never quite clear. It was clear, however, that European anxiety would persist whether new U.S. nuclear weapons were not deployed at all or whether they were deployed and were followed by a Soviet counterdeployment that added to the number of missiles it had already fielded. For the United States then to deploy additional weapons would bring the size of its nuclear arsenal in Europe to a point at which doubt would only grow anew about its willingness to use strategic nuclear forces, as distinct from European-based nuclear forces. One way out for NATO, it seemed, was to achieve negotiated limits on the theater nuclear forces of both sides. Whether those limits were achievable was open to question.

Many of the expressed objections to the 1979 decision masked deeper reservations about the military and political wisdom of NATO's course. The decision underscored the assumption, as prevalent in official circles as in the public mind, that nuclear deterrence alone had preserved the peace in Europe for the past three decades. Because this assumption is not subject to disproof and because it diverts attention from contemplating the consequences of a failure of deterrence, it offers some comfort. Yet it is simplistic, perhaps dangerously so.

Another equally plausible explanation for the durability of the peace in Europe starts with the mutual pledge of the United States and fourteen European states to come to each other's defense and to prepare accordingly through an enduring, possibly permanent alliance. The symbol and embodiment of that mutual pledge are the standing armies—American, British, French, and German—on the central front. These armies are NATO's first line of defense, and it is just as plausible that they, not nuclear weapons, are its principal deterrent to aggression. Both by declared strategy and accepted practice, NATO depends upon initial use of conventional deterrence in the event of attack by Warsaw Pact countries. And even if conventional strength were insufficient by itself to disabuse a would-be aggressor, a robust conventional defense that would make war in Europe more deadly than any that has yet been fought lends the ultimate deterrent—the threat to initiate use of nuclear weapons—whatever credibility it may have.

Those armies and the alliance they defend create a bulwark against two historic sources of war in Europe: a Germany too weak to defend itself against depredation by its neighbors or a Germany too strong to be contained by them. NATO not only guards West Germany against external menace but also weaves it securely into a web of military relationships, giving it no reason and no capacity to act on its own militarily. The alliance thus removes a source of insecurity for all West Germany's neighbors, not the least of them the Soviet Union and its allies. For West Germany to acquire nuclear weapons of its own would revive fears of its strength and would unsettle European security. If it were to loosen its ties to the West, however, and to renounce basing nuclear weapons on its soil, West Germany would raise almost as fearful a prospect of weakness and uncertainty in central Europe. Yet the postwar political settlement, a divided Germany without all the means of securing its own future, remains a historical anomaly. West German security and European security are thereby entwined in the alliance with the United States.

The unity of that alliance, based on members' acceptance of shared risk, remains its fundamental source of strength. America's allies in Europe add formidable military, economic, and political resources to its capacity to secure the blessings of liberty. To be sure, providing for the common defense does bring with it recurrent irritations, but they are minor compared to the distress that would exist if that defense were not sought in common. Nothing so threatens the unity of the alliance, however, as the possibility of a decision to use nuclear weapons. Were those weapons—their stationing or their potential use—to disrupt that unity, their sheer destructive force could not offset the resulting loss of security. Worse yet, nothing so undermines public support for NATO as a strategy that contemplates relying on those weapons for security. Whenever they come to public attention, nuclear weapons are a source of friction in alliance politics and disaffection in domestic politics.

That disaffection is dangerous. Unless a nation's military strategy enjoys widespread public acceptance, its government may well lack the determination to provide the means to sustain it and the will to carry it out. Without political legitimacy, strategy itself collapses, especially in the nuclear era when the sacrifices demanded by what passes for strategy are potentially enormous. That relationship between public approval and military strategy holds as true for alliances as it does for individual nations.

Michael Howard, the distinguished military historian, has rightly called attention to the often neglected social dimensions of strategy. In an address to the 1982 conference of the International Institute for Strategic Studies in The Hague, he noted that "for an appreciable number of Europeans, what was once seen as the prime requirement of deterrence, that is, the commitment of American power to the defense of Western Europe, no longer provides the political reassurance that once it did; in some respects indeed the exact opposite."[1] There is now a rather sharp disjunction between what Howard calls deterrence and reassurance: "The object of deterrence is to persuade an adversary that the costs to him of seeking a military solution to his political problems will far outweigh the benefits. The object of reassurance is to persuade one's own people, and those of one's allies, that the benefits of military action, or preparation for it, will outweigh the costs."[2]

The source of the disjunction between deterrence and reassurance is the mutual vulnerability that nuclear weapons have imposed on the superpowers and their allies. The vulnerability causes enduring contradictions in NATO's military doctrine, its military posture and practices, and its military and political course, contradictions that are harder and harder to ignore. Mutual vulnerability calls into question the very notion of strategy, in Clausewitz's sense of the rational economy of force applied to political ends. Apart from deterring the use of nuclear weapons by NATO's adversary, what political ends could nuclear weapons serve

1. Michael Howard, "Reassurance and Deterrence: Western Defense in the 1980s," *Foreign Affairs*, vol. 61 (Winter 1982/83), p. 315.

2. Ibid., p. 317.

for which their use and the resulting retaliation would not be grossly disproportionate? That question underlies the doubts about NATO's doctrine of first use of nuclear weapons—that NATO is prepared to respond to conventional attack by initiating nuclear war. And the greater the attention paid to the doctrine, the more profound the doubts. The very logic of the doctrine generates a series of dilemmas that the decision to deploy new American missiles, far from resolving, only makes more salient. The consequent tepid public acceptance of NATO doctrine has thus been far from reassuring.

The mutual vulnerability of East and West also has a critical bearing on NATO's military posture and practices. Deterrence alone no longer suffices as the sole criterion for procuring nuclear forces, putting them into the field, and planning for their potential use. An equally important consideration is military stability. NATO cannot amass weapons to deter the USSR and its allies from deliberately going to war without also considering whether the quality or quantity of those weapons might so threaten the Warsaw Pact as to appear provocative. In a crisis, that could give rise to a vicious circle in which both sides would feel compelled to use nuclear weapons before the other side does. NATO must therefore size and configure its forces so that neither side could calculate an advantage from going to war deliberately. At the same time it must avoid a force posture and war plans that would increase the risk of inadvertent war. Under conditions of mutual vulnerability, both deterrence and stability must be criteria for NATO's own security.

Stable deterrence poses no logical contradiction, but it does pose a practical one, a consequence of the forces NATO has chosen to deploy in the past and the way it has postured them. The new missile deployments may not bring NATO much closer to satisfying the requirements of stable deterrence because of the compulsion they exert on both sides to preempt in a crisis. Indeed, the perverse consequences for stability of putting missiles in Europe within range of the USSR have long been recognized by European statesmen. Helmut Schmidt, for one, noted that "everyone capable of objective reasoning must concede that the stationing of enemy I.R.B.M.s, so to speak, on its very threshold (Turkey), must produce the psychological effect of a provocation on any great power. One need only imagine how the Americans would react if the Soviets were to station I.R.B.M.s in Cuba."[3] Those words were published in early 1962, shortly before the missile crisis.

3. Helmut Schmidt, *Defense or Retaliation: A German View* (Praeger, 1962), p. 27.

Mutual vulnerability also underscores what has long been a condition of international relations—that military stability, while necessary, is not sufficient for security. Political stability is also essential. The pressure for mutual political accommodation or détente is acknowledgment of states' interdependence for security and insecurity in the nuclear age. The concern that adding to armaments can only exacerbate political tensions is valid. Just as valid is the concern that too great a preoccupation with political accommodation can jeopardize popular support for the military preparations essential to secure the material basis for that accommodation, a military balance of power. Again the contradiction is not a logical but a practical one. What is the current state of the military balance and what is the proper mix of policy between deterrence and détente under those circumstances? Finding answers to these questions provides an enduring source of friction within the alliance.

The December 1979 decision forced all these military and political dilemmas to the surface. They are addressed in the chapters to come. Chapter 2 examines the logic of NATO's nuclear doctrine and the paradoxes inherent in that logic. Chapter 3 examines the consequent contradictions in the military rationale for ground-launched cruise missile and Pershing II deployments. Chapter 4 discusses the political quandary in which NATO now finds itself, and chapter 5 explores a way out of that quandary through arms control. Chapter 6 examines the difficulties in NATO's short-range nuclear posture and the possibility for unilateral easing of those difficulties.

More than a few participants and observers have wondered whether NATO could ever implement its December 1979 decision and whether the alliance could survive failure to do so. Others have questioned whether its implementation was worth the risk to alliance unity and have called for undoing the Faustian bargain. The decision to pursue both deployment and arms control was not the first occasion on which nuclear choices have opened profound divisions in the alliance, nor will it be the last. A concluding chapter considers where the decision could take NATO.

CHAPTER TWO

Deterrence and Stability: Contradictions in NATO Strategy

Thus it may be that we shall, by a process of sublime irony, have reached a stage in this story where safety will be the sturdy child of terror, and survival the twin brother of annihilation.   Winston Churchill

IN POSSESSING nuclear weapons and threatening to use them, NATO's purpose is to deter war and to preserve military stability in Europe in ways that are politically acceptable to those who must share the burdens and risks of raising the nuclear forces and basing them on their territory. Yet this seemingly simple intention turns out upon reflection to prove exceedingly complex.[1] First, deterrence and stability are both essential for the security of the alliance, but they are not always compatible. Second, the very logic of nuclear deterrence is internally paradoxical, and the paradoxes create dilemmas in practice: inconsistencies in declaratory policy and strategic doctrine, trade-offs among weapons and force postures, predicaments for leaders in crisis and wartime. Most

---

1. It is a commonplace to assert that nuclear deterrence is a complex matter. Too often, however, that assertion is taken to mean that this subject is unfathomable to laymen and, by implication, best left to experts who alone have the wisdom to appreciate its intricacies. Yet, however intimidating or boring the subject may be, it is not beyond the wit of laymen to grasp its essentials. The subject is instead complex in a more fundamental sense. Complexity is present when three conditions hold: an issue raises competing values that cannot be simultaneously satisfied, uncertainty cloaks the consequences of any choice among options embodying these values, and authority over choice-making is dispersed among various individual and organizational actors, each of whom attends to different aspects of the problem. See John D. Steinbruner, *The Cybernetic Theory of Decision: New Dimensions of Political Analysis* (Princeton University Press, 1974), pp. 15–18.

attempts to escape the paradoxes of deterrence merely pose them in new form. Third, there is considerable discordance between strategic logic and political logic, between the superficial elegance of deterrence theory and the political acceptability of deterrence practice. This discordance constrains the public rationales for the choices made, if not the choices themselves.

Before taking a detailed look at the nuclear forces deployed in Europe, it is essential to grasp the complexities of deterrence in order to see why every proposed solution is partial and slights, if it does not ignore, important aspects of the whole.

Stable Deterrence: An Apparent Contradiction in Terms

The logic of deterrence, when it is not maddeningly opaque, can seem deceptively simple. For instance, to equate more nuclear weapons with more deterrence is often considered a truism, but it lacks the virtue of being true. The implicit assumption that the greater the prospective costs of war the more a state will be deterred from starting one is a legacy of prenuclear thought. Once the Warsaw Pact as well as NATO acquired nuclear weapons, it became difficult to raise the cost of war for one side without also doing so for the other. In this situation of nuclear interdependence,[2] deterrence no longer means increasing the cost of war to the enemy but rather manipulating the shared risk of a nuclear war neither side wants.

Since the advent of nuclear interdependence, strategists have become preoccupied with deterring premeditated aggression. Yet the threats posed by deterrents may not suffice to prevent war; indeed, they may provoke it. In August 1914, for instance, the alliance obligations undertaken to deter war helped bring it about, and the mobilization ordered as a precaution against aggression prompted preemption. In December 1941 the United States believed it was deterring a war by building up a sizable fleet at Pearl Harbor. Japan, however, considered war with the United States inevitable, and the U.S. buildup spurred it to war sooner rather than later when the empire might have been relatively worse off

2. The term *nuclear interdependence* captures the sense of mutual vulnerability that is the critical condition of today's nuclear balance. *Strategic parity* is a misnomer for this condition in that it has taken on the connotation of numerical equality in warheads or megatonnage, which is not essential for mutual vulnerability.

militarily. Under conditions of nuclear interdependence, as in a conventional balance of power, the possibility of preemptive or preventive war coexists with that of premeditated war.[3] War can result not only from a failure of deterrence but also from its instability.

Stable deterrence need not be a contradiction in terms. In a fundamental sense, deterrence and stability are mutually compatible. The aim in deterrence is to convince a potential adversary that the risk of seeking political objectives by military means is prohibitively high. If two adversaries deter each other from deliberately resorting to military force, then a modicum of stability, however precarious, exists in the military relationship between them. Yet military stability has always imposed more demanding requirements on armed forces than just the deterrence of premeditated war. Although nuclear weapons have altered the material basis for deterrence, military stability continues to take three distinct but related forms: strategic stability, crisis stability, and arms race stability.

When both sides are secure in the knowledge that each has a second-strike capability—sufficient numbers of survivable nuclear weapons to threaten unacceptable damage to the other side even after suffering a nuclear attack—*strategic stability,* or mutual deterrence, exists.

Even if both sides have enough survivable warheads for a second-strike capability and know they do, either may still worry that a sizable proportion of its nuclear forces may be vulnerable to attack. In a crisis in which nuclear war seems imminent, the side worried about vulnerability might see some advantage in preemptive attack. If either side sees itself in such a predicament, both sides are less secure for fear of preemption. Moreover, once nuclear war seems unavoidable, each side has an incentive to attack first in order to limit the damage it will suffer when the inevitable happens. When neither side has reason to fear a preemptive strike in a crisis, *crisis stability* exists.

3. *Premeditated war* results from coolly deliberate calculations by one side that the gains of war will be worth the costs. *Preemptive war* occurs in a grave crisis when war seems on the verge of breaking out, and one side, because of its narrow margin of security or the dictates of its war plans, feels compelled to strike the first blow. Anticipating this, the other side may want to strike even sooner. *Preventive war* occurs when one side sees war with the other as inevitable, though not necessarily imminent, and deems it better to wage it sooner rather than later because the balance of forces between them looks less and less favorable to it in the longer term. Preventive war thus results from a sense of fatalism, both about the unavoidability of war and about its prognosis. The very act of maintaining a balance of forces to deter premeditated war may trigger preemptive war in a crisis or provoke preventive war.

Each side may continue to test or deploy new weapons under conditions of strategic or crisis stability. Yet some weapons developments may threaten to undermine strategic or crisis stability. If so, they may well give rise to concern that deterrence is likely to fail in the future or, worse yet, that nuclear war with the other side is inevitable. *Arms race stability* prevails when neither side is concerned that its opponent is trying to build weapons that endanger either strategic or crisis stability. Arms race stability damps down mutual fears of aggressive intentions that lead to interpretations of the other side's acts as provocative and undermine attempts at mutual political accommodation.

Strategic stability deters either side from undertaking premeditated war. Crisis stability reduces the chances of preemptive war. Arms race stability minimizes incentives for preventive war.

Strategists do not construe military stability to mean absence of change in the two sides' forces nor to mean a Newtonian mechanical balance on which "heavy missiles" somehow weigh more, as some popular accounts suggest. Under present conditions, having a few hundred nuclear weapons more or less does not necessarily make one superpower better or worse off. What matters more than the quantity of nuclear forces is their quality, particularly their vulnerability to attack and their accuracy for attacking.

Not all weapons, force postures, and targeting plans designed to ensure deterrence also promote stability. For deterrence, one side may need only enough survivable nuclear weapons to cause catastrophic damage to the other side. For strategic stability, however, both sides must have this capability. Crisis stability is even more demanding. It is not sufficient to have some survivable nuclear forces on both sides; some crisis instability will remain as long as either side fears a significant portion of its nuclear weapons or command-and-control are vulnerable or thinks the other side's forces are.

Stable deterrence has become possible in the nuclear era in a way that it was not in previous international systems: survivable nuclear forces would enable the two superpowers to achieve both strategic and crisis stability at the same time. Yet stable deterrence at the intercontinental nuclear level does not ensure stable deterrence at the theater nuclear or conventional level. Even though the two superpowers are deterred from deliberately waging nuclear war with one another, what prevents the Soviet Union from using nuclear weapons against America's allies in NATO or from threatening to do so? By the late 1950s, nuclear interdependence between the superpowers had led to concern about America's ability to extend the protection of its nuclear deterrent to its allies in Europe. And even if extended deterrence sufficed to prevent nuclear attack or nuclear blackmail in Western Europe, what deterred the Warsaw Pact from launching a conventional attack there? Nuclear stability, it seemed, might not preclude conventional instability.

Under conditions of nuclear interdependence between the superpowers, four possible approaches to ensuring stable deterrence at the theater or regional level have been considered. One was to have European states acquire their own nuclear weapons, but that possibility, open to Great Britain and France, was not available to West Germany. West German acquisition of its own nuclear force would undermine the postwar settlement in Europe and jeopardize East-West, intra-European, and intra-German relations. By virtue of its military integration with NATO, West Germany has denied itself not only a nuclear potential of its own, but also a capacity to wage war on its own. Indeed, one of NATO's raisons d'être is to reconcile Western Europe's dominant power to its historically anomalous status of military self-denial. A second possibility for ensuring stable deterrence in the region was a Western European nuclear force, and British or French forces could conceivably evolve in that direction. However, such a force would imply a degree of political community currently absent in the rest of Western Europe. A third approach was somehow to enhance the credibility of U.S. nuclear weapons for extending deterrence to Europe, either by adding to the number of nuclear weapons in the European theater or by augmenting U.S. strategic nuclear forces. A fourth was to strengthen NATO's conventional defenses, relying on them and the risk of escalation to nuclear war to deter attack from the East. It is the last two approaches that have posed most starkly for NATO planners the trade-offs between deterrence and stability.

Extending nuclear deterrence to Europe means, by longstanding NATO policy, contemplating first use of nuclear weapons. At issue is how to do so credibly under conditions of nuclear interdependence. Some strategists feel that first use need only remain a possibility. As long as that possibility exists, they argue, it introduces enough risk into Soviet military calculations to deter them from a deliberate attack on Europe. Other strategists insist that first use must be a near certainty, not just a possibility. Only by making nuclear war seem inevitable, they feel, can NATO be sure of deterring the Soviet Union. What then is to be done about the prospect of Soviet nuclear retaliation for NATO first use? This prospect leads these strategists to two somewhat contradictory conclusions, each problematic. One is to prepare to wage limited nuclear war; the other is to prepare to limit damage to the United States in the event that the war does not stay limited. Yet limiting damage imposes a much more demanding requirement than first use; it requires a disarming first strike to destroy as many Soviet nuclear weapons as possible and some way of protecting the American people and industrial capacity from Soviet weapons that survive that strike. The means to accomplish these tasks do not seem attainable under existing technological conditions. Even if they were attainable they would not be desirable because they pose grave risks for stability.

What distinguishes the two schools of strategists is not a greater or lesser willingness to engage in nuclear war if need be or a desire to have options short of all-out nuclear attack on enemy population centers. Both accept the need to prepare for nuclear war and to have weapons, force postures, and targeting plans capable of attacking targets other than cities. Where the two schools part company is in their degree of readiness to jeopardize stability—all three forms of it—for the sake of supplementing extended deterrence.

Buttressing U.S. nuclear capabilities to make extended deterrence somehow seem more credible carries a heightened risk of instability. At the intercontinental level, acquiring a sufficient number of accurate warheads on MX and Trident II missiles to threaten in theory the entire Soviet land-based missile force would contribute little to extended deterrence, but it would make crisis stability precarious by giving Soviet leaders considerable inducement to launch a preemptive attack if U.S. first use appeared imminent. So, too, would the deployment of anti-satellite weapons to supplement other means of disrupting Soviet command, control, and communications (C^3). Acquiring antiballistic missiles and embarking on civil defense programs might limit damage in the event of Soviet retaliation and thereby increase somewhat the credibility of U.S. first use, but such designs, if ever realized, would endanger all three forms of stability between the superpowers. Were they capable of protecting a sizable portion of the American populace, which seems unlikely, they would undermine the mutuality of deterrence that is at the heart of strategic stability. Anticipating this and uncertain how workable these programs might prove, Soviet leaders might be tempted to start a preemptive or preventive war. That possibility would make the United States less secure.

Not all the efforts to enhance extended deterrence are directed at the intercontinental level; some involve deployments in Western Europe. A few strategists hope to impress the Warsaw Pact with the automaticity of NATO's nuclear response through predelegation of nuclear authority to field commanders. They are prepared to entertain a higher risk of inadvertent nuclear war in hopes of making the threat of deliberate nuclear first use somewhat more certain of execution. Others have sought, as yet unsuccessfully, to deploy enhanced-radiation weapons, short-range nuclear artillery shells (their more familiar designation, "neutron bombs," is a misnomer) designed to reduce collateral damage and thereby seem more usable in the crowded confines of Europe. But they would be stored in a few sites near the front, vulnerable both to being overrun and to being preempted.

Other strategists oppose these efforts as counterproductive because they increase instability without adding much to deterrence. While some have been willing to countenance a modest increase in long-range theater nuclear forces in Europe as symbolic assurance to allies concerned about the credibility of NATO's nuclear deterrent, they have stressed the primacy of redressing NATO's conventional disadvantages. Under nuclear interdependence, they argue, a balance of conventional forces is essential to deter limited threats to peace in Europe. Their focus on the conventional balance allows them by and large to reconcile the competing demands of deterrence and stability. The more robust NATO's conventional defense, the greater the risk that a conventional war might escalate to the nuclear level, they argue, and it is this risk of escalation that deters any war in the first place. Escalation would seem far less plausible if NATO were to suffer conventional collapse at the outset of hostilities.

Not all the sources of instability lie in deployments now under way or contemplated in the future. NATO has been less than fully attentive to sources of instability in its present and past nuclear posture. Its short-range nuclear forces, especially its nuclear artillery, remain vulnerable to attack by either conventional or nuclear means. Adding to their number would not help, nor would dispersing them. Nuclear artillery perhaps best exemplifies the alliance's penchant for making marginal contributions to its nuclear deterrent at considerable cost to stability.

NATO can ill afford such trade-offs, whether at the intercontinental or the theater nuclear levels. And it can do much more to reconcile deterrence with stability.

Paradoxes in the Logic of Deterrence

Although it is possible to reconcile apparent contradictions between deterrence and stability, internal contradictions in the logic of deterrence remain. That logic rests on a central paradox: how can NATO deter the Warsaw Pact by nuclear threats that it manifestly has little or no incentive to carry out? This paradox generates policy dilemmas that put the credibility of NATO's doctrine in doubt.

From the vantage point of Washington, shorter-range or tactical nuclear weapons may appear a more plausible deterrent to war in Europe than strategic nuclear weapons, which invite a Soviet counterattack against the United States. Yet what seems tactical an ocean away from the battlefield seems strategic to those living where the warheads will explode. Allies in Europe may prefer to rely on long-range theater nuclear forces (LRTNF) against the Soviet heartland in the hope of ensuring that any nuclear exchange takes place over, not on, their heads. Precisely this prospect, however, makes the United States no more likely to use its nuclear forces in Europe than its intercontinental systems. Yet extended deterrence, in its most fundamental sense, means committing America's strategic nuclear forces, not just its battlefield or its theater nuclear weapons, to Europe's defense.

Rather than trying to reconcile these differences among the allies, NATO has papered them over with its doctrine of flexible response. Codified in MC-14/3, a document agreed to in 1967, flexible response is less a strategy than an agreement not to disagree over strategy. Should Western Europe be attacked, the doctrine calls for initially meeting the aggression with "direct defense," responding to the attack at whatever level of force it was initiated. This means, in particular, a commitment to meeting conventional aggression with conventional defense. If direct defense should fail to contain the aggressor, it would be followed by "deliberate escalation"—first use of nuclear weapons and, ultimately, if all else fails, general nuclear release. Flexible response was a compromise between American insistence that the alliance treat conventional requirements seriously and European desires to avoid specificity on precisely at what point direct defense would give way to deliberate escalation. The lack of specifics for implementing a flexible response gives further testament to the underlying dilemma of deterrence. NATO has adopted guidelines for initial demonstrative use of nuclear weapons, but ten years of negotiating has brought no agreement on use beyond that.

Were Warsaw Pact forces on the verge of breaking through NATO defenses, NATO doctrine calls for selective nuclear strikes to deter advances on the ground without provoking further escalation. These could take one of three forms: an attack by LRTNF against military installations in the USSR, an attack by medium-range missiles or aircraft against Warsaw Pact force concentrations behind the lines in Eastern Europe, or the use of short-range artillery shells or nuclear bombs against enemy forces on the battlefield.

The first of these responses, against the Soviet Union itself, poses the difficulties of extended deterrence in their sharpest form for the United States because it risks Soviet retaliation not against the site from which the attack was launched but against the source of the attack, the United States or its military forces and installations. The other alternatives pose the same dilemma, if not for the United States, then for its allies in central Europe. At the moment of decision it will be difficult to get allied assent to a nuclear attack on Warsaw Pact force concentrations in Eastern Europe, for that attack would invite retaliation in kind against NATO forces in Western Europe. It will be even more difficult to obtain West German consent to battlefield use of nuclear weapons because the battlefield would likely be the Federal Republic itself. Precisely at the point of utmost peril, therefore, the unity of the alliance might be most threatened—and by a choice of its own devising.

One way out of this dilemma might be to base deterrence primarily on conventional defense, either by posing a conventional threat so robust that the Warsaw Pact would doubt its chances for victory by conventional means alone or by ensuring that any conventional conflict in Europe would be so violent as to become unbridled and make escalation to nuclear war more probable.

Emphasizing conventional deterrence, however, may only pose the paradox in a new form: how can NATO enhance dissuasion by a threat that, however more likely to be carried out, reduces the potential damage to the other side but not necessarily to all NATO members? Geography makes this paradox all the more poignant because it dictates that the battlefield would likely be West Germany, and what threatens to destroy West Germany is not nuclear war but any war. Besides, from the vantage point of U.S. allies in central Europe, any step that reduces the cost of war to the Warsaw Pact would seem to increase the chance of its outbreak, and that is intolerable: conventional weapons have grown so destructive that the prospect of even their use is too grim to bear for those situated near the battlefield. Therefore, as General André Beaufre has written with characteristic bluntness, "Europeans would prefer to risk general war in an attempt to avoid war altogether rather than have Europe become a theatre of operations for limited war."[4] While many U.S. strategists see advantages in waging conventional defense in depth and allowing NATO forces to fall back into West Germany and wage a sustained conventional war, West German strategists have tended until recently to emphasize deterrence and to talk only of forward defense, if they talked of defense at all.

In theory, were NATO to undertake a conventional buildup sufficient to take forward defense to its extreme—a threat to roll deep into Eastern Europe if attacked—that posture might seem more a provocation than a precaution to the Warsaw Pact despite any NATO protestations that its intentions were defensive. If the Pact were to respond with an offsetting buildup or by adopting a strategy of preemption, the result would be an arms race or crisis instability at the conventional level in Europe.

Short of its extreme form, which the alliance shows no present signs of intending to pursue, a stouter NATO conventional posture could strengthen deterrence without jeopardizing stability. The difficulty lies in making the defensive forces more convincing without posing too great an offensive threat to the Warsaw Pact. But even if it is achieved, a stronger conventional force could reinforce the risk that war, once it erupts, may get out of hand—what Thomas Schelling calls "the threat that leaves something to chance."[5]

That threat leaves too much to chance for those strategists who seek to fill every lacuna in NATO doctrine with new forces and more options for waging and "winning" nuclear war. While other analysts insist there is some level of conventional capability and risk of escalation sufficient to deter war in Europe, these strategists see a need for superiority at every level of conflict from conventional war through battlefield and

4. *New Encyclopaedia Britannica,* 15th ed., s.v. "warfare, conduct of."
5. Thomas C. Schelling, *The Strategy of Conflict* (Oxford University Press, 1960), p. 187.

theater nuclear war up to general nuclear war—"escalation dominance" in their parlance. Instead of stressing the need for conventional defense and for holding nuclear weapons in reserve, they want to incorporate nuclear weapons fully into NATO's force posture and battle plans so that there would be no doubt about the ability and will of the alliance to initiate nuclear war.

Yet by this logic these strategists create paradoxes of their own. In multiplying nuclear options to try to enhance nuclear deterrence, they increase the threat of nuclear war. How can they increase the threat of war without also increasing its likelihood? How can they restrain escalation by threatening escalation dominance? How can first use of nuclear weapons followed by threats of further use convince the other side to stop the war and return to its prewar borders and at the same time reassure it that no further harm will come to it if it does accede? How can they threaten first use without also encouraging Soviet preemption? In short, sacrificing stability for deterrence is no way out of the dilemma.

It is only by recognizing the deterrence dilemma and the inevitable trade-offs it imposes on the choice of weapons, force postures, targeting doctrine, and declaratory policy that the analytical problem posed by NATO's nuclear forces comes fully into focus. Simply put, no solution can satisfy all the relevant dimensions of the problem simultaneously. It is possible, however, to eliminate some contradictions by recasting the logic of deterrence to reflect better the conditions of nuclear interdependence. Under these conditions the calculus of deterrence now rests on two fundamentals: the level of risk as perceived by the state to be deterred and the assumption of risk—which side will have to bear the burden of risk in deciding to wage war or to escalate it.

The level of risk is a product of the prospective costs of war and the probability of incurring those costs. With the advent of nuclear interdependence, is it the absolute or relative cost of war that counts? Strategists disagree. Those who believe in "assured destruction" assert that some threshold of damage or punishment exists that is simply unacceptable to the enemy. Those who disagree insist that relative costs still matter in the nuclear age and the states continue to calculate how much better off they will be than their opponents at war's end, regardless of what both sides suffer in absolute terms. This belief, a premise of prenuclear logic, leads these strategists to the conclusion that a nuclear war between the superpowers can be won. Their opponents contend that beyond a point the victors will envy the dead.

Cost alone, however prohibitive, does not determine the calculus of risk. Another factor is the probability of incurring that cost, the likelihood that nuclear threats will be carried out. That probability, or the other side's assessment of it—credibility in strategists' shorthand—has a critical bearing on extending the nuclear umbrella to U.S. allies under conditions of nuclear interdependence. Is it necessary and possible to devise ways of increasing that probability or at least to strengthen the Warsaw Pact's conviction that it is considerably higher than zero? Again, strategists disagree. Some insist that as long as the Warsaw Pact cannot be certain that the United States will not carry out its threats, it will be deterred from initiating nuclear war—a modern version of Pascal's wager. Others add that uncertainty about the chance of escalation deters not only nuclear war in Europe but also conventional war, along the lines of Schelling's "threat that leaves something to chance." Still others, adhering to prenuclear military ideology, insist that the Warsaw Pact will be deterred only if it is convinced that the United States and its allies are prepared to fight and win a nuclear war, that nuclear war must be made more certain and its outcome less in doubt.

Whatever level of risk would dissuade a potential adversary in theory, who bears the burden of risk of having to decide to escalate remains critical in practice. Because the consequences of nuclear war are so catastrophic, deterrence ultimately rests on threats that a state would manifestly prefer not to carry out. Deciding whether to go nuclear means assuming a burden of risk that may be unbearable. To a lesser degree the burden also falls on those taking steps short of nuclear war that could lead to escalation. Thus, placing the burden on the other side, manipulating the risk, is a key to nuclear deterrence.

At no time since the onset of nuclear interdependence was the perception of shared risk clearer than during the Cuban missile crisis. Both President John F. Kennedy and Premier Nikita S. Khrushchev alluded to it in their diplomatic exchanges, and both manipulated it by their military acts. Soviet efforts at secrecy and dispatch in installing the missiles were designed to create a fait accompli, forcing the United States to assume the risk of removing them. The U.S. blockade of Cuba, aimed at barring delivery of additional missiles and showing resolve, made the Soviet Union assume the risk of initiating hostilities by running the blockade. Both sides took precautions to avoid direct engagement after that point. Kennedy ordered the blockade drawn closer to Cuba in order to give the Soviet leadership more time to consider withdrawing.

When his order was not obeyed, a Soviet ship was allowed to pass through the blockade. The precautions did not always succeed in averting direct confrontation—a U-2 intruded into Soviet air space and Soviet submarines were forced to surface—but these incidents took place despite the best efforts of leaders on both sides and did not lead to retaliation. Crisis instability and the chance of inadvertent war remained a concern throughout, however. As Robert S. McNamara, then secretary of defense, testified shortly thereafter, "The greatest danger was not that Khrushchev would deliberately launch nuclear war, but that the situation might have gotten out of control if conflict had started."[6]

Over the course of a crisis or a conventional war the assumption of risk can shift from side to side. In contemplating aggression the Warsaw Pact would initially assume the risk that a conventional war in Europe would escalate. Once the war is under way and both sides consider further escalation, the assumption of risk may fall first on one side then the other. Should one side begin to lose, it may consider using nuclear weapons. At the same time, the side holding the advantage will begin to worry about nuclear attack and consider preempting with nuclear weapons of its own. As both sides face the prospect of nuclear preemption, the burden of risk becomes shared.

Under nuclear interdependence, deterrence no longer depends primarily on increasing the cost of war to the enemy but rather on manipulating the shared risk of a war neither side wants.

Political versus Strategic Logic

Recasting deterrence theory by focusing on the assumption of risk may make compelling strategic logic, but it is unconvincing political logic. Strategically, basing long-range theater nuclear forces on European territory may not increase the likelihood that the United States would initiate nuclear war in response to a conventional attack on Europe, but it does put the Soviet Union in the position of having to eliminate these forces in a war if it is to be certain they will not be used. To the extent that hardening, mobility, and perimeter defenses can

6. *Military Procurement Authorization, Fiscal Year 1964*, Hearings before the Senate Committee on Armed Services, 88 Cong. 1 sess. (Government Printing Office, 1963), p. 85.

secure these missiles against conventional attack and sabotage, the Soviet Union would have to consider using nuclear weapons against them. Because it could not be sure how many NATO missiles would survive to retaliate and whether the United States would refrain from responding with its strategic systems, the Soviet Union would have to assume the risk of starting not just conventional war in Europe but nuclear war between the superpowers. By this reasoning it would be deterred from doing either.

This rationale for basing long-range theater nuclear forces on land in Europe has long been a staple of strategic thought. Helmut Schmidt, discussing the Jupiter and Thor missiles installed in 1959 and subsequently withdrawn, put it succinctly:

What gives rise to the conviction that American missile forces in Britain, Italy and Turkey would inevitably become involved is the prospect that, in the event of a nuclear conflict in Europe, the Soviet forces would feel a compulsion to eliminate these missile bases as early as possible and whatsoever the circumstances. The installation of American IRBMs in Europe also has the object of making it clear that NATO can defend itself against threats of nuclear blackmail exclusively and expressly directed against Europe and Europe alone.

On the other hand the military value of the seven IRBM bases already installed in Europe, or at present under construction, is very small.[7]

That deterrence rests precisely on increasing the shared risk of escalation is a point not lost on the critics of new NATO deployments. To say that the United States shares this risk with the five basing countries or that the assumption of risk falls to the Soviet Union and its allies does not allay popular anxiety in Europe. Such reminders are no more reassuring to Europeans than they were to Americans faced with ABMs or MXs in their own backyard, even though Europe's very security depends on accepting such risks. Nor does the knowledge that stability makes a state more secure leave its citizens very reassured. Political logic is thus somewhat at odds with strategic logic. Strategic logic suggests basing missiles on land in a number of allied countries as visible testament that a war in Europe could go nuclear and that a would-be invader dare not contemplate war without planning to eliminate these weapons first. Political logic suggests avoiding public reminders of nuclear vulnerability. Those who would reduce the visibility of new deployments by moving them out to sea ignore the strategic logic of

---

7. Helmut Schmidt, *Defense or Retaliation: A German View* (Praeger, 1962), p. 77.

widespread land-basing in order to satisfy the political logic of not drawing attention to the risk.

Putting populations at risk thus furthers strategic stability at a cost of political instability. Public anxiety invites cynics to cloak themselves in moralism and denounce strategies based on mutual vulnerability as bloodthirsty, only to propose alternative strategies that make nuclear war more possible. Nuclear disarmers increase the risk of war by denying the possibility of deterrence; some nuclear strategists do so by insisting that NATO be prepared not only to initiate nuclear war but also to fight a prolonged one and somehow prevail. Both take advantage of the difficulty the public has in grasping the idea of stability. Most people continue to think that only numbers matter; they disagree whether NATO would be better off with more or fewer nuclear weapons in Europe or whether equal numbers of weapons or no weapons is the condition most desirable. Those strategists who advocate stable balance try without much success to convince people that numbers matter only insofar as they affect the stability of deterrence. But those who advocate nuclear buildup as well as those who favor disarmament do not challenge the popular faith in numerology; they play the numbers game in public. What strategic logic requires, political logic rejects.

Strategic logic also comes into conflict with political logic when NATO tries to mobilize public support for the weapons and force postures it needs. To do so, it emphasizes the threat from the East. The difficulty is to modulate the emphasis so that the alliance retains the requisite military might to deter war without engendering such unremitting hostility between East and West that war comes to be seen as likely if not inevitable. And there is always the possibility that truculence may arouse fear in NATO's supporters without instilling caution in its enemies.

Military Stability and Political Stability

The conflict between military and political logic runs deeper than mere rhetoric. Trying to stabilize the nuclear balance in Europe may be a necessary condition for reducing the chance of war; it is not a sufficient condition. Military stability is at best precarious without political stability. Unless antagonistic powers can reach some mutual accommodation, war remains a possibility. Moreover, a buildup undertaken to ensure military stability, especially if it threatens to overmatch the other side, can have adverse effects on political stability. As Chancellor Schmidt told the Bundestag in 1979, "Elimination of this feeling of being threatened is possible only if confidence in the other side grows and if the security demands of the other party are included in one's own security considerations."[8]

Experience has taught Europeans that neither deterrence nor détente would alone suffice to keep the peace: the lesson of the years leading up to World War I was that strength without conciliation was a flawed policy; the lesson of the years between the two world wars was that conciliation not backed by strength was no better. These lessons have not been lost on the current generation of Europe's leaders or on NATO itself.

The lessons are embodied in the Harmel report, agreed to by all members of NATO in 1967, which saw deterrence, defense, *and* détente as functions of the alliance. The report emphasized the compatibility among them: "Military security and a policy of détente are not contradictory but complementary. Collective defense is . . . the necessary condition for effective policies directed toward a greater relaxation of tensions."[9] Yet there are incompatibilities as well. Views may well differ in America and Europe on the balance to be struck between deterrence and détente, but trade-offs are unavoidable. Those who deny the necessity for such trade-offs only make it harder to reconcile the differing perspectives.

These differing perspectives inform the positions of Europeans and Americans over arms control. To many Europeans the fascination of American arms controllers for the technicalities of military stability seems misplaced. What counts to them is the political stability imparted by the very process of negotiation.

European dependence on the United States for its security aggravates the deterrence-détente trade-off. Too much accommodation between the superpowers raises Europeans' fears of Soviet-American collusion to their detriment, just as too much antagonism between them tempts European governments to vie for the role of mediator to reassure anxious publics. The Harmel report indirectly acknowledges the delicacy of

8. "Text of Schmidt Speech at Bundestag Security Debate," in Foreign Broadcast Information Service, *Daily Report: Western Europe*, March 12, 1979, p. J10.
9. "Report on the Future Tasks of the Alliance," *NATO Letter*, vol. 16 (January 1968), p. 26.

achieving accord: "Each Ally should play its full part in promoting an improvement in relations with the Soviet Union and the countries of Eastern Europe, bearing in mind that the pursuit of détente must not be allowed to split the Alliance. The chances of success will clearly be greatest if the Allies remain on parallel courses. . . ."[10]

The deterrence dilemma, the apparent contradiction between deterrence and stability, the discordance between strategic and political logic—these form the context for choice among declaratory policies, strategic doctrines, weapons, force postures, and targeting plans for nuclear forces in Europe. To Americans, prone to think of problems with solutions rather than dilemmas without resolution, the temptation is to deny the difficulty, show impatience with those who raise it, and confuse palliatives with panaceas. To Europeans, dependence is the stuff of paranoia; the deterrence dilemma makes reassurance ultimately impossible.

The paradoxes, dilemmas, and compromises required by having nuclear weapons in Europe help account for many features of alliance behavior: persistent differences of interests between the United States and the Europeans that are papered over in NATO decisions; recurrent crises of confidence as the alliance attends first to one aspect of the problem then to another, temporarily resolving but never solving any; and the persistent strain of making choices, which could become intolerable in the event of a military confrontation in Europe. Not the least of the consequences is the difficulty of sustaining any military rationale for new nuclear deployments in Europe.

10. Ibid.

CHAPTER THREE

NATO's Rationale for the Euromissiles

"When I use a word," Humpty Dumpty said, in a rather scornful tone, "it means just what I choose it to mean—neither more nor less."
"The question is," said Alice, "whether you can make words mean so many different things."
"The question is," said Humpty Dumpty, "which is to be master—that is all."
Lewis Carroll, *Through the Looking Glass*

IN THEORY the design of weapons, their deployment in a particular force posture, and the options for using them in the event of war should follow logically as well as chronologically from the formulation of a strategic doctrine. In practice the development of doctrine, especially for nuclear weapons, may come after weapons design. Partly as a consequence, connections between the detailed characteristics of weapons systems, force postures, and targeting plans on the one hand and their military rationale on the other are often tenuous. Plans for NATO to deploy new intermediate-range nuclear missiles in Europe are no exception. Yet even if planners were to start with doctrine and proceed to design, deployment, and operational planning, the paradoxes in the logic of deterrence that were discussed in chapter 2 would make it particularly difficult to devise any consistent military rationale for cruise and Pershing II missiles as instruments for extending deterrence to U.S. allies.

In a general sense the military rationale for all nuclear forces in Europe is to prevent war in Europe and to defend against what they fail to prevent. Moving from the general to the specific, however, points up substantial differences in the missions that nuclear weapons are capable of performing and in the threats they might credibly counter. In part these differences are a function of their technical characteristics and in part a function of the geopolitical positions of the states controlling their use.

24

One technical characteristic commonly used to differentiate nuclear weapons is range, specifically, the maximum range that their means of delivery can project them. Using range to categorize weapons is somewhat arbitrary because delivery vehicles can obviously reach targets closer than their maximum range. In addition, assessments of range are based on extrapolations from test data, while actual ranges can vary depending on flight path, climatic conditions, force loadings (the number of warheads actually carried), and in the case of cruise missiles, fuel capacity and fuel and engine technology. Nonetheless, maximum range remains a meaningful distinction because it is a critical determinant of possible missions. Short-range nuclear systems are defined as capable of maximum ranges of 100 kilometers or less, which limits their use to targets on or near the battlefield (hence their designation, battlefield nuclear systems). Medium-range nuclear systems have maximum ranges of between 100 and 1,000 kilometers. Because such ranges enable them to attack enemy tank and troop concentrations, military installations, or lines of supply well behind the front lines, they are often grouped with shorter-range systems under the rubric of tactical nuclear weapons. Long-range theater nuclear forces (LRTNF), otherwise known as intermediate-range nuclear forces (INF), can travel from 1,000 to 5,500 kilometers. They are capable of reaching Western Europe from bases deep in the USSR, or vice versa, but not of traveling between the continental United States and the USSR (hence their somewhat unfortunate designation, Eurostrategic weapons).

Vulnerability, accuracy, and yield are the other key technical characteristics used by analysts to differentiate nuclear weapons. Vulnerability is obviously important because weapons cannot deter or defeat attacks they cannot survive. Accuracy matters for threatening such targets as missile silos or bunkers to house C^3 facilities that have been hardened to withstand the blast effects of a nuclear explosion. Accuracy can also reduce collateral damage to people and property in the vicinity of the intended target, although this distinction may mean little for targets located in the crowded confines of Europe. Explosive yield, expressed in terms of megatonnage, can compensate somewhat for inaccuracy in threatening hardened targets and can increase effectiveness somewhat against soft targets. Otherwise, whether measured by megatonnage, temperature, or roentgens, varying yields represent differences in degree rather than in kind: all nuclear weapons, regardless of the blast, heat, and radiation they generate, can wreak unprecedented death and destruction.

Another critical distinction to bear in mind is that between American nuclear weapons on one hand and those of Britain and France on the other. Although they have technical specifications similar to their American counterparts, British and French systems are set apart by the geopolitical positions of their owners and hence their conceivable military purposes. Nuclear weapons under American control may not be able to accomplish what the same weapons under British or French control could and vice versa—for instance, in deterring an attack against their possessor.

It is thus useful to examine separately the military rationales for proposed deployments of ground-launched cruise missiles (GLCMs) and Pershing II, present and future deployments of British and French systems, and NATO's present short-range nuclear posture. This chapter looks at the GLCM and Pershing II; chapters 5 and 6 will examine the others.

GLCM and Pershing II Technical Characteristics

Cruise missiles are analogous to unmanned aircraft: like jet planes, they breathe air and consume fuel as they fly. Their fuel capacity thus limits their maximum range (to about 3,000 kilometers in tests of the current generation of GLCMs). Like jet planes, too, they can maneuver en route to their targets, but maneuvering reduces their operational range (to about 2,500 kilometers for GLCMs).[1]

Unlike manned aircraft, however, they rely wholly on an on-board guidance system to change course in flight without missing their preprogrammed targets. They use terrain contour matching (TERCOM) to correct any drift in inertial guidance over the course of flight and to deliver warheads on target with a circular error probable (CEP) of approximately thirty meters when fully operational. TERCOM essentially consists of a radar altimeter, which provides regular updates of the altitude profile of the terrain below, and a computer, which compares these updates to digital maps of altitude profiles made at various locations

1. Department of Defense, *The FY 1981 Department of Defense Program for Research, Development and Acquisition* (Department of Defense, 1980), p. VII-8; *Department of Defense Authorization for Appropriations for Fiscal Year 1980*, Hearings before the Senate Committee on Armed Services, 96 Cong. 1 sess. (Government Printing Office, 1979), pt. 5: *General Procurement, Civil Defense*, p. 2492.

along the intended flight path and stored in its memory. Comparison of the actual readings and the stored profiles permits in-flight course correction as well as properly timed fusing of the warhead. TERCOM works best over highly articulated topography; guiding cruise missiles over featureless landscapes or over sea has proved much more troublesome. A digital scene-matching area correlator (DSMAC) provides final course correction near the intended point of impact for conventionally armed cruise missiles. Early versions of DSMAC compared a stored photographic negative to a photograph of the ground taken in flight; even more advanced versions have not fully overcome the limitations of night, smoke, dust, or inclement weather.[2]

Unlike most modern military aircraft, cruise missiles are presently capable of flying only at subsonic speeds. The GLCM's cruising speed is Mach 0.7 (roughly 550 miles per hour) and its maximum speed is Mach 0.85.[3] This low speed saves fuel but increases vulnerability to Soviet air defenses. It also puts the USSR one to three hours away from basing sites in Western Europe, too far to make GLCMs useful for strikes against time-urgent targets such as missile silos and C^3 facilities, especially those at a distance. The critical factor is not the GLCM's penetrativity or accuracy but the potential Soviet ability to detect its launch, allowing some time for counteraction.[4]

Cruise missiles are presently less vulnerable to Soviet air defenses than are aircraft. They can fly close to the earth—as low as 50 feet above water, 150 feet above land, and 300 feet over mountainous terrain— under Soviet radar or masked amid ground clutter. Their shape gives them a small radar cross-section; proposed use of stealth technology, such as an airframe designed to deflect radar signals, materials which absorb those signals, and electronic countermeasures, could further enhance their ability to avoid detection and penetrate air defenses.

2. Kosta Tsipis, "Cruise Missiles," *Scientific American,* vol. 236 (February 1977), pp. 20–29; John C. Toomay, "Technical Characteristics," in Richard K. Betts, ed., *Cruise Missiles: Technology, Strategy, Politics* (Brookings Institution, 1981), pp. 36–41.

3. David Hobbs, *Cruise Missiles: Facts and Issues,* Centre Piece 3 (Aberdeen: Centre for Defence Studies, 1982), p. 20.

4. Some Soviet commentary suggests that the USSR may not have high confidence in their capability to detect the launches. If so, remedying any such deficiency would be possible, but it would take time and money to do. In the interim, the GLCM would present many of the same problems for the USSR—and hence for NATO—that Pershing II does.

Cruise missiles can be armed with conventional or nuclear warheads. Their high accuracy permits them to carry smaller nuclear warheads, and the reduced weight lowers fuel consumption and increases the missile's range. The smaller warhead, of variable but relatively low yield (10 to 50 kilotons), can be said to limit blast effects and collateral damage, but only in comparison to current multimegaton weapons: the Hiroshima bomb had a yield of 12.5 kilotons. Conventional ordnance, by contrast, weighs much more than nuclear warheads, increasing fuel consumption and cutting down considerably the maximum range.

Cruise missiles can be air launched (ALCMs) from bombers or other aircraft, sea launched (SLCMs) from standard torpedo tubes or vertical launch tubes aboard surface ships or submarines, and ground launched (GLCMs) from transporter-erector-launchers (TELs), tractor-trailer trucks specifically configured for the purpose. The GLCM, an air force program, originated as a variant of the navy's SLCM. Unlike the ALCM, which acquires its initial velocity from inertia when dropped from fast-moving aircraft, both the SLCM and the GLCM are propelled for the first few seconds of flight by a solid-fuel booster rocket, which is then jettisoned. Once in flight, GLCMs and SLCMs, whether conventionally or nuclear armed, are indistinguishable: they have identical airframes, 18.25 feet long and 21 inches in diameter with an 8.6-foot wingspan.

Present plans call for GLCMs to be mounted four to a TEL. A flight, or fire-control unit, consists of four TELs, or sixteen missiles, and two launch-control centers (a primary and a backup unit). Seven GLCM flights would be based at Comiso, Sicily; six at Greenham Common, Berkshire, sixty miles west of London; four at Molesworth in the east Midlands sixty miles north of London; three each at bases at Florennes, Belgium, and at Wönsdrecht, the Netherlands; and six at Wüschheim, West Germany, in the Rhineland-Palatinate near the Luxembourg border. NATO would draw on infrastructure funds to construct reinforced concrete caserns on the bases to garage each flight and to house command-and-control facilities; the caserns are supposed to withstand conventional bombing. To guard against attacks by paramilitary forces, base security would have to be bolstered. Neither would offer much protection against nuclear attack.

In contrast to the GLCM, Pershing II is a ballistic missile, an improved version of the older Pershing I-A presently deployed in West Germany both with U.S. units and with West German forces under a program-of-cooperation agreement. Although Pershing II is virtually indistinguishable externally from the older model, the resemblance between the missiles is only skin deep. At 7,200 kilograms, Pershing II is more than 50 percent heavier than the I-A. Two other changes make it far more formidable, at least on paper. It has more than double the range of its predecessor and close to pinpoint accuracy. Yet the improved version is somewhat jerry-built, and testing was compressed by some eighteen months to meet the political schedule of an initial operating capability in December 1983: even though Pershing II was deployed by that date, it will still need more than a little tinkering to meet its technical specifications.

Pershing II emerged as a by-product of an army program to modernize Pershing I-A by improving its accuracy at shorter ranges. It has a redesigned reentry vehicle incorporating a new radar area-correlation guidance, RADAG for short, which supplements inertial guidance in the terminal phase of reentry. As the reentry vehicle descends, an on-board radar scans the target area. A computer converts the radar output to digital format and compares it to a radar image of the target area stored in its memory, determining errors in position and updating its inertial guidance. Pershing II can be deliberately programmed to overshoot and use its terminal guidance to maneuver back on target. The maneuverable warhead, or MARV, is intended to defeat potential antiballistic missile defenses. The improved accuracy, a CEP of twenty-five meters, would, if achieved, make it possible to reduce the explosive yield of its nuclear warhead to as low as five kilotons, though it can carry a warhead with a yield in excess of fifty kilotons, which would be needed if the requisite accuracy proves unattainable.[5] The combination of accuracy and yield, together with its flight time of ten to fourteen minutes, makes Pershing II capable of attacking time-urgent targets such as strategic C^3 and ICBM silos in the western USSR.

Pershing II's range has never been officially estimated in public, but informed guesses put it at 1,800 kilometers when armed with a nuclear warhead, enough to fall just short of Moscow if based in West Germany

5. F. Clifton Berry, Jr., "Pershing II: First Step in NATO Theater Nuclear Force Modernization?" *International Defense Review*, vol. 12, no. 8 (1979), pp. 1303–08; Kevin N. Lewis, "Intermediate-Range Nuclear Weapons," *Scientific American*, vol. 243 (December 1980), p. 64; "Pershing 2 Completes Test Series," *Aviation Week & Space Technology*, vol. 112 (June 16, 1980), p. 290; *Department of Defense Appropriations for 1983*, Hearings before the Subcommittee on the Department of Defense of the House Committee on Appropriations, 97 Cong. 2 sess. (GPO, 1982), pt. 1, p. 325, and pt. 4, pp. 412–14, 443.

but not enough to reach much of the USSR from elsewhere in Europe. Equipping it with a new front end capable of delivering multiple independently targeted reentry vehicles, or MIRVs, which weigh less than MARVs, would further boost its range relative to the MARVed version, though not with a full payload. The increased range came about through a cumulation of marginal improvements rather than by design to army specifications. Pershing I-A and its short-range follow-on, Pershing I-B, were designed by Martin Marietta to satisfy an army requirement to target tactical C^3 with conventional payloads. The weight of an earth-penetrating warhead and associated guidance added to its conventional ordnance meant that Pershing I-A would have had to have more thrust than was needed to hurl a nuclear warhead at its target. The improved guidance on Pershing II enables it to use a smaller nuclear warhead, conserving space for more fuel. Improved propellants also give it more thrust. Finally, the payload is intended to be brought down in a steeper trajectory, although that has required the addition of a heat shield to protect the guidance system during the initial phases of reentry. The shield makes the reentry vehicle more detectable and possibly vulnerable to electronic countermeasures. Thus, when civilian officials began casting about for an alternative to cruise missiles that would satisfy NATO's urge for a new LRTNF missile, Martin Marietta had something to sell, however improvised it may have been.[6]

Pershing II can be launched from a TEL similar to the one used by Pershing I-A but modified to accommodate the missile's greater weight. Each TEL can carry one missile. A Pershing platoon consists of three TELs, a launch-control truck, and other ground-support equipment. Three platoons constitute a battery—the unit designation is a legacy of army artillery—and four batteries a battalion. Pershing II battalions are scheduled for deployment at three West German bases, Schwäbisch Gmünd, Neu-Ulm, and Neckarsulm.

One battery in each battalion is to be placed on quick reaction alert (QRA), reportedly at Kleingartach near Heilbronn, at Mutlangen near

6. Berry, "Pershing II: First Step in NATO Theater Nuclear Force Modernization?" pp. 1306–08; "Pershing 2 Completes Test Series," p. 290; Christopher Paine, "Pershing II: The Army's Strategic Weapon," *Bulletin of the Atomic Scientists*, vol. 36 (October 1980), pp. 25–26. Paine wrongly attributes the Pershing II's range to an army desire for acquiring strategic missions; see pp. 28–30 of the article for relevant counterevidence from Senate hearings. A 4,000-kilometer variant was not funded, according to Robert A. Moore, "Theater Nuclear Forces: Thinking the Unthinkable," *International Defense Review*, vol. 14, no. 4 (1981), p. 407.

Schwäbisch Gmünd, and at Inneringen.[7] Present plans call for Pershing IIs on QRA to be left out in the open, armed with their warheads and ready to deploy at a moment's notice to presurveyed sites in surrounding areas. The remaining Pershing IIs will be garaged in reinforced concrete caserns.

Both GLCMs and Pershing IIs have low likelihoods of surviving a nuclear attack on their caserns.[8] Although reinforced concrete does provide some protection against conventional bombs, present technology is incapable of ensuring invulnerability against a nuclear explosion, even a near miss. Moreover, both guidance and command-and-control systems may well be susceptible to the effects of the blast and the electromagnetic pulse it generates. The systems will remain vulnerable even after current efforts to improve redundancy and survivability are complete, which means the missiles could be unusable even if they did survive. Vulnerability also limits their flexibility. Both GLCMs and Pershing IIs can be programmed to strike a variety of targets with different yields. But their computers must be preprogrammed with digital images of specific targets and data on the choice of target and the missile's location fed in just prior to launch.[9] The effects of a nuclear blast might preclude not only reprogramming but also transmitting and receiving the signal to launch and feeding the critical data into a missile's computer and launch control.

To increase the missiles' chances of survival, NATO intends to rely on mobility and concealment. Yet mobility has problems of its own. Traffic in the vicinity of some bases can be congested in the best of times, not to mention in a war or near-war crisis. The TELs' off-road mobility is limited by terrain. They cannot climb a grade steeper than thirty degrees and cannot achieve even that if weather impedes traction. In addition, all firing sites have to be presurveyed so that accurate data on a missile's location can be fed in before launch. Once out of their caserns, moreover, the missiles and associated C^3 become more vulnerable to conventional bombing or a near miss by nuclear weapons.

7. Uwe Zimmer, "Das falsche Spiel mit den Raketen," *Stern Magazin*, no. 42 (October 14, 1982), pp. 275–77.

8. On Pershing survivability, see *Department of Defense Appropriations for 1979*, Hearings before the Subcommittee on the Department of Defense of the House Committee on Appropriations, 95 Cong. 2 sess. (GPO, 1978), pt. 4, pp. 347–50.

9. Berry, "Pershing II: First Step in NATO Theater Nuclear Force Modernization?" p. 1306; Bruce A. Smith, "Tomahawk Ground Control Evaluated by Air Force," *Aviation Week & Space Technology*, vol. 116 (June 21, 1982), p. 48.

Security against special operations, sabotage, or terrorism may be especially difficult to preserve. The convoys, twenty-two vehicles, including four TELs fifty-five feet long in the case of GLCMs, are unlikely to escape notice. Adding to their small complement of security forces would only attract more attention. Finally, unless mobility is routinely exercised, any move out of garrison in a crisis could be mistaken as a sign of hostile intent and would be likely to prompt Soviet preemption if war appeared imminent. Yet peacetime exercises to make movements out of garrison routine may well arouse local animosity and draw protesters, even if the missiles are not armed with nuclear warheads at the time. Frequent exercising would also affect the reliability of the missiles, which are subject to damage from "shake, rattle, and roll." Spare missiles may only partly offset the problem, if they are available.

Just as overly optimistic claims of ensuring survivability through mobility and concealment must be put into perspective, so too the picture of vulnerability should not be overdrawn. Although the missiles' chances of surviving a nuclear attack are low if they remain in their caserns and the survivability of NATO C^3 is even more in doubt, the ability of GLCM and Pershing II TELs to run and hide does mean that the Warsaw Pact cannot be wholly confident of targeting and eliminating all these forces if NATO has warning and can deploy off base.

Taking advantage of warning may be politically difficult to accomplish under pressure of a crisis, however, and it is under crisis conditions that the trade-off between deterrence and stability becomes most palpable to political leaders. Relocation might enhance the missiles' survivability, thus reinforcing deterrence, but it could also hasten enemy preemption. The decision to move missiles off base would be difficult enough to make if conventional war were imminent but not yet under way; if a conventional battle were already joined, the risk of escalation might make the strain of decision almost unbearable. Getting the allies, with their diverse interests and varying propensities for taking risks, to agree on a decision is far from a foregone conclusion. The temptation to wait on events, to seek better intelligence, and above all to avoid provocation may well carry the day.

Decision procedures for nuclear release are also cloaked in secrecy. The missiles are deployed to each NATO host country under a program of cooperation. None of these agreements involves so-called dual-key arrangements, whereby the host government owns and controls the missiles while the United States owns and controls their warheads.

Although an American offer of such arrangements was considered at the time of the NATO deployment decision, it was rejected by host governments. The British and Italians did so primarily on grounds that owning the missiles meant paying for them. Whatever added physical control would be provided was judged not worth the cost. The West Germans did not seek such arrangements for political reasons: the symbol of a putative German finger on the nuclear trigger was deemed too provocative, and not just to the East.

These technical and operational characteristics of the GLCM and Pershing II are critical factors in the military rationales for building and deploying them.

GLCM and Pershing II Contributions to Defense and Deterrence

Any military rationale for nuclear forces in Europe should specify what effects their deployment would have both on stable deterrence and on defense if war should nonetheless erupt.

Constructing a military rationale based on the contributions that additional American nuclear weapons can make to European defense is straightforward: theoretically, in the event of nuclear war there might be a number of critical targets that existing nuclear forces are incapable of attacking or insufficient to cover fully. The quality and quantity of the forces needed would be a function of the number and kind of enemy targets and the probabilities that the forces could survive enemy attack, respond reliably, penetrate enemy defenses, and destroy targets. Although estimates of each of these variables are a matter of some contention, at least the factors that enter the assessment are knowable in theory.

The targets that the GLCM and Pershing II could conceivably attack are largely covered by existing NATO aircraft, the 400 U.S. Poseidon SLBM warheads dedicated to NATO, and U.S.-based intercontinental weapons. As Walter Slocombe, deputy under secretary of defense, testified in 1979, "the requirement for theater nuclear force modernization is not principally an issue of hitting new targets."[10] The new missiles

10. Quoted in William M. Arkin, "Pershing II and U.S. Nuclear Strategy," *Bulletin of the Atomic Scientists,* vol. 39 (June–July 1983), p. 12.

are therefore somewhat redundant for fighting a nuclear war. However, proponents of their deployment insist they are more effective than existing weapon systems for attacking four classes of Soviet targets: strategic and tactical C^3 in the case of Pershing II and troop or tank concentrations and airfields in rear echelons in the case of the GLCM.

By virtue of its increased range and accuracy and its basing location, Pershing II could attack strategic C^3 in hardened sites in the USSR's western military districts with little if any warning. Launched in coordination with ICBMs targeted against Soviet land-based missile silos, it could thus preclude a coordinated Soviet launch on warning, something U.S.-based ICBMs cannot do because they take too long to reach the USSR. American SLBMs, especially after the deployment of Trident II, might be capable of accomplishing the same mission, but in using them NATO could not ensure as coordinated an attack. Pershing II is also designed to attack Soviet tactical C^3—field headquarters and associated communication facilities—that are of special concern to the army. Its longer range permits it to attack such sites deeper inside the USSR than Pershing I could.

The enemy troop and tank concentrations that would be vulnerable to the GLCM are also susceptible to conventional bombing by the deep-interdiction-strike aircraft already deployed with NATO. To use nuclear weapons for such a purpose shows a lack of proportion that would make sense only in the context of general war. And while GLCMs may be more cost effective than aircraft for penetrating enemy air defenses, they may also be too slow to reach targets before they disperse.

That lack of speed would not pose as much of a problem for attacking airfields deep in Eastern Europe because neither GLCMs nor aircraft would be likely to surprise enemy planes on the ground. Using GLCMs could therefore free some dual-capable NATO aircraft, especially those assigned to quick reaction alert, for conventional roles and missions. Reassigning these aircraft would strengthen NATO's conventional capabilities and overall deterrence posture and should be considered on its own merits (as chapter 6 argues). How much incentive the new missiles would provide to make this necessary change is questionable, however. Flying nuclear missions is a source of prestige for the air force's Tactical Air Command (TAC) and not one it will relinquish without a fight. TAC pilots are likely to concentrate their criticisms on the GLCM's inferiority to manned aircraft in performing selective employment truly selectively, its unsuitability for performing deep

interdiction strikes against mobile or dispersing targets, and the imprac-
ticality of firing a GLCM salvo from an airfield while leaving aircraft
behind on the runways or of keeping them in conventional roles once
the war has gone nuclear.

To recognize that nuclear weapons might be used in a war and that
some are marginally better than others for this purpose is not to construct
a convincing military rationale for producing and deploying additional
weapons in Europe. Regardless of their political persuasion or military
expertise, nearly all Europeans know the consequences of nuclear war
would be so catastrophic that no military rationale for nuclear weapons
based solely on their contribution to fighting a war as distinguished from
deterrence is politically sustainable; deterrence, not defense, is their
only military rationale. What these weapons do for stable deterrence is
thus critical to the military rationale for the GLCM and Pershing II.

NATO confronts a variety of threats in Europe, and its doctrine of
flexible response subsumes various ways in which nuclear weapons
might deter these threats. American nuclear weapons conceivably have
at least six different roles as deterrents in Europe:

(1) to deter Soviet use of nuclear weapons against Western Europe;
(2) to deter Soviet use of chemical or biological weapons in Western
Europe;
(3) to deter Soviet conventional attack against Western Europe by
    (a) threatening limited or selective use as a signal to warn of the
risk of further escalation;
    (b) threatening use on or near the battlefield, which carries with
it the risk of further escalation; and/or
    (c) threatening use to defend Western Europe in ways likely to
bring about the defeat of enemy forces; and
(4) to deter Soviet use of nuclear weapons against the United States
in connection with the threat by the United States to use nuclear weapons
for any of the purposes enumerated above.

The weapons, force posture, targeting plans, and declaratory policy best
suited for any one of these uses are not necessarily compatible with
those for the other uses. There is no all-purpose deterrent. Deterring
Soviet use of nuclear weapons against Western Europe, for instance,
requires nuclear forces that can strike targets on Soviet territory after
surviving a nuclear attack—invulnerable long-range theater nuclear

forces or intercontinental systems. Short-range battlefield nuclear weapons, which cannot reach the Soviet border, are no deterrent against this threat; indeed, they may be an inducement to it because of their own vulnerability.

The GLCM and Pershing II add little to existing capabilities for preventing Soviet use of chemical or biological weapons in Western Europe. NATO's already sizable chemical stockpile, along with appropriate defensive countermeasures, should suffice to deter limited use of chemical or biological weapons. In the event of large-scale or indiscriminate attacks, nuclear weapons would come into play, and the GLCM and Pershing II, by virtue of their physical location, are suitable for this purpose. They are also redundant, however, because NATO aircraft and British and French systems are available.

For deterring nuclear attack on the United States, Pershing II's accuracy, range, and speed pose a threat to many Soviet C^3 facilities as well as to a small number of Soviet ICBMs. And plans laid out in the Fiscal Year 1985–89 Defense Policy and Planning Guidance call for increased integration of theater nuclear forces with central systems to facilitate "their effective, coordinated employment."[11] Yet the United States can threaten these targets with its own central systems without taking the political risk of having to arrange European basing for so small an increment to its strategic forces—108 warheads on top of the thousands already aimed at these installations. The GLCM, with its long flight time to Soviet targets, is even more redundant for this purpose. Moreover, deterring nuclear attack on the United States hardly provides an adequate rationale for European-based weapons. Were it not for some presumed deterrent value that they might have for Europe, the alliance would hardly have assumed the substantial political costs of deploying these missiles.

The military rationale for deploying GLCMs and Pershing IIs as deterrents rests entirely on their marginal utility in preventing nuclear or conventional war in Europe. As deterrents against Soviet nuclear attack they add little to the capabilities of American, British, and French nuclear weapons already in place and of U.S. strategic nuclear forces. They could supplement those deterrents only if they could survive a Soviet nuclear attack, but according to present plans, they will not be so

11. Richard Halloran, "New Weinberger Directive Refines Military Policy," *New York Times*, March 22, 1983.

postured. Moreover, the accuracy and speed of Pershing II poses a threat for Soviet C^3 that may compel preemption in a crisis.

Internal Military Rationales

As deterrents against Soviet conventional attack, what cruise and Pershing II missiles would add to existing NATO and American capabilities is open to question. Quantitatively, what difference would 572 warheads make, when the United States already has many thousands targeted on the USSR? Qualitatively, how would they add to the perceived likelihood that the alliance is prepared to initiate nuclear war in response to conventional attack? Faced with these questions NATO developed two internal military rationales for the weapons. These rationales were not only too complex for proponents to grasp but also too nebulous to pin down and scrutinize: they seemed to float away before anyone could see through them.

Filling the "Gap in the Continuum of Deterrence"

Deployments of GLCMs and Pershing IIs are essential, proponents argue, to fill a "gap in NATO's continuum of deterrence." Prior to the advent of nuclear interdependence, the rationale goes, any threat by the USSR to use its intermediate-range missiles against Europe was deterred by an American counterthreat to respond with its intercontinental nuclear forces. Once the Soviet Union acquired sufficient strategic nuclear forces to survive an American attack and retaliate, however, this was no longer so. Under conditions of nuclear interdependence, it is argued, Soviet leaders could come to believe, no matter how incorrectly, that they may use or threaten to use their intermediate-range forces, especially ballistic missiles, against Western Europe while their intercontinental forces deterred any American response. NATO's doctrine of flexible response, which calls for deliberate escalation to the nuclear level if necessary, requires options so graduated that the alliance would not be forced to respond disproportionately to any level of attack or threat. NATO thus needs some equivalent to Soviet IRBMs, though not necessarily in equal numbers.

This reasoning is dubious at every point. First, nuclear interdependence has been a fact of life at least since the early 1960s, a development that did not pass unnoticed in Europe at the time. Yet, at that very time the United States withdrew its Jupiter IRBMs in Italy and Turkey and did not replace them. A less vulnerable alternative, a multilateral force of sea-based missiles, found little favor in Europe. The United States did provide Polaris SLBMs to the British under arrangements that permit their independent use and later assigned some 400 of its own Poseidon SLBMs to NATO.

Second, GLCMs and Pershing IIs are American owned and cannot be used without American approval. If Soviet leaders conclude, however incorrectly, that their threat to strike the United States precludes an American response to their use or threatened use of IRBMs against Western Europe, how could the GLCM or Pershing II alter that conclusion? Their location is of less consequence than the fact that they are unambiguously American, and no president contemplating their use could ignore the possibility that the USSR might respond by attacking the United States. How does the location of American missiles change Soviet perceptions of American will to authorize nuclear attacks on the USSR?

Third, the idea of a "continuum of deterrence" or a "spectrum of options" exemplifies the fallacy of misplaced concreteness. In a blurred way, both constructs presuppose a ladder of escalation—another NATO analogy—with discrete rungs perceptible to both sides and discernible in battle. These rungs supposedly correspond to weapons classified according to range. The ladder analogy inadvertently suggests, however, that the safest place is at its foot, that climbing up is easier than climbing down, and that the only other way to get off is to fall. NATO has various options for using nuclear weapons, but the illusion of a continuum, spectrum, or ladder of escalation only begs the question of what other options, if any, it may need for threatening nuclear war.

Capabilities for Selective Nuclear Employment

At this point, NATO introduces a second military rationale for its new deployments, the need to increase its capabilities for selective employment plans (SEPs) because the threat of general war or massive retaliation is no longer a credible response to conventional attack. SEPs entail "limited" use of nuclear weapons to signal escalation. Deployment of SS-20 missiles and Backfire bombers, the argument goes, greatly augments Soviet capabilities for carrying out SEPs against Western

Europe. New NATO missiles are necessary so that Soviet leaders are under no misapprehension that they could carry out these options without risking a proportionate response from NATO, that NATO would be unable to retaliate with the weapons at its disposal without taking too great an escalatory step. MIRVed SLBMs will not suffice, NATO insists, because their lower accuracy and higher yields would make their use less selective even if fewer than a boatload were fired at once. But use of land-based missiles in Europe for this purpose would carry with it less risk of further escalation because their unique signature, the telltale pattern of trajectory and yield, would be distinguishable from that of weapons in U.S. central systems.

This rationale, too, has its shortcomings. First, it is hard to imagine circumstances in which the USSR would use its nuclear forces in an SEP against Europe. Even in the most bizarre scenarios, Soviet use could hardly be too selective because most NATO targets lie near population centers. While by comparison to the older SS-4s and SS-5s the SS-20 is accurate enough to carry a lower-yield warhead, its yield is still 150 to 500 kilotons. Collateral damage would be unavoidable.

Second, the possibility of Soviet preemption calls into question the utility of GLCMs and Pershing IIs for SEPs. Even if the USSR were not to preempt, any selective use of these weapons would surrender the initiative and invite Soviet retaliation against the remainder of the force. The vulnerability of the missiles and their associated C^3 makes prompt reprisal especially attractive. Knowing this, NATO commanders have little incentive to leave much residual force on the ground. At a minimum they would want to include their full complement in any single SEP package—4 TELs or 16 warheads for each GLCM flight and 3 TELs or 3 warheads for each Pershing II platoon. More likely, they will insist on expending the 27 Pershing IIs assigned to quick reaction alert and all the missiles assigned to a given base—27 Pershing IIs or a squadron of 48 GLCM warheads (as many as 112 at Comiso and 96 at both Greenham Common and Wüschheim) as well as any collocated aircraft. In either event the number of warheads in a package would not make SEPs very selective. And allied insistence on risk sharing might only add to the packages: basing countries may be reluctant to go it alone and may demand that SEPs include missiles from others as well. For the purpose of SEPs, ALCMs in bombers might be preferable to land-based missiles. Yet any SEP package using cruise missiles, regardless of their launching platform, would have to be sizable to ensure penetration of Soviet defenses.[12] The more conservative the estimate of penetrativity, the larger the package. The larger the package, the greater the collateral damage and the less discrete it may appear to Soviet observers.

Third, using SEPs to justify deployment of new missiles has distressing political connotations for Europe because it raises fears that the intention is to confine nuclear war to Europe, that the missiles are intended to substitute for American strategic nuclear forces. That assumes, of course, that Soviet leaders either will not return nuclear fire or will retaliate only against European basing countries and will not respond to the state that owns the attacking missiles and controls their use.[13] Soviet propaganda plays to these fears in artfully ambiguous statements about the true targets of its retaliatory strikes in the event that GLCMs or Pershing IIs are used. And repeated American reassurances have not calmed those fears.[14] However unwarranted European fears may seem to Americans, all talk about needing missiles to conduct SEPs is bound to prompt questions about U.S. willingness to commit strategic systems if necessary.

The Public Rationale: Countering the SS-20

While the foregoing rationales are esoteric enough to confound even NATO strategists, a third has a simplicity tailored for popular consumption: that GLCMs and Pershing IIs are needed to counter the threat

12. Bruce Bennett and James Foster, "Strategic Retaliation against the Soviet Homeland," in Betts, ed., Cruise Missiles, pp. 166–67.

13. That possibility has been ruled out, both in Soviet military doctrine and in authoritative statements from Soviet leaders. For instance, President Leonid Brezhnev denied that limited nuclear war could occur: "Once begun—in Europe or somewhere else—a nuclear war would unavoidably and irrevocably take on a worldwide character." What the USSR would do in practice is, of course, unknowable. Interview with Der Spiegel; see "Excerpts from Brezhnev's Replies to Questions on East-West Arms Issues," New York Times, November 4, 1981.

14. In an unusually explicit discussion of this issue on September 23, 1981, in Brussels, Richard Burt, director of the Bureau of Politico-Military Affairs in the State Department, noted that "the United States took this step [deciding to deploy new missiles] in the full knowledge that the Soviet Union would most likely respond to an attack on its homeland by U.S. systems in Europe with an attack on the United States. Thus the emplacement of long-range U.S. cruise and ballistic missiles in Europe makes escalation of any nuclear war in Europe to involve an intercontinental exchange more likely, not less. This is why our allies asked for such a deployment. This is why the United States accepted."

posed by Soviet deployment of the SS-20. While the USSR was negotiating SALT and thereby codifying parity, the NATO argument goes, it
was taking advantage of Western forbearance and deploying new missiles
considerably more threatening than the ones it already had in Europe.
The deployment of the SS-20, with its increased accuracy, mobility, and
improved readiness, upsets the military balance in Europe. Deployment
of the GLCM and Pershing II would supposedly redress that balance.

This rationale has little to recommend it beyond simplicity. As Soviet
propagandists have been quick to point out, the genesis of NATO's
LRTNF decision antedates deployment of the SS-20s. Site preparations
for the first SS-20s did not begin until 1976; the first bases became
operational late the following year.[15] Flight testing had begun in 1974–
75, about a decade after the design bureau started work on the missile,
although the existence of an intercontinental look-alike, the SS-16, may
have initially confused assessments. NATO's LRTNF, meanwhile,
emerged from a prolonged process of internal deliberations that had
begun with meetings of the Nuclear Planning Group as early as 1974,
although a decision to deploy did not become a real possibility until
1978.[16] The start of research and development on a Pershing I-A follow-
on and on cruise missiles preceded these deliberations. Nonetheless,
without the deployment of the SS-20s, political agreement on NATO's
December 1979 decision would have been considerably harder to achieve.

As with many Soviet-American strategic interactions, evidence of
only a simple action-reaction process is spurious. Both sides, it seems,
were adjusting to a diet of SALT, which whetted their appetites for new
weapons. Faced with a continuing strategic threat from nuclear forces
in Europe and a growing threat from the MIRVing of U.S. central
systems, the Soviets needed a missile capable of surviving and of
blanketing regional targets, especially nuclear ones, in Europe, the Far
East, and the Middle East. They wanted an IRBM that was free from
SALT limitations to replace those missiles previously targeted on Europe
(most notably the SS-11s) that were capable of intercontinental ranges
and hence were SALT-accountable.[17] The Americans, negotiating a

15. Raymond L. Garthoff, "The Soviet SS-20 Decision," *Survival*, vol. 25 (May–
June 1983), p. 113.

16. J. Michael Legge, *Theater Nuclear Weapons and the NATO Strategy of Flexible
Response*, R-2964-FF (Santa Monica, Calif.: Rand Corp., 1983), pp. 32–38.

17. Robert P. Berman and John C. Baker, *Soviet Strategic Forces: Requirements
and Responses* (Brookings Institution, 1982), pp.102–03.

treaty that would codify strategic parity with the USSR, sought an "evolutionary upward adjustment" in LRTNF to reassure those Europeans whose doubts about the U.S. nuclear commitment to its allies were revived by SALT. Politically, they found it useful to call attention to the SS-20 threat, but that threat was only one of many stimuli for the NATO decision.

While marginally improving Soviet intermediate-range capabilities, the SS-20 did not appreciably alter the threat to Europe. Indeed, the missile itself represented little more than a quick fix, allowing force posture to adjust to changing strategic realities in the light of continuities in Soviet military doctrine and within limits imposed by available options—those generated by ongoing research and development processes that were unconstrained by SALT.

Military doctrine gave shape to perceptions of threat. While American strategic doctrine is preoccupied with somehow squaring strategic stability and extended deterrence, Soviet doctrine shows more concern with countering possible American first use of nuclear weapons. In the event of a European crisis verging on war, Soviet military doctrine has a strong presumption for seizing the initiative. Should nuclear war seem imminent, Soviet doctrine calls for preemption—"striking first in the last resort"—and for protecting Soviet assets against enemy preemption.[18] Interpreting this presumption by their own lights, many American strategists see in it a Soviet attempt to acquire the means for a deliberate disarming first strike—as a threat to strategic stability instead of a precaution against American first use. From a Soviet perspective, American practice exposes both American pretense and Soviet vulnerability. The U.S. strategic buildup in the early 1960s, the subsequent deployment of MIRVed launchers accompanied by promulgation of Schlesinger's doctrine of limited counterforce options in the early 1970s, and improvements in Minuteman III accuracy and the funding of the MX, Trident II, and Pershing II against a backdrop of a restatement of strategic doctrine in PD-59 and talk of "protracted" nuclear war in the early 1980s—all called into question the mutuality of deterrence implied in strategic stability while underscoring concern about the survivability of Soviet forces in a crisis.

If Soviet doctrine defined the threat, Soviet research and development dictated the response. Between 1965 and 1968 when Soviet design work

18. The phrase is Malcolm Mackintosh's, quoted in an admirably succinct discussion of Soviet strategic doctrine by John Erickson, "The Soviet View of Deterrence: A General Survey," *Survival*, vol. 24 (November–December 1982), pp. 242–51.

began, reported American interest in the WS-120A, a precursor of the MX that combined massive throwweight with improved accuracy, stimulated Soviet concern about the vulnerability of its missile force.[19] The WS-120A was not built, but it helped encourage Soviet interest in mobility as a way to lower the likelihood of a successful U.S. counterforce attack. By the time that SS-20 flight testing began, the United States was rapidly MIRVing its strategic forces, adding enough warheads to target Soviet missiles, aircraft designated for theater use, and ICBMs many times over. With improvements in accuracy, these warheads had considerable potential for counterforce strikes. At the same time, SALT was under way, limiting the options that the Soviets had for coping with potential vulnerability, and the Vladivostok Accord of 1974 set limits on the number of new launchers the Soviets could construct. That left hardening, mobility, and higher alert rates as possible responses. Soviet design bureaus were having trouble perfecting the necessary solid-fuel technology, however. One design did show promise, but it came in two versions that would have been hard to distinguish for purposes of SALT verification, the SS-16 ICBM and its IRBM counterpart, the SS-20. Perhaps because the SS-16 had a smaller payload than other ICBMs then under development and was reportedly experiencing problems during testing, the Soviets agreed to a ban on it in SALT and went ahead with SS-20 field tests.[20]

From these diverse decisions, the Soviet SS-20 threat emerged. Its longer range allowed it to be based deeper inside the USSR than the SS-4s and SS-5s, out of reach of some American ICBMs. Its mobility and improved readiness also made it less vulnerable to attack and therefore suitable for holding in reserve as a retaliatory force. Its somewhat better accuracy and longer range made it a greater threat to all Western European nuclear installations and C^3 facilities, which were just minutes away. The fact that it was MIRVed obviously added somewhat to Soviet target coverage but did not quadruple it as the simple calculations of some analysts suggest, since SS-4s and SS-5s were being dismantled as SS-20s were being deployed.[21] Moreover, solid fuel enabled the SS-20 to maintain higher alert rates for launching preemptive strikes than did

19. Berman and Baker, *Soviet Strategic Forces*, p. 66. Throwweight is a measure of how much the missile can project. A high throwweight means that it is capable of carrying more warheads of higher yield.

20. Ibid., pp. 66–67.

21. Garthoff, "The Soviet SS-20 Decision," p. 115 and p. 118, note 8, shows the decline in SS-4s and SS-5s.

the liquid-fueled SS-4s and SS-5s, which took hours to ready for launch. It is not, however, more capable of maintaining high alert rates than the SS-19 ICBMs, some of which probably have been and remain targeted on Europe. And the long time it took for the Soviets to deploy a substitute for the SS-4s and SS-5s suggests that the SS-20 was somewhat improvised and not quite the calculated threat of nuclear blackmail that NATO makes of it. A successor system to the SS-20 might be considerably more capable of performing theater missions because of further improvements in reliability, accuracy, and mobility.

As the SS-20 program developed, its size exceeded initial Western estimates. Some bases were added within range of Europe, no doubt to offset new NATO deployments and to provide bargaining chips that might be traded away in negotiations. Others were added in the eastern USSR, virtually out of range of Europe. Four possibilities could account for this growth in Central Asian deployments. First is a shift in targeting responsibility for the Far East and south to bases out of range of Western Europe in anticipation that any arms control agreement would constrain if not reduce deployments within range of Europe. As one Soviet military theoretician put it, "The SS-20 is not a European problem; it would be scientifically correct to consider it only a global problem. Look at the map. Bear in mind the defense problems in the Far East at the seam of three power blocs."[22] Second is an attempt to increase extra-European deployments in the expectation of a numerical constraint on IRBMs regardless of basing location. Third is an anticipated growth in targets in the Middle East and Persian Gulf in the expectation of expanded American presence there, including deployments of nuclear land-attack SLCMs. Fourth is the preparation of bases to receive SS-20s redeployed as part of an agreement to reduce the threat to Europe, the least likely reason of the four in view of the expressed Soviet intention to dismantle any missiles in excess of a ceiling negotiated in Europe and to freeze deployments in the Far East.

As of December 1983 the Soviet Union had 41 operational SS-20 squadrons in all, each with 9 missiles capable of carrying up to 27 warheads. Three more bases with 27 SS-20s were under construction in the east. Of the total 369 missiles already operational, 252 were judged to be within range of Europe, including the 72 based east of the Urals

22. Robert Held report from the *Frankfurter Allgemeine*, June 11, 1981; see "FRG, USSR Experts Discuss Armament Problems," in Foreign Broadcast Information Service, *Daily Report: Western Europe*, June 18, 1981, p. J6.

near Omsk that are more likely intended for targets to the south and east. Another 117 SS-20s were based in the eastern USSR (east of eighty degrees longitude). Those at Drovynaya and Olovynaya as well as those south of the eighteenth parallel near Novosibirsk are almost certainly aimed at China, Japan, and Korea and are capable of reaching other targets in Asia and as far south as the American naval base at Subic Bay in the Philippines.[23]

The rationale that GLCMs and Pershing IIs were intended to offset the Soviet SS-20 is a political argument parading in military uniform. Politically, it may seem unacceptable for NATO to tolerate deployment of a new Soviet weapon without responding in kind. But militarily, for the GLCM or Pershing II to serve as a counter to the SS-20 presumes either that both sides have comparable strategies and thus require equivalent forces, which they do not, or that the GLCM and Pershing II are capable of surviving an SS-20 attack and of targeting SS-20 sites in return, which they cannot. The Soviet strategy of preempting imminent nuclear attack requires missiles that have the accuracy to destroy nuclear forces in Europe but that are themselves not vulnerable to preemption. NATO's strategy is to deter conventional or nuclear war in Europe, in part by threatening to strike targets in the USSR with nuclear weapons. This strategy does not require weapons capable of destroying Soviet nuclear forces, but it does require weapons capable of surviving Soviet preemptive strikes. Neither the GLCM nor Pershing II presently satisfy that requirement. The GLCM cannot threaten the Soviet SS-20 force on its own; it takes too long to arrive on target. The Pershing II force, however, though it lacks the range and numbers to threaten more than a fraction of the total SS-20 force per se, has the speed and accuracy to disrupt much of Soviet C^3. With C^3 knocked out, the Soviets might be unable to mount a coordinated counterattack, and remaining missiles would be vulnerable to further U.S. attack.

The rationale of countering the SS-20 is also vulnerable to Soviet rebuttal. The SS-20 program, as Moscow never tires of reiterating, is merely a modernization of obsolescent SS-4s and SS-5s, which were first deployed in 1959 and 1961, respectively. With the retirement of

23. John Barry, "Geneva Behind Closed Doors," *The Times* (London), May 31, 1983. A range estimate of 4,400 kilometers puts Omsk but not Novosibirsk within range of Western Europe; an estimate of 5,000 kilometers for the SS-20 would encompass both areas. The December 1983 data are in "Weinberger Puts SS20 Total at 369," *Washington Post*, December 14, 1983.

these missiles the USSR will have fewer IRBMs targeted on Europe than it did a decade ago, about 250 SS-20s compared with 649 SS-4s and SS-5s in January 1970.[24] Even allowing that each SS-20 missile can carry up to three warheads, and some do, the number of warheads aimed at Europe will remain about the same as it was a decade ago or slightly greater. Perhaps there could be fewer if all SS-4s and SS-5s are eventually retired and some variable-range SS-11s and SS-19s are retargeted against the United States.

NATO also argues that new deployments would restore the military balance in Europe. The USSR insists they would upset it. Both claims are somewhat disingenuous because both take advantage of the ambiguity in the concept of "military balance." A *balance of power* exists when both sides are deterred from initiating any war, not just from waging nuclear war. By this standard the new missiles make little difference; the critical conditions remain the relative conventional capabilities of both sides and the risk of escalation to nuclear war between the superpowers. Some strategists identify the balance of power with an *operational balance*, the relative capabilities of the two sides for waging nuclear war and the likely outcome of such a war. Yet the outcome of nuclear war in Europe is not likely to be affected much one way or the other by the new deployments. For public perceptions, what matters more than the military calculations of exchange ratios is a *symbolic balance* focusing on static "bean counts" of the number of comparable weapons on each side. Yet any notion of having equal numbers on each side in Europe leaves the United States out of the equation. Because of the decoupling implications of such a Eurostrategic balance, the NATO decision carefully avoids any numerical definition of the threat and specifically disavows matching the USSR on a warhead-for-warhead basis. Numerical equality is the stuff of propaganda, not military strategy.

A Possible Rationale, Largely Unstated

The rationales that NATO invokes for deploying new missiles start with the premise that the alliance might have to initiate use of nuclear weapons to deter conventional war in Europe. But in contemplating first

24. Garthoff, "The Soviet SS-20 Decision," p. 118, note 8.

use, NATO takes upon itself a burden of risk that, under conditions of nuclear interdependence, is best left to the other side.

An alternative rationale acknowledges the vulnerability of NATO's new missiles to Soviet nuclear preemption but regards that vulnerability as potentially helpful in deterring conventional war in Europe. Prudent Soviet planners, uncertain whether these weapons would be used against their homeland in the course of a war in Europe, would have to eliminate them. If GLCMs and Pershing IIs could be rendered invulnerable to other than nuclear attack, then Soviet planners would have to employ nuclear weapons. In so doing they would also have to contemplate striking first at U.S. strategic nuclear forces, thereby putting the United States as well as the European basing countries at risk. In this sense the deployment would reinforce coupling of the American deterrent to European security. And by forcing Soviet leaders to consider initiating use of nuclear weapons as part of any attack on Europe, it would increase immeasurably the risk associated with that attack, a risk they might not care to assume. European-based missiles would thus contribute to deterring the Soviet Union from starting any war.

If NATO has a case for proposed deployment on these grounds, it is largely an unstated one; alliance members barely allude to this line of reasoning when they talk about risk sharing and demonstrating resolve. Characteristically elliptical is an American rationale paper, prepared in 1979 just before the decision to deploy, which notes, "Land-based systems reinforce the credibility of NATO's deterrent because their physical location in the European theater makes manifest their direct role in the defense of NATO Europe, thus advancing deterrence."[25] This rationale is too impolitic to state publicly because it casts the basing countries in the unenviable role of becoming even more inviting targets for nuclear attack than they already are. Yet that very exposure is essential for extended deterrence under conditions of nuclear interdependence. The rationale also tacitly acknowledges the uncertainty of U.S. commitment to initiate use of nuclear weapons on Europe's behalf. In this respect, deploying GLCMs and Pershing IIs has an ambiguous effect on coupling.

Coupling is neither tangible nor mechanical, and arguments about it often suffer from terminal vagueness. In its broadest sense, coupling is

25. U.S. Rationale Paper, "Modernization and Arms Control for Long-Range Theater Nuclear Forces" (Washington, D.C.: October 16, 1979), p. 9.

synonymous with political commitment, and the very presence of American troops in Europe is the physical embodiment of coupling because their fate is linked with that of their host countries. This presence is not sufficiently reassuring, however, to those who want to be certain that a U.S. president would be willing to use nuclear weapons in Europe's behalf. Yet it is not at all clear why having nuclear weapons on the ground in Europe would make a president any more certain to use them.

Proponents of the new deployments sometimes seem to reduce coupling to a question of numbers: too small or too large a U.S. missile force in Europe might imply a diminished role for U.S. central systems and hence appear to suggest decoupling, an issue that preoccupied French strategists at the time NATO was considering the deployments. Yet how small is too small and how large is too large? And what is so special about 200 to 600 missiles let alone 572, the numbers that figured so prominently in NATO deliberations? Finally the success of coupling depends on Soviet perceptions of American willingness to use nuclear weapons. The effect of any deployment or withdrawal of American forces, whether nuclear or conventional, on coupling is ultimately unknowable. Yet such perceptions are likely to be deeply rooted and very resistant to change, responsive to fundamental political transformations, not to marginal military adjustments.

Apart from its effects on the politics of coupling, the military rationale imposes requirements that neither the GLCM nor the Pershing II is especially well suited to satisfy. Both are presently vulnerable to other than nuclear attack. If they could be eliminated by conventional or paramilitary attack, they would not present a would-be aggressor with the choice of either eliminating them by using nuclear means or forgoing any attack on Western Europe. Were the GLCM less vulnerable to nonnuclear attack, it might fit the specifications of this rationale. Pershing II is another matter. Its accuracy, speed, and proximity would pose a threat to Soviet targets that exceeds any requirement for deterring conventional war. What little it adds to deterrence of conventional war in Europe comes at a considerable cost to military stability.

The New Missiles and Stable Deterrence in Europe

Soviet missiles have long imperiled some of NATO's nuclear forces in Europe, in particular its aircraft and artillery, although the bedrock of NATO's deterrent, at sea in submarines, remains invulnerable. Yet extending deterrence to Europe may well call for putting some American missiles on land, where they are inevitably more vulnerable. As long as the Soviet Union has missiles within striking distance of Europe—ICBMs and SLBMs as well as missiles of shorter range—and as long as some NATO nuclear forces and C^3 remain vulnerable to attack, NATO will have some incentive to preempt once it perceives nuclear war to be imminent, and hence some crisis instability will persist in the European theater.

The SS-20 adds little to the crisis instability already present as a result of Soviet SS-11 and SS-19 ICBMs and SS-4 and SS-5 IRBMs targeted on Western Europe. In one respect the SS-20 is marginally more stabilizing: its mobility makes it less vulnerable to attack than the Soviet ICBMs in fixed silos or than the movable though not very mobile SS-4s and SS-5s. But because the SS-20 is solid-fueled and can be readied for launch much more quickly than SS-4s or SS-5s, it can preempt more quickly, thereby adding somewhat to the crisis instability in Europe already posed by Soviet ICBMs.

If the vulnerability of NATO nuclear forces to Soviet attack contributes to crisis instability in Europe, so does the vulnerability of Soviet nuclear forces to NATO's nuclear arsenal. NATO's doctrine of first use has always encouraged the Soviet doctrine of preemption, but until now NATO forces in Europe have not been so configured that they could strike quickly at Soviet nuclear forces and C^3 installations. The GLCM does not alter that condition: it is potentially accurate enough for this use, but it would take long enough to reach the USSR that it would give ample warning for Soviet missiles to launch. It thus does not compel Soviet preemption in a crisis, which in turn would compel NATO preemption—the vicious circle of crisis instability. Pershing II, however, does just that. Its accuracy and short flight time pose a worrisome new threat to C^3 facilities as well as to some missile sites in the western military districts of the USSR. That, plus its own vulnerability, would make it a prime target for Soviet preemption once nuclear war seemed about to erupt. Its offensive potential and its own vulnerability to Soviet attack make it destabilizing in a crisis.[26]

---

26. Much attention has been given to Soviet hints about being driven to a policy of "launch on warning" or "launch under attack." Apart from the technical feasibility of such a policy, it is incompatible with long-standing Soviet command-and-control practices that put a premium on centralized authority for nuclear use. Much more likely is greater reliance on preemption in anticipation of an attack, which is consistent with long-held Soviet strategic beliefs but no less a concern for crisis stability.

If the Soviet Union, in deploying the SS-20, may be adding to crisis instability, some may wonder why NATO should refrain from responding in kind. Even if all SS-20s were removed, however, NATO would still have to live with the significant threat to its nuclear forces and C³ from remaining Soviet missiles, which would give NATO some reason to preempt in a crisis. Nothing likely can be done to coerce or negotiate away that danger. But to react by deploying Pershing II, thus posing a significant threat to Soviet nuclear forces and C³, is perverse. To cope with crisis instability by compounding it is contrary to NATO's own security interest in stable deterrence. The only way for the alliance to reduce crisis instability is to enhance the survivability of its own nuclear forces to the extent that is feasible—by removing some weapons from Europe altogether and by increasing the mobility and hardening the shelters and storage facilities of the weapons that are left. It is more prudent for NATO to live with some residual crisis instability than to add to it by destabilizing deployments of its own.

A Loose Fit between Rationale and Weapon

None of the principal military rationales NATO invokes publicly for deploying the GLCM and Pershing II can stand close scrutiny. None calls for weapons of their particular character or number. All suggest the need for a more survivable force posture. Indeed, the fit between the military requirements of NATO strategy and detailed specifications of these weapons is loose enough that the existence of any military rationale for the NATO decision is open to doubt. A brief review of the origins of the decision strengthens such doubts. It suggests that political considerations were the primary reasons behind the December 1979 decision.

There were always some planners in the Pentagon and in Brussels who saw a military need for new LRTNF in Europe, but their views had little high-level political sanction until 1978. Doctrinal justifications had been circulating among military experts in NATO headquarters for some time, but the experts did not agree on the preferred justification. Moreover, no analysis of the cost effectiveness of alternative weapons received interagency or alliance consideration until after NATO's High Level Group had taken a decision in principle for "an evolutionary upward adjustment" in LRTNF.

Although the supreme allied commander in Europe, General Alexander Haig, was an enthusiast, the U.S. armed services on the whole felt lukewarm at best about the need for new missile deployments in Europe. In their view it was a "national program," one with high-level political interest but not one they were prepared to support out of their budget shares. Indeed, the Joint Chiefs of Staff posture statement for 1978, entered into the record during congressional testimony four months after Chancellor Schmidt's speech at the International Institute for Strategic Studies in London and over a year after Soviet SS-20 deployments got under way, discussed modernization as a way to maintain American nuclear superiority in Europe, not to reverse any imbalance in the Soviets' favor: "On balance, the United States currently retains an advantage in theater nuclear forces, but must continue development and deployment of modern systems to meet the challenge of Soviet modernization efforts."[27]

The particular weapons chosen to be deployed were symbolically rather than militarily suited to the task: the GLCM and Pershing II could be launched on land and had the range to reach the USSR from Western Europe. Moreover, they would be available within four years of the decision. Their availability was less a function of any conscious design to satisfy strategic requirements than the happenstance of research and development processes. When NATO decided to deploy new LRTNF, it plucked the GLCM and Pershing II off the shelf. There were few alternatives.[28] European concern that the SALT treaty would bar European access to cruise missile technology required that cruise missiles, in one form or another, be offered. ALCM numbers were already limited by SALT. SLCMs were ruled out: sea basing lacked the symbolic connection needed for coupling, and submarines dedicated to theater nuclear missiles would be vastly more expensive to build than land-based TELs, prohibitively so when they added not very much of symbolic value to the Poseidon missiles already dedicated to NATO. That left GLCMs. The Pershing II, the extended-range version of the

27. Testimony of General George S. Brown in *Department of Defense Authorization for Appropriations for Fiscal Year 1979*, Hearings before the Senate Committee on Armed Services, 95 Cong. 2 sess. (GPO, 1978), pt. 1, pp. 406–07.

28. The High Level Group considered five options: four missiles (GLCM, SLCM, and extended-range Pershing II, and a medium-range ballistic missile) and the FB-111 H, a variant of the FB-111 A, presumably to be based in Europe and to carry higher payloads over a somewhat longer range. David N. Schwartz, *NATO's Nuclear Dilemmas* (Brookings Institution, 1983), p. 226.

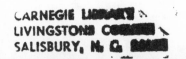
CARNEGIE LIBRARY
LIVINGSTONE COLLEGE
SALISBURY, N. C.

Pershing I-B, could be portrayed as mere modernization of an existing system, the Pershing I-A, which was already deployed in West Germany. An alternative, a medium-range ballistic missile called the Longbow, was judged not to be available in time for deployment late in 1983, although the dates for its and Pershing II's initial operating capacity were fixed largely through political judgment of need rather than technical judgment of availability.

The number of weapons to include in the deployment was a matter of political rather than military arithmetic: it bore no relationship to any relevant Warsaw Pact targets nor to considerations of survivability, reliability, penetrativity, and kill probability. The only military factors that counted were the standard operating procedures of the armed services. The 108 Pershing IIs scheduled for deployment equaled the number of U.S. Pershing Is in West Germany. A one-for-one replacement was thought to be politically palatable, leaving aside the issue of reloads and spares. The 464 GLCMs decided upon was a number derived in part from the standard operating procedures of air force programmers: four GLCMs fit on a TEL and four TELs constitute a single flight, as was the case with the GLCM's predecessor, the Matador cruise missile. In part, too, the number satisfied a political desideratum in the alliance for widespread basing: it was a NATO premise that risks be shared and a West German precondition that it not be the sole continental basing country. Once five countries accepted basing, political bargaining decided how many GLCM flights each took, leaving some room for any negotiated reductions to be shared. Targets for the weapons were chosen only after the December 1979 decision, and even then with a view toward armed services' interests in covering the targets of the systems the weapons would replace.

The military rationales offered are hard to defend in terms of NATO strategy. The specific character of the weapons to be deployed fits the requirements of these rationales loosely. The only rationale consistent with the logic of deterrence was that the Soviet Union, uncertain whether these weapons would be used and unable to ensure their destruction by conventional means alone, would have to contemplate using nuclear weapons to destroy them as part of any premeditated attack on Europe, something they would be unwilling to risk. But that rationale was deemphasized because it was politically unacceptable. The military rationales chosen to justify placement of the weapons are themselves political constructs to satisfy the need for some military reason for an ostensibly military program.

The logical contradictions in the doctrine of extended deterrence and the policy dilemmas that flow from those contradictions lend an Alice-in-Wonderland quality to the rationales for cruise and Pershing II missiles in Europe. The only question seems to be whether Alice or Humpty Dumpty will be proved right.

No matter how artificial their military rationales, however, the deployments would be real in their effects. Were it invulnerable to conventional preemption, the GLCM could arguably add to NATO deterrence by shifting the burden of risk onto the Soviets for initiating not just war but nuclear war in Europe. Pershing II shifts the burden of risk, too, but in a way that would be dangerously destabilizing in a crisis. By threatening Soviet C^3 as well as some SS-20 bases and part of the Soviet ICBM force, yet remaining vulnerable to attack itself, Pershing II virtually compels preemption in a crisis. Its deployment makes sense only if NATO had a strategy of preemption and damage limitation, in short, a first-strike instead of a first-use strategy. NATO, however, has always disavowed such a strategy. The doctrine of flexible response involves the possibility of using nuclear weapons first in the event of conventional attack, but in a limited way not designed to eliminate Soviet nuclear forces on the ground. To counter the Soviet strategy of preemption by acquiring preemptive capabilities of its own only aggravates crisis instability in Europe. Pershing II is the antithesis of the stable deterrent NATO requires.

CHAPTER FOUR

The Politics of the Euromissiles

It is not possible to step into the same river twice.
Heraclitus

THE POLITICS of nuclear weapons, like a river, is always in flux, and as in some rivers, the flows are tidal. No consensus has ever existed on the place of nuclear weapons in NATO strategy. There have been, instead, periods of public and parliamentary quiescence, punctuated by occasional outcry. This recurrent ebb and flow of public opinion is a manifestation of the underlying structure of the issues involved. Even if most people do not follow the logic of deterrence in all its tortuous complexity, they do grasp the nub of the strategic dilemma posed by nuclear weapons—that in order to prevent war, states threaten to unleash forces that could lead to Armageddon. Some try to escape that dilemma, acknowledging only the necessity of nuclear threat or the fear of nuclear holocaust. Others, upon reflection, shift from horn to horn, sometimes emphasizing the threat, other times the fear. In the course of public controversy over nuclear weapons, this response has manifested itself in both the persistent ambivalence of individuals and in the mood swings of publics as a whole. This erratic pattern may reflect another characteristic response to dilemmas fraught with anxiety—denial. Denial is evident in the persistent refusal of many people to think about nuclear weapons and in the lack of salience the subject has for publics at large. Encouraged by inevitable news media distraction and neglect, denial allows most people to forget and controversy to subside. In every past outbreak of nuclear controversy, popular acquiescence and parliamentary acceptance were eventually restored.

Alliance politics is always subject to the crosscurrents of domestic politics—all the more so when the dominant mood differs from state to state. The differences in mood aggravate the inevitable conflicts in the alliance that stem from the contradictions of coupling. Narrowly construed, coupling is the term of art in NATO circles for the credibility of America's commitment to use nuclear weapons, if need be, in Europe's behalf. In a broader sense, coupling binds America to Europe and vice versa; the contradictions inherent in coupling affect both sides of the Atlantic. The United States, for example, experiences a tension between the desire to act as a guarantor of European security and the desire to exercise global influence. Coupling can thus embroil reluctant Europeans in unwanted involvement outside Europe as well as draw a distracted America into permanent entanglement in Europe. The ties binding both feel even more constricting because of the ever-present risk of nuclear escalation and NATO's reliance on that very risk for its security. And when domestic politics pulls allies in different directions, it is no wonder that those bonds begin to chafe.

Europe in Flux, 1977 to 1983

The current nuclear distemper in Europe is but the latest recurrence of a lingering malaise. Transatlantic and domestic politics impelled a decision to deploy new missiles in Europe in 1979, but political currents have since shifted. The change in mood is symptomatic of NATO's inability to sustain political support for its nuclear strategy. The latest phase began with Chancellor Helmut Schmidt's speech to the International Institute for Strategic Studies in London in October 1977. The speech elevated to political prominence a concern that until then only military experts in NATO circles had been brooding about: the nuclear balance in Europe in the context of nuclear interdependence. When Schmidt spoke, center-left governments in Bonn, London, and Washington were attempting to cover themselves against anticipated attacks from the right over a "missile gap" in Europe. Six years later, these governments had fallen from power, and antinuclear tremors were sending shock waves through the polities of Western Europe, threatening to destabilize regimes, exposing fault lines within political parties on the center-left, and setting off a scramble for solid ground among politicians of all persuasions.

What Schmidt said in October 1977 is a matter of record, and what he meant is subject to conflicting interpretations. But he did give public voice to private unease in a way that required some politically visible American response. In the aftermath of the so-called neutron bomb debacle, that response gradually assumed a tangible form—deployment of new nuclear missiles in Europe. Yet, if the GLCM and Pershing II seemed a source of reassurance in December 1979, they no longer did four years later. Although the full history of that decision before and since need not be rehearsed, it is nonetheless essential to understand the political dynamic it set off and the reasons for the reaction in order to see where the current controversy may be heading.

Four events formed the context for the Schmidt speech: a modest campaign, starting in 1974, by a handful of civilians in the American defense community to encourage modernization of NATO nuclear forces and, in particular, to stimulate European interest in the potential of cruise missiles; Germany's reluctance to be seen welcoming deployment of enhanced-radiation warheads on its soil, a factor in President Carter's abrupt reversal on that issue in April 1978; signs of the start of SS-20 deployments in the USSR; and above all, American readiness to conclude a SALT II agreement that did little to constrain the Soviet nuclear threat to Europe. In addition, the Carter administration failed to still rumors circulating in Europe, fanned by American opponents of SALT and their allies on the European right, that the United States was preparing to sacrifice allied interests in nuclear modernization by accepting stringent restrictions on the transfer of new technology and a ban on the deployment of cruise missiles.

According to Schmidt, by codifying strategic parity between the superpowers, SALT neutralized their strategic nuclear capabilities. From his vantage point, the effect was to cast new light on an old problem: "In Europe this magnifies the significance of the disparities between East and West in nuclear tactical and conventional weapons." He did not question the principle of parity, only its application to a limited category of weapons: "Strategic arms limitations confined to the United States and the Soviet Union," he argued, "will inevitably impair the security of the West European members of the Alliance vis-à-vis Soviet military superiority in Europe if we do not succeed in removing the disparities of military power in Europe parallel to the SALT negotiations." In the meantime the balance had to be maintained, by new nuclear deployments if necessary: "The Alliance must, therefore, be ready to make available the means to support its present strategy, which is still the right one, and to prevent any developments that could undermine the basis of this strategy.''[1]

From the outset, then, two tracks, modernization and arms control, were immanent in the Schmidt approach. But although these tracks were in principle parallel, it has proved impossible for modernization and arms control to stay abreast of one another, posing an ever-present risk of derailment.

Initially, modernization forged ahead. Among the ten task forces NATO set up in 1977 as part of its Long-Term Defense Program was one to study nuclear issues. Even before Schmidt's speech, the Carter administration had proposed that the nuclear task force be a High Level Group consisting of defense experts from the various capital cities rather than those already in Brussels so that the program's emphasis on conventional force improvements would not be interpreted in Europe as intended to downplay the role of theater nuclear forces and thus to decouple the U.S. strategic deterrent. Convening regularly from November 1977 on, the experts in the High Level Group, to the surprise of their political masters at home, soon reached agreement. Their recommendation to NATO defense ministers meeting in the Nuclear Planning Group (NPG) in April 1978 called for new long-range nuclear weapons to be based in Europe without specifying either their type or their quantity. In Washington, formal interagency study of the issue had yet to be completed, but the High Level Group recommendation had been prefigured in a closely held letter from British Defence Minister Fred Mulley to Defense Secretary Harold Brown the previous August. So, too, was the form and the rationale for nuclear modernization. In reply to a question raised by Brown at the June 1977 NPG meeting in Ottawa about the adequacy of NATO's present nuclear posture, Mulley wrote of the need for new land-based deployments in Europe that would be more visible than the Poseidon SLBMs dedicated to NATO and more capable than the American medium-range aircraft then in Europe. The rationale he offered for the deployments was the so-called emerging gap in NATO's spectrum of deterrence.[2]

1. Helmut Schmidt, "The 1977 Alastair Buchan Memorial Lecture," *Survival*, vol. 20 (January–February 1978), pp. 3–4. It is fully consistent with views he has long expressed; see, for instance, *Defense or Retaliation: A German View*, p. 147.

2. On the origins of NATO's nuclear modernization, see J. Michael Legge, *Theater Nuclear Weapons and the NATO Strategy of Flexible Response*, R-2964-FF (Santa Monica, Calif.: Rand Corp., 1983), pp. 51–55; on events after the formation of the High Level Group, see John Barry, "Revealed: The Truth about Labour and Cruise," *The Sunday Times* (London), February 6, 1983.

Modernization had few enthusiasts at senior levels of the American government. Reluctance was evident when Deputy National Security Adviser David Aaron was dispatched to Europe in late 1977 to dissuade European governments from that course. He was unsuccessful, but some American skeptics consoled themselves with the thought that NATO had considered deploying nuclear weapons before without ever actually doing so. By the spring of 1978, however, the outcry against the neutron bomb had been politically damaging in the United States as well as in Europe, and senior American officials became sensitive to the need to be seen exercising leadership in the alliance and toughening up the administration's image on defense. Deploying new missiles in Europe was seen by governments on both sides of the Atlantic as a way of mollifying right-wing critics. Although firm commitments on deployments were yet to be made, an abrupt change of course at this point would have exposed the Carter administration to renewed criticism from its right, further jeopardizing prospects for SALT ratification. Center-left governments in Bonn and London had to anticipate comparable challenges from their right, however unpalatable deployments might prove to be to their left.

Momentum for modernization picked up over the summer of 1978.[3] U.S. bilateral conferences with France on June 21 and with West Germany on July 31 revealed their disquiet at the state of the nuclear balance in Europe and at the results of SALT II and the prospects for SALT III. The Germans sketched the outlines of the two-track approach, seeing the question of nuclear weapons in Europe as primarily a political one to be resolved through negotiations, if possible, with a modest nuclear buildup as a bargaining chip. Were negotiations to stall or break down, then new weapons, tentatively a mix of aircraft and an extended-range Pershing, would have to be deployed. An American interagency study, Presidential Review Memorandum 38 (PRM 38), was completed, and an August 23 meeting of the Special Coordinating Committee of the National Security Council endorsed its conclusions. PRM 38 identified the critical issue: whether to base new nuclear weapons in West Germany that were deliberately designed to put a substantial part of the USSR at risk. Its assessment was that the British and French would ultimately overcome their reluctance to deployments in West

3. These events are described in Barry, "Revealed," and in Raymond L. Garthoff, "The NATO Decision on Theater Nuclear Forces," *Political Science Quarterly*, vol. 98 (Summer 1983), pp. 202–06.

Germany but were in no hurry to do so. It anticipated German insistence that the risk of basing be shared with other countries, and it saw some tension between the need for a visible presence to reassure Europeans about the U.S. nuclear commitment to their defense and the greater survivability of a sea-based force. PRM 38 accomplished three principal tasks: it endorsed a need for some "evolutionary upward adjustment" in long-range theater nuclear forces, which was then under consideration in the High Level Group, while downplaying more alarmist projections of the nuclear balance in Europe and eliminating even greater additions to U.S. nuclear forces in Europe; it melded the idea of negotiations with the deployment of additional hardware along the lines suggested by the Germans; and it devised a military rationale for that additional hardware along lines the British had suggested. PRM 38 was a political solution to political problems posed by both the right and the left—so long as it held together.

Yet arms control and modernization were getting out of synchronization as arms control failed to keep pace, a point made by the State Department in meetings on PRM 38 and underscored by Bonn. London and Paris had their doubts about the utility of arms control, but by the January 1979 summit meeting in Guadeloupe they were reconciled to it as necessary, if only for reassuring their publics and satisfying West German political requirements. In a series of working-level conversations in late 1978 and early 1979, the Special Consultative Group, a counterpart to the High Level Group, was set up to design NATO's approach to arms control. Starting in April 1979 it met once a month to draft a set of principles intended to guide the United States in negotiations. By November the work of the two NATO bodies was ready to be integrated into a single decision document for formal submission to NATO defense and foreign ministers in December.

Now there was ample time for arms control negotiations to move ahead: it would be four years before the missiles were scheduled for deployment. But the talks got off to a faltering start. First the framework for the negotiations, the opening of SALT III following ratification of SALT II, was put in doubt when the Senate suspended ratification at the request of the Carter administration following the Soviet invasion of Afghanistan. The Russians also balked, insisting that NATO's December decision had destroyed the basis for negotiations. Under prodding from Chancellor Schmidt to enter negotiations, Moscow came around in July 1980, but the Carter administration, still reacting to the invasion of

Afghanistan and in the midst of an election campaign against Ronald Reagan, was in no hurry to negotiate. Finally, under allied urging a preliminary round of talks took place in Geneva during October, but nothing more happened until November 30, 1981, when allied insistence finally overcame the Reagan administration's reluctance to resume negotiating.

The slow pace of the talks may have been more of a problem for managing public perceptions in Europe, however, than it was for expediting results in Geneva. Obtaining a timely agreement was a difficulty intrinsic to the two-track approach, a point as apparent to proponents as to critics of the December decision. Until deployment, though not necessarily under way, was at least considered a sure thing politically, the Soviet Union would have little incentive to bargain in earnest. Yet the absence of visible progress at the negotiating table could keep modernization in jeopardy because its opponents would have an easier time of rallying and sustaining support than would its proponents.

The political predicament would have persisted for a while regardless of how prudently or impetuously the Reagan administration chose to conduct itself in public, but administration officials exacerbated unease among Western European publics by their all-too-apparent lack of regard for negotiating and their excessive zeal for arming. In May, under close questioning by a BBC correspondent, Secretary of Defense Caspar Weinberger acknowledged the possibility of a limited nuclear war confined to Europe while insisting that the object was to prevent it. Later that month, administration officials disclosed the 1984–88 Defense Guidance, which talked about "prevailing" in the event of nuclear war and called for forces to endure "protracted" nuclear war and plans to ensure that U.S. strategic nuclear forces could "render ineffective the total Soviet military and political power structure." Taken out of context, such talk was unsettling to Europeans.

Partly as a result, protests against the missiles gained strength, and the mood in Europe shifted from seeming unconcern in 1977 to manifest opposition by 1981. In 1977, for instance, Great Britain had accepted without public outcry the addition of ninety nuclear-capable F-111s to American bases there, an addition that more than doubled the American fighter-bomber force stationed on British soil. Also in 1977 the so-called neutron bomb controversy erupted in the American press. Although European governments, anticipating trouble, had shown little enthusiasm for deploying the enhanced-radiation warheads, public reaction was in fact quite mild everywhere in Europe except the Netherlands. Yet the December 1979 decision aroused mass movements against nuclear weapons throughout Western Europe that swelled and intensified with the passage of time. In June 1980 a Labour party rally in rainswept Hyde Park drew 20,000 people, the largest nuclear protest in England since the ban-the-bomb marches of the late 1950s and early 1960s.[4] By October 1981 a London demonstration drew as many as ten times that number. The same day, an equally large demonstration took place in Rome, the biggest there in a decade by some estimates, while others in Milan, Venice, and smaller Italian cities brought the total turnout in Italy that day to perhaps half a million.[5] The following day saw the protests spread to Brussels and Paris, where marches each drew over 50,000 participants.[6] A month later, over 350,000 jammed the narrow streets of Amsterdam to protest the missile deployments, the largest demonstration in Dutch history.[7] In June 1982, President Reagan's visit to Bonn for a NATO summit prompted well over 300,000 protesters to gather across the Rhine from the meeting site to oppose the nuclear buildup.[8] And in the fall of 1983, just one month before the scheduled arrival of the first of the American missiles, rallies across Europe drew the most massive outpouring of all. Over 200,000 protesters assembled in London, exceeding the largest rally of two decades ago.[9] Demonstrations in Brussels, The Hague, and Rome were larger still, and more than 600,000

4. Leonard Downie, Jr., "A-Bomb Opponents Resurface in Britain," *Washington Post*, June 25, 1980.

5. Leonard Downie, Jr., "Thousands in London Protest Nuclear Arms: NATO, Soviet Missiles Assailed," *Washington Post*, October 25, 1981; William Borders, "150,000 in London Rally Against Bomb," *New York Times*, October 25, 1981; Henry Tanner, "In Italy, the Bomb's a Political Issue for the First Time," *New York Times*, November 14, 1981.

6. Edward Cody, "Antinuclear Protest Spreads in Europe," *Washington Post*, October 26, 1981; Frank J. Prial, "50,000 March in Paris to Protest Weapons Buildup," *New York Times*, October 26, 1981.

7. "350,000 in Amsterdam Protest A-Arms," *New York Times*, November 22, 1981.

8. Bradley Graham, "300,000 Demonstrate During Bonn Summit," *Washington Post*, June 11, 1982.

9. James M. Markham, "Vast Crowds Hold Rallies in Europe Against U.S. Arms," *New York Times*, October 23, 1983; R. W. Apple, Jr., "Missile Protestors Jam Central London," *New York Times*, October 23, 1983; Peter Osnos, "Rally in London Draws Crowd of 200,000," *Washington Post*, October 23, 1983; Priscilla Painton, "Record Crowds March in Brussels to Protest New NATO Weapons," *Washington Post*, October 24, 1983; and William Drozdiak, "More Than a Million Protest Missiles in Western Europe," *Washington Post*, October 23, 1983.

protesters, perhaps over a million, took part in rallies throughout West Germany, the largest turnout there in postwar history.

Support for NATO continued to hold firm, but polls registered mounting opposition to the missile deployments as well as rising fear that war seemed more imminent. By 1981 they showed majorities in Britain, West Germany, and Italy against basing in their respective countries; a 1980 poll of Belgians indicated 42 percent disapproval for deployments there.[10] Poll data reported by the U.S. International Communication Agency in the spring of 1981 suggested the dimensions of disaffection; among Italians, 54 percent expressed unconditional opposition to accepting the missiles in Italy, another 22 percent would accept them only if arms control talks failed, 12 percent favored proceeding simultaneously with deployment and talks, and 6 percent supported basing unconditionally. Comparable data for West Germany were 40, 27, 19, and 9 percent, respectively; for the Netherlands, 40, 15, 16, and 8 percent; and for Britain, 31, 20, 19, and 15 percent.[11] Without corresponding data from opinion samples taken before and since and without meaningful measures of the salience of this issue, it is difficult to assess how much leeway governments will have beyond 1983, but the lukewarmth of the support is evident.

To dismiss the public campaign against the missiles as the work of an impassioned but unrepresentative minority or to view the shift in public opinion as an aberration from longstanding support for NATO strategy, as some American observers have tried to do, is to overlook the significance of what has been happening in Europe. Issues of war and peace, as political leaders well know, differ in kind from other public

10. "Majority in a British Survey Oppose U.S. Nuclear Stands," *New York Times*, November 8, 1981; Heinz Vielain, "90 Prozent für besseren Draht zu USA," *Die Welt*, April 30, 1980; "La Majorité des Belges ne Veulent pas des Missiles," *Le Soir* (Brussels), October 19–20, 1980; Connie de Boer, "The Polls: Our Commitment to World War III," *Public Opinion Quarterly*, vol. 45 (Spring 1981), pp. 130–32. On the war scare and confidence in American leadership, see Bruce Russett and Donald R. DeLuca, "Theater Nuclear Forces: Public Opinion in Western Europe," *Political Science Quarterly*, vol. 98 (Summer 1983), pp. 179–96.

11. U.S. International Communication Agency, "Italians Largely Oppose LRTNF and Increased Defense Spending, But Still Support NATO," *Foreign Opinion Note*, June 1, 1981. More recent polls show little erosion in this opposition; see "Polls Show Majority Against Missile Deployment," in Foreign Broadcast Information Service, *Daily Report: Western Europe*, September 28, 1983, p. J3 (hereafter FBIS, *Daily Report: WEU*); and "Reportage on Developments in Euromissile Issue: Majority Opposes Deployment," in FBIS, *Daily Report: WEU*, October 17, 1983, p. L2.

policies: they bear a heavier burden of popular acceptability. This is especially so for issues of nuclear war and peace because they raise the prospect of mass annihilation. Even if the mechanism of denial deflects most people's attention from the nuclear issue and the majority becomes acquiescent, antinuclear sentiment may be slow to subside, and the quantity and intensity of opposition voices can affect the outcome of political controversy in any democratic state. A large and passionate minority prepared to go to tactical extremes can make any NATO military strategy bureaucratically unmanageable and legislatively unsupportable.

The heat of the demonstrations and the tepid public support have already been felt. Although no government has yet fallen over the missile issue alone, it has been a precipitating factor in changes of government in Belgium and the Netherlands and has at least contributed to the decay of the Social Democratic party (SPD)–Free Democratic party (FDP) coalition in West Germany. Deep splits have developed within British Labour, the German SPD, and most Belgian and Dutch parties on the moderate left. At its September 1982 conference, the British Labour party reverted to the unilateralist stance it had abandoned twenty years ago as delegates voted to include in the party's official program a commitment to cancel GLCM and Trident deployments and to close all nuclear bases, British and American alike.[12] By coming out in favor of a delay in deployments at a special party congress in November 1983, the German SPD showed signs of moving in a similar direction. So did other social democratic parties from the Netherlands, Belgium, Denmark, Norway, and Luxembourg.[13] Were this trend to continue, it would narrow considerably the hitherto broad-based party support for NATO strategy, threatening to turn the alliance into a right-wing club.

Europe's Dependence and the Antinuclear Mood

What accounts for the shift of mood on nuclear weapons? Popular aversion to them, some say; yet this obvious explanation is insufficient

12. R. W. Apple, Jr., "Labor Party Reinforces Stand on Disarmament by Britain," *New York Times*, September 30, 1982; "Labour Asserts Unilateral Pledge in New Policy Paper," *The Guardian*, June 18, 1982.

13. See "NATO Social Democrat Parties Oppose Deployment," in FBIS, *Daily Report: WEU*, September 26, 1983, pp. P1–2.

because proposals for adding to Europe's nuclear arsenals have in some instances and some places aroused widespread and passionate opposition but not every time and everywhere. Moreover, to judge from poll data, ambivalence rather than aversion characterizes the present state of public opinion in Western Europe and, indeed, the attitudes of most individuals there.

Some see opponents of nuclear deployments as victims of manipulation by a propaganda campaign from the East, but while evidence of such a campaign is incontrovertible, evidence of its success is not. Antinuclear sentiment is by no means confined to the left in Europe; it extends across the political spectrum to embrace Christian Democrats, Liberals and center party members, and Social Democrats, all of whom are historically unreceptive if not downright hostile to Communist appeals. Indeed, it is a sign of their self-confidence that some leaders in these parties have opposed the missile deployments in spite of the Soviet campaign. Moreover, Soviet propaganda has proved notably uninspiring among the one group from which it might have expected to command allegiance, Italy's Communist party.

The presence of nuclear weapons on European soil is more a symptom than a cause of political unease there, for the weapons symbolize Europe's dependence on the United States for its ultimate security. Dependence breeds paranoia. A Europe caught between the superpowers can never feel wholly secure. As hostility rises between the two rivals, so does the chance of war and with it the fear that the threat of nuclear retaliation may be invoked. As hostility subsides, so does the chance of war and with it the assurance that the threat of nuclear retaliation remains reliable. A dependent Europe swings from one anxiety to the other, with the swings most pronounced in West Germany where no illusion of political control can ease the anxiety of dependence. This anxiety is the source of the current distemper in Europe, no less than of similar moods over the past thirty years.

Yet the basis of dependence has undergone significant change over the course of those thirty years. Although Europe remains ultimately dependent on the American nuclear deterrent, that dependence seems more remote than ever before. The change came about with mutual vulnerability, which has been a fact of life for the superpowers since the mid-1960s. While Charles de Gaulle and other Europeans had long anticipated this development, SALT brought it home to everyone. The shock of recognition led some Europeans to conclude that the American

presence was less a source of reassurance, committing America irrevocably to Europe's defense, than a source of peril that could embroil
Europe in Soviet–American rivalry. A second change was the postwar
economic recovery in Europe, which restored its self-confidence. If the
basis of dependence had eroded by 1983, so, too, had the feeling. But
dependence would remain as long as Europe could not provide wholly
for its own security. For some Europeans the implication was that
European states had to have nuclear forces they could call their own;
for others, that a European defense of Europe could not be nuclear
alone, that conventional defense was the way to ease the anxiety of
dependence.

Amid these crosscurrents lies the Federal Republic of Germany.
Precluded by recent history from having nuclear forces and thus ultimately dependent, yet deriving little reassurance from new American
nuclear deployments on their soil, West Germans wish to raise the
nuclear threshold without putting it out of reach. Many are prepared to
do more for conventional defense but are worried about the budgetary
cost and the political commitment of others. And although West Germany
is moving toward greater cooperation with France in defense, it is doing
so within the framework of NATO, seeking to be more European without
seeming less Atlanticist, perhaps to ensure against too close an embrace
with America, yet without feeding American doubts or loosening American ties. Whatever direction West Germany heads, the conflicting
demands of coupling and commitment will remain a constant preoccupation.

American Challenges to NATO's Working Premises

While the current disquiet in Europe is largely symptomatic of conflicts
among enduring security demands, it has been aggravated since 1979 by
a dramatic if perhaps impermanent shift in America's stance. The United
States has been posing a rather direct challenge to three working premises
of military cooperation with Europe.

One premise is that NATO is a military alliance for common defense
in Western Europe. The United States has recently sought to expand
NATO's mission to Poland and Eastern Europe and to the Middle East
and the Persian Gulf. Yet allied involvement outside Europe has always
been divisive, whether it has been Franco-British intervention over the

Suez Canal, American engagement in Vietnam and Central America, or differences over the Middle East. Despite talk of a division of labor, setting a common course of action has seldom been possible. As Henry Kissinger observed in 1965, "Sharing our burdens would give impetus to Atlantic cooperation only if our Allies have the same view as we of what is at stake outside of Europe and if they believe that the United States would curtail its commitments but for their assistance. Neither condition is met today."[14] Or has been since, one might add. American efforts to foster those conditions after the events in Afghanistan and Iran, whether by lectures on the common cause or threats of unilateral action, have only exacerbated relations.

A second challenge from the United States is to the alliance's shared image of the Soviet threat. American officials argued that Soviet military power grew at an accelerating rate in the late 1970s and early 1980s, even though evidence indicated that growth had leveled off. They attributed the growth to an expansionist impulse, rather than a desperate attempt to preserve the status quo or at worst opportunism. American hyperbole about the magnitude and imminence of that threat was greeted with incredulity in much of Europe, where exposure to Soviet power has been a constant since World War II. Nothing short of a drastic overturning of the military balance is likely to alter the perceptions of most Europeans very much. Indeed, many have sensed a diminution of the threat as a result of the erosion of the Soviet position in Eastern Europe, the diversion of military resources to the Far East and Afghanistan, and continuing economic weaknesses at home. There have, of course, been some notable exceptions in the conservative press and among experts, many of them with a sympathetic ear in Washington. Generally, however, the discrepancy between European and American assessments has aroused more suspicions about American than about Soviet intentions. Suspicion is not allayed when the United States rationalizes its attempts to expand NATO's mission beyond Europe by attributing security threats elsewhere to Soviet manipulation and by proclaiming the "indivisibility" of détente. European support for countervailing pressure against the USSR has continued to be forthcoming; enthusiasm for an anticommunist crusade has not. Americans who see an inflated image of the Soviet menace feel let down by the European response. If

14. *The Troubled Partnership: A Re-appraisal of the Atlantic Alliance* (McGraw-Hill for the Council on Foreign Relations, 1965), p. 231.

the past is prologue, exaggerated assessments of the Soviet threat may discourage European defense efforts, which in turn may stimulate American impatience and pressures to withdraw from the Continent. Unilateralism in America and neutralism in Europe feed on each other.

Third and more fundamental is the American challenge to the alliance policy of deterrence and détente. Western Europe has few war fighters, nuclear or otherwise. To most Europeans the only rationale for NATO's military capability is deterrence, a rationale rooted in the European experience during this century. That experience, Fritz Stern has pointed out, has not been one of "the triumphant use of power" but "of brute and futile power, blindly spent and blindly worshipped."[15] The experience informed the reaction of many Europeans to strategic parity when they came to recognize U.S. nuclear superiority to be a thing of the past and extended deterrence as less than certain. They became skeptical of American attempts to restore superiority. Most are prepared to live with less than certainty. Loose talk from Washington about limited nuclear war, exchange ratios, and protracted nuclear conflict only arouses their fear of war without reassuring them of its outcome. American harping on the need for capabilities to fight and win a nuclear war seems like so much whistling in the dark and does no more to put Europeans at ease. Those who do not dismiss this rhetoric as meaningless deem it unduly provocative.

From a European perspective, Americans talk all too much about moving beyond nuclear deterrence but have too few words to say about détente, none of them very kind. While continuing to sell its own wheat to Moscow, Washington accused Europeans of being bought off by the gas pipeline and other commercial deals with the East. Apart from its blatant inconsistency, to trivialize and demean the European conception of détente in this way was an affront. To some "great simplifiers" in America, détente is an unspeakable French word; to many sophisticated Europeans, détente reinforced by deterrence holds the most hope for survival against an implacable foe in a nuclear world. As the Harmel report noted in 1967, "Military security and a policy of détente are not contradictory but complementary."[16] For Europeans, détente means more than trade with the East; it also signifies a gradual evolution in the two Europes, perhaps leading to a partial restoration of historic ties. For

15. "A Shift of Mood in Europe," *New York Times*, September 2, 1981.
16. "Report on the Future Tasks of the Alliance," *NATO Letter*, vol. 16 (January 1968), p. 26.

some Germans it holds the possibility that the division of Europe is not permanent; for others it makes permanent division more tolerable, enabling families separated by the postwar partition to resume normal contacts as well as commerce.

In Europe the effect of all three American challenges to accepted NATO premises is to heighten the risk of war. American attempts to expand NATO's mission raise the prospect that Europe might be dragged into an escalating war on the periphery. American exaggeration of the Soviet threat arouses fears of preventive war or of an arms race in Europe. American talk of fighting a nuclear war stirs latent European anxiety of a war somehow limited to Europe, and American depreciation of détente does nothing to allay that anxiety. Coming as it does in the context of these other challenges to NATO premises, the decision to deploy new American missiles takes on an added political burden. European fears of reckless abandonment are being laid to rest only to reawaken fears of needless entrapment.

The contradictions that arise from Europe's dependence on the United States and the dilemmas posed by deterrence account for the persistent European anxiety about nuclear weapons and the recurrent mood swings there. Because the contradictions cannot be avoided, however, neither the deployment of new missiles nor the withdrawal of all U.S. forces from the Continent could put an end to that anxiety. The decision to deploy new intermediate-range nuclear missiles forced to the surface the latent fear that the threat of nuclear retaliation may be invoked. Yet U.S. failure to respond at all in 1977, if it came to be seen in Europe as an attempt to avoid sharing the risk of war, could have given rise to the contrary fear—that the threat of American nuclear retaliation could not be counted on. The persistence of the underlying dilemmas, moreover, suggests that simply reversing the December 1979 decision in order to ease present European anxieties might give rise to contrary anxieties a few years hence.

Domestic Differences over Nuclear Strategy

If the underlying security dilemmas are common to all European nations, the play of politics is not. Treating Europe as an undifferentiated mass or treating separate nations as if they were subject to the same pressures risks obscuring significant differences among antinuclear movements and their effects on publics and parliaments. The task of analysis is to account for the differences as well as the similarities from country to country.

Why is public sentiment in the Netherlands, West Germany, and Great Britain so much more antinuclear than it is in France? Popular feelings about NATO are not the reason: the Dutch, for instance, have remained more staunchly pro-NATO than either the British or the French. Ownership of the weapons does seem to matter, however. In the Netherlands and in West Germany, nuclear weapons are symbols of an alien intrusion, whatever the arrangements for their use; in France, they are not. In Great Britain, no matter how much more new Trident submarines may cost in terms of alternative defense or social programs, it is cruise rather than Trident missiles that have thus far borne the brunt of animosity from the antinuclear movement, if not from the rest of the public.

The size and intensity of the antinuclear movements vary from place to place. Public support may be a factor in the variation, but opposition to cruise missile basing is as strong if not as salient in Italy as it is in the Netherlands, even though the Italian antinuclear movement is comparatively weak. The institutional independence of the movements themselves may be a source of significant difference: in the Netherlands, where it has a broad base of support in the churches and is not the province of any single political party, the peace movement is strong. In Great Britain and West Germany the movements are somewhat dominated by leading Labour and SPD figures, and their potential base is narrower. In Italy, the Communist party has tried to take control from more independent leaders and may suffocate the movement in its embrace.

How the antinuclear issues are joined also varies from country to country. Despite its common roots, the nuclear controversy branches off in different directions across Europe. That the bonds of coupling still chafe, for instance, may be evident in the contorted rationales that British and French governments offer for their nuclear deterrents and in the parties' flip-flops on their value. The chafing may be evident in the renewed debate among British, Italian, and even a few German parliamentarians over so-called two-key arrangements for nuclear release of cruise missiles, the desire for at least a symbolic finger of their own on the trigger. And the discomfort may also manifest itself in the visits by Chancellors Schmidt and Kohl to Moscow to talk about the new missiles, preceded in each instance by pilgrimages to Paris and Washington and followed in each instance by allies' expressions of nervousness and by the gibes of opposition parties. The underlying concern may be the same, but the terms and forms of discourse differ.

Antinuclear Movements

The pool of antinuclear activism is fed by various streams emanating from different sources and flowing in diverse directions. Among the movement activists are a considerable number of pacifists who renounce the use of force on religious and ethical grounds. Although they attach special moral opprobrium to nuclear weapons as indiscriminate, they want all weapons out of Europe. Others active in the movement are specifically antinuclear. The environmental wing is broadly so, bearing as much animus toward nuclear power as toward nuclear weapons; the Greens in West Germany are a case in point. A small minority of others within the movement, mostly parliamentarians, strategists, and the handful of arms controllers in Europe, harbors doubts about NATO strategy and wants to reduce its reliance on nuclear weapons.

Some activists have joined with antinuclear groups as a means to other ends. For many that end is to dissociate Europe from America. In West Germany, for instance, there is some feeling that the only chance for German reunification lies in loosening ties to NATO and the United States. In the Low Countries, for quite different reasons rooted in a history of neutrality, nationalist neutralism is also associated with the drive for denuclearization. For radical leftists in the antinuclear movement, U.S. presence in Europe forecloses the possibility of a thorough restructuring of domestic political and economic relations along socialist lines. For still others, the motive is little more than the visceral anti-Americanism often associated with European populism.

The association of antinuclear sentiment with other motives is clearly recognizable in French and West German attitudes. In France, where the antinuclear movement is weak, populist anti-Americanism on the right and left is associated with pronuclear views: the French favor nuclear arming—in the form of the *force de frappe*—as a way of distancing France from the United States. In West Germany, by contrast, where having nuclear forces of its own is out of the question and where nuclear weapons are physical embodiments of the American presence, anti-

Americanism and antinuclearism are conjoined in the minds of many in the peace movement.

Differences within antinuclear movements may affect their staying power. Lacking leaders and structure, indeed even somewhat antagonistic to both, they may be unable to direct and sustain the drives of their diverse adherents in an organized effort that avoids collapsing in cynicism or erupting in violence at unmistakable signs of failure.

However mixed the motives of antinuclear activists and whatever the limits of their appeal, their opposition to deploying Pershing II and cruise missiles could not have developed so broad a base if it were not for genuine doubts about the usefulness of these weapons and for plausible alternatives to the direction the alliance is taking. To describe this opposition as the work of unilateral disarmers or fellow travelers and the widespread sympathy they have elicited as an expression of European pacifism, self-Finlandization, or Protestant angst, as some American officials have done, is to confuse political epithets with political analysis.

To dismiss the antinuclear movements is to misread the political undercurrents in Europe; to assume that the movements will succeed in blocking the deployments is also to misread those undercurrents. Public receptivity to these movements varies from place to place in Europe, but everywhere there are limits to their pull. Some limits are generated by crosscurrents. For every European who wants to cut the tie that binds Europe to America by preventing deployment, there is another who wants to strengthen the connection, by deployments if that seems unavoidable. For every European who conceives of these weapons as an incitement to war, there is another who conceives of them as deterrents to it. Other limits are structural—institutional dikes and dams that channel the flow of public sentiment into policymaking and limit the play of security issues in party and parliamentary politics. European states are not plebiscitary democracies. While it may be that, as E. E. Schattschneider said, "the outcome of every conflict is determined by the extent to which the audience becomes involved,"[17] bureaucracies, parliaments, and party systems can all erect barriers to that involvement.

West Germany

Both the possibilities and the limits of protest are nowhere more evident than in the Federal Republic. There, the party system creates

17. *The Semisovereign People: A Realist's View of Democracy in America* (Holt, Rinehart and Winston, 1960), p. 2.

both a pathway for the antinuclear movement and a barrier to its success. And the political culture sets restrictions on permissible tactics. The movement may be incapable of adhering to these restrictions but violates them at its peril.

The foot soldiers of the West German peace movement are predominantly under thirty-five years old and middle class, drawn from social groups that would normally be expected to vote for the Social Democratic (SPD) or liberal (FDP) parties. However, a substantial minority of potential conservative or Christian Democratic Union (CDU) party members are also supporters.[18] The movement itself consists of some two dozen groups that band loosely together in umbrella organizations to stage demonstrations. It has no formal affiliations with the churches, unions, or political parties, but memberships do overlap. Many in the movement who do vote back the Greens, an environmentalist, antinuclear party, and its antiestablishment partner, the Alternative List, a confederation of single-issue groups with a strong local base in some areas, most notably West Berlin. The Greens and the Alternative List are self-styled antiparties, ambivalent about the very idea of party organization, not to mention participation in the parliamentary game. They occasionally go out of their way to violate the rules of that game and to breach parliamentary decorum in order to assert their distinctiveness from the established parties. Their political style both attracts and repels, which raises a question about their political future. Yet their very presence also raises a question about the future of the established parties, especially the Social Democrats, and perhaps even about the stability of the political system.

For the movement itself and the two parties loosely associated with it, there is a question of tactics: how militant should they be? Only the outrageous can convey their outrage, some activists believe. Whether it is disruption in the parliament or violence in the streets, they urge extreme expression to display the depth of their opposition to and contempt for the positions on nuclear weapons taken by the established parties. And some small groups on the fringes of the left are prepared for physical confrontation once the missiles arrive at their sites. Most activists, however, especially those closest to the churches and estab-

18. The movement's appeal to the rank and file of every party is suggested by polls showing that most CDU–CSU, FDP, and SPD supporters oppose missile deployments. See, for instance, "Polls Show Majority Against Missile Deployment," in FBIS, *Daily Report: WEU*, September 28, 1983, p. J3.

lished parties, believe the German tradition of civil disobedience is too brief and too shallow to tolerate the militancy of a minority, no matter how numerous its ranks or how respectable its background. They believe that physical confrontation over the missiles will mark the failure of the peace movement, not its apotheosis. Yet in any mass demonstration, organizers find it difficult to rein in the intemperate few or to distract public attention from their acts. Although they have tried to redirect the movement's activities away from demonstrating at the basing sites and into more decentralized petitioning and educational efforts, they have not succeeded in heading off confrontations. Nor can they hold out much prospect of success through nonviolence. To those whose watchword is "Be reasonable; demand the impossible," all they can do is recall Max Weber's counsel of caution, "Politics is made with the head, not with other parts of the body or soul."[19] In the heat of the moment the frustration of the disaffected could boil over, causing public sympathy for the movement to evaporate. With little organization to hold off the centrifugal forces at work, the peace movement could break up over tactics.

For the established parties, the movement, if it holds together, presents both a threat and an opportunity. As antagonist of the political norms, way station for the politically disaffected, and alternative rallying point for political allegiance, the movement seems threatening. Yet its constituents are attractive, perhaps fatally so, to the established parties, who want to woo them back into the political system. This ambivalence is especially evident in the stance of the Social Democrats, whose leadership was prepared by 1983 to permit deputies to take part in protest marches, an act Helmut Schmidt had taken vigorous exception to just two years earlier. In 1983 the SPD executive issued a statement referring to the peace movement as "a sometimes awkward companion who on occasion blurs the borderline between reality and wishful thinking," a mild reproof compared to Schmidt's earlier denunciation of the movement as "damaging the established parties and the Western Alliance."[20]

Left-wing Social Democrats, particularly those active in the party's youth organization, generally agree with the Greens and Alternative List on the question of nuclear weapons. They favor hosting no cruise and

19. "Politics as a Vocation," in H. H. Gerth and C. Wright Mills, eds., *From Max Weber: Essays in Sociology* (New York: Oxford University Press, 1958), p. 115.
20. Anna Tomforde, "German Peace Movement Plans Biggest Protest Yet," *The Guardian*, June 15, 1983.

Pershing II deployments on West German soil, eventual elimination of the 6,000 allied nuclear warheads currently based there, and some loosening of ties with the United States. Others, like former Chancellor Willy Brandt and SPD deputy Egon Bahr, architects of *Ostpolitik,* do not agree, but they are anxious to preserve a climate of comity with the East in which expanded contacts can be preserved if not extended. They also fear the impact of the movement parties on the political system. Were the Greens to maintain the 5 percent of the vote necessary to hold seats in the Bundestag, they might hold the balance between the Christian Democratic Union (CDU)–Christian Social Union (CSU) and the Social Democrats, particularly if the Free Democrats were unable to muster the necessary 5 percent. That would force the two major parties to bargain with the Greens in order to form a coalition, to install a minority government, or to form a grand coalition with one another as Kurt Georg Kiesinger did with Willy Brandt in 1966–69. None of these alternatives augurs well for West German political stability. Even if they did not come to pass, and they did not in the 1983 federal elections, they remain a possibility in future Länder and municipal elections. Moreover, since the Greens draw more heavily from the SPD than from its rivals, they threaten to relegate that party to the role of permanent opposition. That would be worrisome to SPD strategists, even if the Greens were unable to sustain themselves. The movement parties would then have served as a stepping-stone for some young Germans, many of them prospective SPD voters, to leave the political system and remain a permanently alienated minority available for mobilization for extraparliamentary action. Those in the SPD who share this analysis want the party to bridge some of its differences with the Greens, putting itself in position for Green supporters to return should the Green party fall apart.

This strategy requires the Social Democrats to shift leftward on the nuclear issue as well as on some socioeconomic questions. Yet the strategy has its pitfalls. Too sharp a leftward lurch could shatter the party's image of moderation and respectability so carefully built up by Brandt and Schmidt. As a member of the "Bürgermeister group" in the 1950s, Brandt helped push the party to adopt the Godesberg program at the 1959 party conference in Bad Godesberg that renounced its Marxist legacy and embraced democratic socialism less as credo than as a general orientation. That platform gave the SPD the aura of a party capable of assuming responsibility for governance in the eyes of many West Germans. Schmidt solidified the other facet of the SPD's image as

POLITICS OF THE EUROMISSILES

a responsible party, the subtle mix of loyalty to and independence from the American alliance. Too close an identification with the Greens, many Social Democrats feel, risks driving away centrist voters and conceding the government to the CDU–CSU, much as it did in the 1950s. Too warm an embrace of the protest movement, moreover, is out of keeping with the SPD's history. It has never been a populist party; it is a parliamentary faction. Even its Marxist heritage was the work of intellectuals, not trade unionists. Reflecting the leadership's uneasiness about associating with the protesters, Karsten Voigt, the SPD spokesman on foreign policy, has been quick to reject calls on the party's left for a general strike in response to the missile deployments, and Hans-Jochen Vogel, Schmidt's successor as party leader, has drawn a clear line on the issue of alliance membership; "For us, the Alliance is not up for discussion, let alone discontinuation."[21]

One way out of the party's quandary is a negotiated solution in Geneva. Arms control, unless it obviates the need for any new missiles, is unlikely to placate the millenarians among the peace movement, but it is a unifying theme in a party divided over the wisdom of deployments. It has been a continuing refrain for the SPD leadership, sounded as often if not as subtly by Vogel as it was by Schmidt. Yet the SPD has continued to drift leftward on the missile issue, drawn by the need to hold onto its left and repelled by Washington's doctrinaire stance.

The FDP, which brought down the Schmidt government by joining forces with the CDU and its Bavarian wing, the CSU, in the fall of 1982 to form the Kohl government, is also haunted by the peace movement. While its left is not as receptive to the antinuclear appeal as the SPD's, it does not have as much margin for error. A loss of just some of its younger supporters could drop the FDP below the critical 5 percent threshold, precluding the party from the balancing role it has played in the Bundestag for the past two decades. (The erosion of support has already had that effect in several Land parliaments.) The FDP and its chairman, Hans-Dietrich Genscher, barely survived its reversal of alliances, garnering just 6.9 percent of the returns in the March 1983 voting, down from 10.6 percent in the 1980 election. While Genscher

21. Voigt took issue with Oscar Lafontaine, an outspoken member of the party's left wing, at a European disarmament conference in Berlin in May 1983; see "Disarmament Conference Opens in West Berlin," in FBIS, *Daily Report: WEU*, May 13, 1983, pp. J4–5. Vogel's remark came in Bundestag debate; see "FRG Consensus Urged in Disarmament Issue," in FBIS, *Daily Report: WEU*, May 13, 1983, p. J3.

stayed on as party chairman and as foreign minister in the new coalition, he felt compelled to press openly for changes in the American negotiating position, first in the course of the 1983 election campaign and again in the fall as the date for deployment approached.

For the CDU, the SPD's bridge to the peace movement is a tempting target. By questioning the party's allegiance to NATO or its patriotism, it could force the SPD to rally to defend the bridge in hopes that this stance will alienate enough SPD voters to make the CDU a majority party again. There are others, especially in the CSU, who are itching to confront the demonstrators in the expectation that the resulting violence will attract support to the government. Many in the CDU question these tactics, however. The new missiles, they feel, are too unpopular for the coalition to take full political responsibility for deploying them. They prefer having some SPD backing to having a unified SPD in opposition to deployments, so that they would not draw too sharp a partisan line and put the CDU on the wrong side of it. They also want to minimize violent confrontations for fear that they might set off social unrest or evoke painful memories of the political instability of the Weimar Republic. Moreover, to seem overly compliant with American wishes without showing any signs of independence might discomfort some of the nationalist or Gaullist elements in the party, not the least of them followers of the CSU's Franz Josef Strauss. Helmut Kohl, though relatively inexperienced in foreign policy, has mastered the intricacies of intraparty maneuvering. He seems to have found, as did his predecessor as chancellor, that the missile issue is more a matter of fancy footwork than of firm stances. He waged a campaign of reassurance in the 1983 elections and has recently shown signs of looking for a negotiated way out of deploying Pershing II, if not cruise missiles.

The play of party politics has been reflected in public positions taken by the West German government from the start of the missile controversy. Maneuvering toward a decision on enhanced-radiation warheads, Chancellor Schmidt refused to issue an open invitation to deploy the artillery rounds in the Federal Republic. Whipsawed by opposition on both his right and left—the CDU–CSU in the Bundestag and the SPD left—he made his priorities clear at a November 1977 party congress: "All attempts to drive a wedge between myself and my party are without purpose: they result from naive illusions. I stand in the middle of my party."[22]

22. *Parteitag der Sozialdemokratischen Partei Deutschlands, Protokoll der Verhandlungen, von 15 bis 19 November 1977* (Bonn: Vorstand der SPD, 1977), p. 177.

In 1977 and 1978 the CDU began raising the specter of a missile gap. With the start of SS-20 deployments in a context of strategic parity, the party's defense spokesman, Manfred Wörner, somberly warned that "Western Europe finds itself all of a sudden, and for the first time, in the role of nuclear pawn of the Soviet Union." Even worse, "now the United States is for the first time susceptible to nuclear blackmail on account of its commitment to the Alliance. . . ."[23] This domestic challenge to the SPD line of détente within the framework of the alliance formed the context for Schmidt's speech at the International Institute for Strategic Studies. Having answered the challenge from the right, he moved to placate his left by emphasizing that arms control might vitiate the need for deployments. Others in the SPD were prepared to go further. Egon Bahr spoke of a decision to produce that was separate from a decision to deploy, with the missiles to remain in the United States pending results of negotiations. Still others envisioned a second decision point in December 1983 to reconsider deployments in the light of arms control progress to that point.[24] Both stands were antithetical to NATO's formulation of the 1979 decision, which spoke only of adjustment in the light of arms control results without saying when that adjustment might be made. Some CDU members began muttering about Finlandization and openly questioned the SPD's allegiances. The refrain was soon picked up across the Atlantic. Finlandization was always taken as a partisan gibe in Bonn if not in Washington, and Schmidt's rejoinder was characteristically blunt: "That notion is being nurtured by people who for domestic reasons either fight my government in Bonn or fight the Carter Administration in Washington."[25]

Having taken the initiative in 1977 and again in early 1979 for a two-track approach, Schmidt was now content to assume a less visible role in NATO's decision. He took refuge in the Four Power Pact committing West Germany not to go nuclear: "As far as I can see into the future, any German Federal Government must abide by this situation under international law. Consequently, on questions concerning nuclear armament it can neither take initiatives nor assume key roles. But it can

23. "Abrüstung nur bei Gleichgewicht der Kräfte—Westeuropa braucht mehr Mitsprache bei strategischen Fragen," *Deutschland Union Dienst,* January 10, 1978.

24. *Der Spiegel* interview in "SPD Leadership Assesses Brezhnev Disarmament Proposal: Federal Manager Bahr," in FBIS, *Daily Report: WEU,* October 18, 1979, pp. J3–6. For a moderate left SPD view, see Alfons Pawelczyk interview in *Frankfurter Rundschau* in "SPD Armament Expert on Procedures for Arms Balancing," in FBIS, *Daily Report: WEU,* November 29, 1979, p. J2.

25. "An Interview with Helmut Schmidt," *Time* (June 11, 1979), p. 39.

take initiatives indeed if arms control and disarmament are involved. This is what we have certainly done."[26] He rejected any dual-key arrangement for controlling the use of the weapons: "We do not want to become a nuclear state, nor do we want to share in determining, or to determine, the nuclear strategical decision-making of the nuclear weapons states even through a back door."[27] He also insisted that West Germany not be the sole Continental ally to accept new missiles on its soil and that all the allies join in the December decision. He worked hard to bring the others along.

The reticence on deployments and the insistence on nonsingularity sprang from similar sources. One was self-protection at home: having other European governments on board, some of them left-of-center coalitions, would make it easier for the SPD to go along. Another was recognition of West Germany's place in the world. Putting long-range theater nuclear missiles there was "a hard decision," Schmidt often reminded Americans: "Think of a situation where an American Administration puts 5,000 nuclear rockets into Oregon and makes plans for adding some hundreds that could hit the Soviet Union and thereby make Oregon a great target area for Soviet missiles."[28] Still another was recognition of West Germany's place in history, which made nuclear weapons there a sensitive subject for Europeans, both in the East and in the West. Initiatives could all too easily be mistaken for self-assertiveness. To the insistence of Franz Josef Strauss that the Federal Republic be prepared to accept the new missiles unconditionally—"We must learn to bear responsibility on our own and not always hide behind others"—Schmidt rejoined, "We must not want to grow bigger here than our other European allies." Militarily as well as politically, this was an "essential prerequisite" to "the psychological balance in Europe."[29] To Schmidt the Federal Republic's exposed geographical position and

26. "Schmidt Discusses NATO Defense, Domestic Issues," in FBIS, *Daily Report: WEU*, November 28, 1979, p. J6.

27. "Schmidt Speech in Bundestag Security Debate," in FBIS, *Daily Report: WEU*, February 16, 1979, p. J4.

28. "Excerpts from Schmidt Interview on Key Issues," *New York Times*, January 3, 1982.

29. "Strauss Interviewed on NATO Arms Plan, Gromyko Visit," in FBIS, *Daily Report: WEU*, December 5, 1979, p. J8; "Chancellor Schmidt Responds to Bundestag Criticism," in FBIS, *Daily Report: WEU*, March 4, 1980, p. J13. Further elaboration of Schmidt's views appears in "Schmidt on International Role, Ties with U.S., Domestic Issues," in FBIS, *Daily Report: WEU*, August 8, 1980, pp. J1–9.

its status as a part of a divided Germany in a divided Europe conveyed a sense of importance yet vulnerability that could only be assuaged by sharing military and political burdens and risks.

Yet within a month of the December decision, Soviet insistence that SALT II be ratified and the deployment decision be revoked as preconditions for entering into negotiations and the Carter administration's request to suspend ratification in the wake of the invasion of Afghanistan were undoing the premises on which the SPD had accepted the two-track approach. Schmidt was scheduled to go to Moscow in early summer, where he intended to urge the opening of talks on theater nuclear weapons without preconditions. At an SPD campaign rally in Essen on April 12, he highlighted positive signs for détente: an agreement with the German Democratic Republic about to take effect on traffic between Berlin and the West and a meeting the next month in Vienna between Secretary of State Cyrus Vance and Foreign Minister Andrei Gromyko. Then he addressed the buildup of SS-20s and Backfires:

The Soviet Union says it is prepared to negotiate, but only if the West will rescind its decision. In the meantime, it wants to continue building a missile every week and two-and-a-half planes a month. That will not do. A first possible step for solving this crisis could be for both states simultaneously to renounce for a certain number of years the production of new additional or more modern medium-range missiles, so that this interim period of years can be used for negotiations on bilateral limitation—limitation to a balance on a lower level.[30]

While Schmidt's suggestion was read by some in Washington as accepting the Soviet idea of a moratorium, it was equally consistent with the interpretation Bonn later gave that it called for a unilateral moratorium on additional Soviet deployments because NATO's new missiles would not be ready to go into the field for another three-and-a-half years.

The subtlety was lost in the ensuing noise. The right was quick to pounce on the proposal. Franz Josef Strauss, then the leading CDU–CSU candidate for chancellor, called it "an open affront against NATO and an undisguised provocation against the United States" and denounced Schmidt as "a security risk."[31] It was campaign rhetoric with a harshness that opponents of Strauss had every reason to expect.

30. "Chancellor Defines Stance on International Problems," in FBIS, *Daily Report: WEU,* April 18, 1980, p. J8. Earlier press reports have a slightly different version, "Schmidt Analyzes World Situation in 11 Apr Speech," in FBIS, *Daily Report: WEU,* April 15, 1980, p. J5.
31. "Strauss Views Schmidt's Negotiations Proposal," in FBIS, *Daily Report: WEU,* April 17, 1980, p. J10.

Insisting he would "stick to his guns," Schmidt restated the proposal in modified form before an SPD party congress in Essen June 9.[32] At this point Washington intervened. A brusque note from President Carter, drafted at the behest of National Security Adviser Zbigniew Brzezinski, warned against any departure from the NATO decision. The letter was promptly leaked in Washington to a German magazine, *Stern*. Schmidt, who had already expressed indignation at American sniping, was outraged.[33] Calling the Carter letter "astonishing," he told a *Washington Post* interviewer he "found it difficult to understand" why his suggestion "should have created such a fuss in Western circles." And he pointedly stood behind the need for some independence of action: "It has been my habit for twenty years to voice my ideas without asking anybody else." Influence in the alliance did not flow one way across the Atlantic: "It is a false conception to believe European governments don't have a right to voice their concern, don't have a right to make their proposals."[34]

Schmidt did not renew his suggestion in Moscow on June 30 and July 1, but he did come home with a Soviet commitment to drop its two preconditions to opening talks. He was greeted by ridicule from Strauss, who questioned the attempt by him or any other West German to mediate between Washington and Moscow: "That hat is too big for us and those boots [are] too big." Strauss said that he did not want to compare Schmidt's role to that of Chamberlain and Daladier, but he did charge that his trip came "against the background of an endangered alliance, as a unilateral action and without a mandate from the alliance partners."[35] To those who govern in Bonn—or want to—loyalty to the alliance is a hallmark of responsibility. It is possible for a West German to play the role of loyal opposition inside the alliance, but within limits. Domestic opponents were always ready to attack too great a show of independence; they are now willing to question too small a show as well. As Schmidt

32. "Chancellor Schmidt Addresses SPD Congress 9 Jun in Essen," in FBIS, *Daily Report: WEU*, June 13, 1980, p. J1.

33. Just days before receiving the letter, he reportedly told a visitor, Senator Joseph Biden, "I want you to know that the United States can depend on the bloody Germans." Bradley Graham, "U.S., W. Germany Tangle on Issue of Stationing Missiles in Europe," *Washington Post*, June 19, 1980; "Public Discussion Continues over Carter Letter to Schmidt," in FBIS, *Daily Report: WEU*, June 20, 1980, pp. J4–7.

34. Bradley Graham, "Schmidt Defends His Missile Proposals: Carter Letter 'Astonishing,' " *Washington Post*, June 21, 1980.

35. "Soviet Reported Willing to Drop 2d Bar to Talks," *New York Times*, July 4, 1980; "Strauss Response to Government Statement on USSR Trip," in FBIS, *Daily Report: WEU*, July 9, 1980, pp. J2–3.

declared repeatedly during his chancellorship and since: "The one who suppresses criticism of a friend cannot remain a good friend in the long run. Whoever doesn't represent his own interests to his friend, can thus lose respect and friendship. For the very reason that I have been a critical partner of four American presidents and administrations, I profess my support for German–American friendship once more at this time."[36]

The Reagan administration presented the Schmidt coalition government with new challenges; its openly hostile rhetoric about arms control, its accelerated program of strategic force modernization, and its talk of nuclear superiority threatened to derail the two-track approach and further erode SPD support for the December decision. When Reagan became president-elect, Schmidt moved to embrace him: "I believe that the decisive thing is that Reagan does not want to negotiate on all parts of SALT II, but that primarily—according to everything I have heard—he is firmly determined to promote the SALT process as a whole."[37] These and similar remarks infuriated SALT opponents in the Reagan camp. In the face of Reagan's announced policy of not meeting with foreign leaders until inauguration, Schmidt paid a courtesy call on the president-elect and returned home to pronounce him back on the track. In March, Foreign Minister Hans-Dietrich Genscher met with Secretary of State Alexander Haig and won a grudging commitment "to continue close consultations" on implementing both tracks of the December decision.[38]

Nonetheless, by May the Reagan administration's delay in returning to Geneva and its bid to reopen the possibility of deploying enhanced-radiation warheads in Europe had the SPD seething with dissent. A regional party congress in Baden-Württemberg, where the Greens had shown strength in 1980, proposed renouncing NATO's counterarming if there were a corresponding reduction in already deployed SS-20 missiles. It called on the party to review its endorsement of the dual decision at the next party congress: "Questioning one part of the dual decision is also questioning the other," the resolution warned. "We will not

36. "Schmidt 'Personal Statement' to Bundestag 1 Oct," in FBIS, *Daily Report: WEU*, October 4, 1982, p. J6.
37. "Chancellor Schmidt Interviewed on U.S. Visit, NATO Issues," in FBIS, *Daily Report: WEU*, November 18, 1980, p. J1. Right-wing Reaganauts vented their displeasure to Rowland Evans and Robert Novak, "An End-Run Around Reagan," *Washington Post*, November 28, 1980.
38. "Agreed Background Summary of the United States and the Federal Republic of Germany Talks," Washington, D.C., March 9, 1981 (mimeo).

participate in a policy which is aimed at military superiority.''[39] SPD
organizations in South Hesse, Saarland, Lower Saxony, Schleswig-
Holstein, Bavaria, and Hamburg all took exception to the party's support
of the 1979 decision. A position paper drafted by members of the security
policy commission of the SPD executive board invoked the party's
heritage in underscoring the possibility of a moratorium on nuclear
deployments put forth at the Berlin party congress in 1979: ''Without
the longing for peace, antimilitarism and an active peace and disarmament policy, the SPD would lose its identity as a social democratic
party.''[40] Even as staunch a supporter of the December decision as Peter
Corterier, chairman of the SPD's foreign and security policy working
group in the Bundestag, was openly critical of actions and statements of
the Reagan administration, complaining that they had ''made things
more difficult than they need be'' in Western European politics.[41] At the
same time Defense Minister Hans Apel moved to allay suspicions that
the Reagan administration was intent on confining a nuclear war to
Europe. ''Let no one believe,'' Apel declared, ''that war is going to
break out in Europe while the Americans are watching it [on] NBC in
color.''[42] Schmidt himself tried to bring SPD backbenchers into line by
threatening the ultimate recourse of a prime minister in any parliamentary
system, a resignation that would likely force new elections.[43] Meanwhile,
his coalition partner and foreign minister, the FDP's Hans-Dietrich
Genscher, was warning of a collapse of the coalition if the SPD were to
back away from endorsing the December decision: ''It would not be the
Free Democratic party—which sticks to the policy of the Federal
Government—which would leave the government, but the SPD would
be departing from the government if it proposes to deviate from the
policy of the government.''[44]

39. ''Baden-Württemberg SPD Opposes NATO Decision,'' in FBIS, *Daily Report:
WEU,* May 20, 1981, pp. J9–12. It had the support of four ministers in Schmidt's own
cabinet.
40. Text of position paper, ''SPD Representatives Define Stance on NATO Decision,'' in FBIS, *Daily Report: WEU,* May 29, 1981, pp. J1–4. Quote is from p. J1.
41. John Vinocur, ''Bonn Official Openly Critical of Reagan Approach,'' *New York
Times,* February 13, 1981.
42. ''Defense Minister Comments on U.S. Missile Policy,'' in FBIS, *Daily Report:
WEU,* July 13, 1981, p. J3.
43. John Vinocur, ''Schmidt Asserts He Might Resign on Missile Issue,'' *New York
Times,* May 18, 1981; ''Schmidt Discusses NATO Decision, Disarmament,'' in FBIS,
Daily Report: WEU, July 1, 1981, p. J1.
44. ''Leaders Comment on Schmidt Threat, NATO–SPD Issue: Foreign Minister,''
in FBIS, *Daily Report: WEU,* May 20, 1981, pp. J6–7.

Nothing short of a resumption of the Geneva talks by those the left called the "nuclear cowboys" could slow the erosion of SPD support for the December decision. In a visit to Washington in May, Schmidt pressed for movement on arms control. On September 24 the United States and the Soviet Union announced that the negotiations would resume November 30. On November 18 the president himself formally unveiled the so-called zero option in a speech televised live in Europe. "The United States," he pledged, "is prepared to cancel its deployment of Pershing 2 and ground-launched missiles if the Soviets will dismantle their SS-20, SS-4, and SS-5 missiles."[45] Accompanying background briefings for the press made it clear that at least some administration officials doubted the proposal's negotiability but stressed its appeal to European publics by holding out hope for no new Western deployments. Schmidt joined other NATO leaders in welcoming the offer, but there were indications soon thereafter that he did not expect the zero option to dissipate antinuclear pressures within the SPD. While taking credit for his part in formulating the approach and in persuading a reluctant United States to adopt it, he also noted that differing assessments of the military balance by the two sides were inflated for propaganda reasons and that their opening positions in the talks were far apart but that both were flexible, which had the obvious implication that the zero option was not the take-it-or-leave-it proposition senior Pentagon civilians intended it to be. He also moved to establish himself in a visible role as interlocutor if not mediator with Moscow at a meeting with Leonid Brezhnev in Bonn a week after Reagan's announcement.

In August 1982 the FDP joined forces with the CDU and CSU to bring down the Schmidt government. The reversal of alliances nearly shattered the FDP, and the bitter election campaign that followed in early 1983 threatened to eliminate the party from the Bundestag. With the public overwhelmingly in favor of postponing deployments, SPD leader Hans-Jochen Vogel campaigned on a platform of accepting new missiles only under extreme circumstances. Less than six weeks before the March 6 election, with polls showing the FDP below the critical 5 percent level, Foreign Minister Genscher attempted to reassert his party's role as a moderating force in any coalition government it joined. One of the vehicles he chose for doing so was to move openly against the zero option and to advocate an "interim solution" in the negotiations.[46] He was not alone in spurning the American negotiating position. Four days later, Franz Josef Strauss, who was himself seeking the foreign minister's portfolio in the next government and whose claim to it would be immeasurably strengthened by the elimination of the FDP from the coalition, joined Genscher in attacking the zero option as "unattainable and absurd." Asked in an interview why Kohl continued to back the option publicly throughout the election, Strauss remarked, "I say what Kohl thinks and he thinks what I say."[47] The day before, SPD leader Vogel had visited the White House and begged the administration to change its position, but the Reagan administration held its ground; to shift at that time, it was claimed, would legitimate the SPD's opposition to deployments. Less than a week after the election in which the CDU–CSU–FDP coalition was returned to power, Kohl publicly came out for a move away from the zero option.[48] He did not propose a specific alternative, even in private, however; he was not yet prepared to define his own acceptable outcome for the negotiations and to insist on putting it on the table.

By the summer of 1983 pressures were mounting in all three major parties to alter their stands on the missiles. Party leaders across the spectrum, from Karsten Voigt, the SPD spokesman on foreign affairs, to Hans-Dietrich Genscher, the FDP leader and foreign minister, and even to Chancellor Kohl himself, began publicly hinting at the desirability of a return to the so-called walk-in-the-woods formula (discussed in chapter 5), which envisioned cancelling Pershing II deployment in return for a reduction in Soviet SS-20s within range of Europe.[49]

In the face of the continuing protests, tepid public support, and the Greens' call for a referendum on deployments, the government scheduled

46. William Drozdiak, "Bonn's Ruling Coalition Strained," *Washington Post,* January 20, 1983.

47. Robert J. McCartney, "Key W. German Conservative Dismisses U.S. 'Zero Option,' " *Washington Post,* January 24, 1983; William Drozdiak, "Deployment of Missiles in Europe is 'Unavoidable,' Strauss Says," *Washington Post,* February 17, 1983.

48. William Drozdiak, "Kohl Urges U.S. to Make Interim Offer on Missiles," *Washington Post,* March 13, 1983.

49. For the respective party leaders' comments, see "Voigt Pleads for 'Walk in Woods' Compromise," in FBIS, *Daily Report: WEU,* August 1, 1983, p. J2; "Genscher Comments on CSCE, Missile Issue," in FBIS, *Daily Report: WEU,* July 19, 1983, pp. J1–2; "U.S. Doubts on Bonn's Missile Stance Grow," in FBIS, *Daily Report: WEU,* July 28, 1983, pp. J3–4.

a Bundestag debate and vote on the missiles for November 21–22 to ratify and lend legitimacy to the deployments. But special party congresses convened prior to the debate gave further testament to the misgivings of West German political elites. In its 1983 election program and again in a June policy declaration by parliamentarians, the SPD had gone on record as pledging that "if the Geneva negotiations should not achieve a result because one side is not prepared to show understanding, this will decisively influence our decision" on deployments.[50] In November, spurning an impassioned appeal by Helmut Schmidt and repudiating its 1979 endorsement of the two-track decision, the party congress by a 383–14 vote rejected stationing new missiles in West Germany in the absence of arms control results. At the FDP congress, Foreign Minister Hans-Dietrich Genscher managed to carry the day for the governing coalition, but one delegate in three backed opposition motions to postpone the deployments or to eliminate Pershing IIs from the package. Amid clashes between demonstrators and police outside and the Greens' warnings of a campaign of civil disobedience within, the Bundestag voted 286–226 to endorse the start of deployments. Only one FDP member broke party discipline and abstained. An earlier SPD motion to delay deployments lost 294–169 with 39 abstentions, mostly Social Democrats and among them Helmut Schmidt. Perhaps the most telling moment came as Willy Brandt was calling upon West Germany "to break down the East-West confrontation and to make the transition to a European peace order." Schmidt, sitting on a back bench, fashioned airplanes out of paper, labeled them Pershing II, and winged them at SPD colleagues.

No less than Schmidt, Kohl is acutely aware of West Germany's exposure in the event of deployments. A Soviet counterdeployment is worrisome enough, but West Germany has lived under the threat of Soviet missiles for nearly three decades. The greater worry is that East-West political tensions could restrict the flow of people, communications, and goods across the inner German border. "You know," Schmidt used to remind Americans, "the United States of America is not a divided nation; there are not sixteen million Americans living in a place where the Soviet Union is present with a great army and another two million Americans living even [farther] eastward. But this is true of the German

50. "SPD Document on Detente Policy, Peace Talks," in FBIS, *Daily Report: WEU*, June 14, 1983, pp. J3–10. Quote is from p. J8.

nation."[51] If anything, Kohl has been more emphatic on the point: "It is important for America and for other countries all over the world to realize that the majority of the Germans have not given up the idea of German reunification."[52] East Germany has played to this concern in warning of the consequences of basing missiles in West Germany. Party Secretary Erich Honecker warned Schmidt during a three-day visit to East Germany in December 1981 that "good neighborliness cannot flourish in the shadow of American nuclear missiles."[53] Soviet Party Secretary Yuri Andropov was just as explicit about the consequences of deploying the missiles on West German soil when Kohl visited Moscow in July 1983: "The military threat for West Germany will grow manifold. Relations between our two countries will be bound to suffer certain complications as well. As for the Germans in the Federal Republic of Germany and the German Democratic Republic, they would have, as someone [*Pravda*] recently put it, to look at one another through thick palisades of missiles."[54] The political consequences of that outcome are ones that Kohl no less than Schmidt would prefer to avoid if he could. Yet unlike his predecessor, the chancellor has remained reluctant to prod the United States to adopt any specific negotiating position.

Italy

The barriers between popular sentiment and official policy are much less permeable in Italy than in West Germany. While military matters have occasionally been the subject of partisan maneuvers within the cabinet or the parliament, nuclear weapons have not. They remain the jealously guarded prerogative of those who have continued to run Italy through the forty-odd changes of government since the end of World War II—the permanent government of career bureaucrats. The lineup of party support and the constraints on party opposition have further

51. "Schmidt on East-West Issues," in FBIS, *Daily Report: WEU*, June 24, 1980, p. A7.
52. "Excerpts from Interview with Chancellor Kohl," *New York Times*, November 11, 1982. He was even more pointed in a 1983 report to the Bundestag; see "Report on Kohl's State of the Nation Speech," in FBIS, *Daily Report: WEU*, June 23, 1983, p. J7.
53. Michael Getler, "E. German Leader Warns Schmidt on Missile Deployment," *Washington Post*, December 13, 1981.
54. Serge Schmemann, "Soviet Invokes German Partition in Warning Kohl on New Missiles," *New York Times*, July 6, 1983.

insulated policymaking from public influence. So, too, has the nature of the peace movement in Italy.

When the government of Prime Minister Francesco Cossiga put the question of Italian basing to the test in parliament in October 1979, he was assured of support from his own Christian Democrats as well as from some of his coalition partners—the Republicans, Liberals, and Social Democrats—and from the rightist Social Movement party. But on a secret ballot, with a number of coalition members abstaining in order to provoke a government crisis, the key votes came from the Socialist party (PSI), not then in the government. Later, a divided PSI central committee qualified the endorsement by emphasizing the arms control track over deployments.

Under the leadership of Bettino Craxi the PSI was in the process of abandoning its doctrinaire heritage and adopting a more moderate stance, much as the German SPD had done two decades earlier. Over the sometimes bitter resistance of some on the party's left, Craxi was determined to distance himself from the Communist party (PCI) in hopes of putting the PSI into a pivotal role as the maker and breaker of governments and of demonstrating its—and his own—capacity to govern Italy some day. Because responsibility for governance in Italy is still partly synonymous with an ability to get on with NATO and in particular with the United States, Craxi wanted the PSI to back the December decision.

What gave him the leeway to do so was the stance taken by the Communists. The Socialist left was unhappy at the prospect of endorsing the basing of cruise missiles in Italy. Moreover, Craxi intended to woo PCI voters in ensuing elections. Had the PCI been outspoken in its refusal to countenance the missiles in Italy, Craxi would have been in danger of being outflanked. The Communists were not. *Embourgeoisment* of its rank and file was slowly eroding support for the Communists, much as secularization seemed to be eating away at the Christian Democrats, and while the trends were not marked, they had been consistent since the mid-1970s. Stressing the newfound respectability and responsibility, based on its independence from Moscow, a dedication to Eurocommunism, and a reputation for efficient municipal management free of corruption, the PCI leadership hoped to stave off decline by helping to form a coalition government. The Christian Democrats continued to hold out that possibility to the Communists, partly as a way of keeping the Socialists in check. For the PCI the hallmark of independence from Moscow was its willingness to tolerate Italy's membership in NATO, albeit combined with opposition to NATO policies.

At the end of November 1979 when Moscow was insisting that a military balance existed in Europe, that a moratorium be declared on all new nuclear deployments there, and that no negotiations would be possible if NATO proceeded with its decision to deploy, the PCI party directorate took the line that Soviet as well as NATO deployments were upsetting the military balance and demanded that NATO postpone its decision for six months or more and that the two sides "open negotiations immediately on fixing a lower ceiling for the military balance."[55] The ideas were identical to those being put forward by center-left parties across Western Europe, a point PCI leaders underscored. The PCI also emphasized the "Euro" in Eurocommunism by treating Europe as a third force between Moscow and Washington. "We are not questioning the policy of alliance with the United States pursued by Italy and other European countries," declared PCI General Secretary Enrico Berlinguer, "but we are convinced that, in order to be really useful, a West European initiative must be free of any spirit of hostility or enmity toward either the United States or the USSR and must develop autonomously and, we maintain, as a task of mediation."[56] While Prime Minister Cossiga praised the PCI for the independence, if not the substance, of its stand during parliamentary debate on the missile question, Moscow dispatched Boris Ponomarev, the Politburo member responsible for relations with nonruling Communist parties, to Rome to try to bring the recalcitrants back into line.

The PCI distanced itself further from Moscow shortly thereafter. It bluntly condemned the Soviet invasion of Afghanistan and then openly refused an invitation to attend a Moscow-inspired conference of European Communist parties on the NATO missiles. In so doing, it again stressed its commitment to Eurocommunism. Questioning whether a conference of Communists alone was a suitable forum for dealing with

55. "PCI Issues Statement on Euromissiles," in FBIS, *Daily Report: WEU*, November 29, 1979, p. L1. Craxi's reply was to wonder why a six-month delay was necessary when deployments would not begin for four years. PCI directorate member Gian Carlo Pajetta later credited the PCI stance with forcing a shift by the PSI Central Committee away from its endorsement of the government's missile resolution. "PCI's Pajetta Justifies Decision to Forego Paris Meeting," in FBIS, *Daily Report: WEU*, April 10, 1980, p. L6.

56. "Berlinguer on Peace Proposals, Government Participation," in FBIS, *Daily Report: WEU*, January 25, 1980, p. L6.

the topic, *L'Unita* noted the "vast debate" already under way "involving not only the communist parties but also socialist and social democratic parties, Christian movements and organizations (mainly Catholic in our country) and groups of other leanings. . . . A conference such as the one planned would give the impression that the communist parties are being isolated from this range of forces."[57] At first Moscow reacted defensively, but when the PCI condemned Soviet pressure on Poland, *Pravda* excoriated its stance as "monstrous" and "truly sacrilegious." *Pravda*'s bill of particulars extended well beyond the PCI stance on Poland: it accused PCI leaders of "actually deny[ing] the contribution of the socialist community to the cause of protecting peace," while crediting Western European states with "a bigger role" in détente. Worse yet, "Matters went to such lengths that even the Soviet-U.S. negotiations on medium-range nuclear means in Europe (negotiations which the USSR is known to have been persistently pressing for since the beginning of the seventies) are being declared by the leaders of the Italian Communist Party to be—an achievement of West European diplomacy!"[58]

By 1983, a month before the Italian election, the PCI again shifted its position on the missiles, rejecting the automatic deployment scheduled for December 31, 1983, if the Geneva negotiations had not yet reached a positive result. It proposed instead that the issue again be brought before parliament for a vote and that work on the basing site at Comiso be suspended in the meantime. The outcome it sought at Geneva was not only no Western deployments but also "an adequate reduction and destruction" of Soviet SS-20s.[59] By fall, just before the first missiles were due to arrive, the PCI finally came around to seeking postponement of deployments—only after many European socialist parties, though not the PSI, had adopted that stance.

A decision to resist missile deployments in Italy by strikes and other extraparliamentary means could make the country ungovernable and jeopardize its participation in the NATO program. Yet the PCI has thus far shown little inclination to take to the streets on the issue. What could move it to action is homegrown antinuclear protest. An independent peace movement was slow to form in Italy, but when it did by 1981, it

57. "L'Unita Questions Method, Essence of Euromissiles Forum," in FBIS, *Daily Report: WEU,* April 4, 1980, p. L3.

58. "Pravda Excoriates Italian CP Leadership," in FBIS, *Daily Report: Soviet Union,* January 25, 1982, pp. G1–2.

59. "Berlinguer Comments on Euromissiles Issue," in FBIS, *Daily Report: WEU,* May 12, 1983, p. L3.

took the established parties by surprise. The PCI saw the movement gaining support and quickly moved to supply most of the foot soldiers who swelled the demonstrations. Apart from PCI supporters the anti-nuclear forces are small and diverse—ecologists, pacifists, feminists, a few religious groups, and youth groups and leftists of various stripes. The Catholic church has stood apart, although two leading bishops did speak out against the basing of cruise missiles in Italy.[60]

The peace movement is at some tactical disadvantage in Italy. The basing site at Comiso in southeastern Sicily is sufficiently isolated both geographically and socially to keep antinuclear protesters at a distance. In choosing the site, officials were counting on centuries of Sicilian resignation in the face of Roman imposition. The major local concern has been that the land acquisition and construction would attract Mafia interest in an area it has long ignored, a concern that events seem to have borne out.[61] With little prospect for direct confrontation at the site, the protesters started a nationwide petition drive to demonstrate the strength of their cause. Officials and politicians are privately contemptuous of the nonbinding gesture and of the movement itself—"anxiety for the rich" that Italy cannot afford, one called it. Perhaps the biggest constraint on the growth of Italy's peace movement, however, is the PCI's embrace of it, which limits its attractiveness to Italians of a more independent political persuasion.

As long as the PCI keeps its opposition pro forma, the Socialists and the government will be able to content themselves with statements stressing the need for a negotiated settlement at Geneva. But the missiles are unpopular in Italy, and if the protests pick up steam, the PCI may be forced to become more active. "Even if things seem quiet now," warned one member of the PCI central committee in mid-1983, "I don't think the actual installation of the missiles will go so quietly."[62] If it does not, the PSI and its newly installed prime minister, Bettino Craxi, are likely to become much more insistent on progress at the negotiating table.

One aspect of the deployments that has aroused contention among

60. Bishop Dante Bernini of Segni, president of the Justice and Peace Commission of the Italian Bishops' Conference, and Bishop Luigi Bettazzi of Ivrea, president of Pax Christi, expressed "solidarity with the American bishops" and "perplexity" about the installation of missiles in Comiso. "Italian Bishops Rap Plan to Put Missiles in Sicily," *Washington Post,* December 1, 1982.
61. This concern contributed to construction delays at Comiso, forcing the missiles to be based temporarily at the U.S. naval air station at Sigonella, Sicily.
62. Giuseppe Boffa, interviewed by Henry Kamm, "Italian Communists Press Arms Issue," *New York Times,* June 2, 1983.

bureaucrats and politicians across the party spectrum is the arrangement for nuclear release. To most proponents of the missiles, basing in Italy is less a token of reassurance than a source of prestige. Basing without control, however, does not fully satisfy that desire. When U.S. Jupiter missiles were stationed in Italy twenty years ago, Italians manned the missiles and Americans controlled the warheads. In order to launch, both had to receive commands to do so. Italy now wants some form of two-key arrangement again instituted to ensure a share in the control of nuclear release for the cruise missiles. Defense Minister Lelio Lagorio, a Socialist, has remained somewhat imprecise in public, however, telling interviewers that Comiso "will be a NATO base, but Italy is demanding the right to have the final word on the use of the Comiso weapons."[63]

Great Britain

Arrangements for nuclear release have also set off rows in the British Parliament as Labourites, Liberals, Social Democrats, and some Conservative backbenchers have sought to exploit government evasions on the point. As with other parliamentary clashes, there was less to this one than met the ear; dual-key arrangements for nuclear release was one of the few issues involving cruise missiles that united the opposition parties while dividing the Tories. Understanding the divisions on the left and the right is critical for assessing the limits of antinuclearism in Great Britain.

Antinuclear sentiment among the British people is not new, nor is the antinuclear movement. Between 1955 and 1961, opinion polls showed a substantial minority, ranging from 19 percent to a high of 33 percent, who opposed British manufacture of hydrogen bombs.[64] During those years the Committee on Nuclear Disarmament (CND) spearheaded a movement favoring unilateral British renunciation of nuclear weapons that held ban-the-bomb rallies and engaged in civil disobedience throughout the country. While some CND supporters were pacifist, or more precisely, unilateralist by conviction, the movement attracted many in the middle class who were critical of other aspects of British society and who found nuclear weapons a convenient rallying point against the

63. "Lagorio on Euromissiles, NATO, Spain, Sarzana," in FBIS, *Daily Report: WEU*, January 17, 1983, p. L1; Walter Pincus, "Allies Split on Touchy Problem of Who Controls Nuclear Launches," *Washington Post*, November 16, 1981.

64. William P. Snyder, *The Politics of British Defense Policy, 1945–1962* (Ohio State University Press, 1964), pp. 59–60.

establishment. Some were religiously inspired to join, and the movement was able to draw on a tradition of pacifism within the Christian churches. Even so, some pacifists took issue with a unilateralist stance against nuclear but not conventional weapons. Moreover, Christian protest was motivated not only by moral anguish over the bomb but also discontent with the Church, Anglican as well as Nonconformist, for its reluctance to address the critical social and political issues of the times.[65]

Political parties were another channel of recruitment to the cause. Communist influence was marginal; although party members did join the CND, they did so as individuals rather than in response to party directive. In embracing unilateralism they opposed the party line, which concentrated on attacking NATO, American bases in Europe, and German militarism rather than on British possession of nuclear weapons.[66] The movement did, however, draw considerable strength from the left wing of the Labour party. Unilateralism had its appeal to the more doctrinaire sects within the party, not only on ideological grounds but also as a platform for attacking the leadership of Hugh Gaitskell and other centrists accused of abandoning Labour's socialist faith. Especially after the party's defeat in the election of 1959, when Gaitskell sought to redirect its program away from nationalization of industry and redistribution of income toward modest extensions of the welfare state, the left charged him with pursuing me-too policies and tried to wrest control of the party away from him and fellow moderates. The high point of the left's challenge came when the 1960 party conference at Scarborough adopted a unilateralist plank and Gaitskell along with most of the Parliamentary Labour party defied the conference mandate. Unilateralists tried to reaffirm the authority of the conference, which had been conferred in the party's constitution. Gaitskell was just as eager to exploit opposition to unilateralism to beat back his rivals and establish his own and the Parliamentary Labour party's supremacy. At the 1961 party conference he triumphed. To non-Labour CND leaders the use of unilateralism in partisan struggles seemed a perversion of the true faith and a diversion of needed energies. Berating the Labour left for refusing to support the CND's campaign of civil disobedience in 1960–61, one CND leader complained that "because we were not attacking the

65. Frank Parkin, *Middle Class Radicalism: The Social Bases of the British Campaign for Nuclear Disarmament* (Praeger, 1968), pp. 63–64.
    66. Ibid., pp. 86–87.

leadership of Mr. Gaitskell it was not your campaign.''[67] With some justification he accused both the left and the moderates in Labour of using unilateralist slogans ''as a means of covering up a struggle which has very little to do with disarmament or defence and a great deal to do with an internal struggle for power.''[68]

The origins of the current antinuclear resurgence are somewhat comparable to those of the earlier period; so too, are the links between the antinuclear movement and Labour's left. But there are important differences in the breadth and depth of current opposition to Britain's nuclear policy that CND's unilateralism obscures. There are also differences in the social underpinnings of Labour support. These differences suggest an outcome different from the earlier one, though not one necessarily more favorable to the unilateralist cause.

Once again, young people make up the bulk of CND's foot soldiers, and churchmen have played prominent roles. And once again, intellectual impetus has come from Marxists—in this case, from the movement for European Nuclear Disarmament (END) and its preceptor, historian Edward P. Thompson. Grappling with the immobility of Marxism on nuclear matters, Thompson attempted to translate into Marxist terminology the irrationality of deterrence and to define the material and social bases of nuclear weapons development. In order to confront what he called ''exterminism''—the economic, scientific, political, and ideological support systems promoting ''technology creep'' in weaponry—Thompson argued for ''unequivocal rejection of the ideology of both blocs.'' This meant not just disarmament but neutralism for England. Other disarmers would settle for less.[69]

The antinuclear resurgence became visible when CND took to the streets to protest nuclear weapons in Britain. Six months after NATO's decision, 20,000 people marched to Hyde Park in a downpour to hear speaker after speaker, many of them prominent Labourites, call for, in the words of Michael Foot, ''a new campaign in which we can give the lead to the people of Europe and the world.''[70] By 1983 the ranks of the protesters had swelled to ten times that number.

67. Ibid., p. 122.
68. ''The Meaning of Aldermaston,'' The New Statesman, vol. 61 (March 31, 1961), p. 501.
69. ''Notes on Exterminism, The Last Stage of Civilization,'' New Left Review, no. 121 (May–June 1980), p. 30.
70. Downie, ''A-Bomb Opponents Resurface in Britain.''

A substantial minority of the British public, between 20 and 25 percent, has continued to back unilateralism. Support peaked at 41 percent in November 1980 soon after a unilateralist plank passed at the Labour party conference with a vote just short of the two-thirds majority required for inclusion in the party's program.[71] But even as support for the principle of unilateralism was declining, opposition to basing American cruise missiles on British soil and to replacing Polaris with Trident missiles was continuing to command majority support, 10 to 15 percentage points ahead of unilateralism. There was, moreover, considerable tolerance for a campaign of civil disobedience: of those polled, 39 percent felt that breaking the law was justified to block the deployments; the figure rose to 57 percent among Labourites, 49 percent among Social Democrats and Liberals, and 45 percent of all Britons between eighteen and forty-four years of age.[72]

Even more than it did two decades ago, Labour's embrace of unilateralism enhances the antinuclear movement's appeal but may ultimately limit its impact. Structural changes in the party's rules and demographic changes in its rank and file have combined to give the unilateralists disproportionate influence over its program, but the same changes have reduced the likelihood that Labour will ever be in a position to implement that program because moderates have defected to form the new Social Democratic party. The party conference has long amplified the voice of the left in Labour's program, and new rules now strengthen the control of constituency organizations over the selection and unseating of candidates for Parliament. Packing a caucus has also long been a favored tactic of intense minorities, but demographic changes have now further augmented the unilateralists' ability to do so in the Labour party. As some skilled workers, the backbone of Labour, have become more affluent, they have converted to Toryism (in 1983 they defected to the Social Democratic–Liberal Alliance in droves).[73] Many more have moved out of their old neighborhoods in city centers, leaving the caucuses

71. U.S. International Communication Agency, "Limited Public Support for Unilateral Nuclear Disarmament in Britain," *Foreign Opinion Note,* June 3, 1981.

72. "Women Voters Pose Problem for Alliance," *The Guardian,* February 7, 1983.

73. Ivor Crewe, "The Disturbing Truth Behind Labour's Rout," *The Guardian,* June 13, 1983; and Crewe, "Dealignment and Realignment in the British Party System: The 1983 General Election," unpublished paper presented at the annual meeting of the American Political Science Association, Chicago, September 1–4, 1983. The Conservative party base has also been eroding over the past decade, but at a far slower pace than Labour's.

there more open to packing. The net effect has been a long-term decline in the strength of Labour's rank and file.

Sensing this trend, some left-wingers want to see Labour become less a broad church of a party and more a narrow sect true to its socialist creed. They want their candidates to speak the rhetoric of conviction and to mean what they say. The unilateralists among them intend never again to admonish a Labour government, as they did in the 1976 party program—"We have yet to see any progress towards the removal of American nuclear bases"—only to have that government move to add nuclear weapons to those bases. If their strategy means a less appealing party, it may still be large enough to hold the balance between the Conservative party and a growing Social Democratic–Liberal Alliance. Yet even under these circumstances the unilateralists are unlikely to have their way with government policy because only a minority within the Social Democratic–Liberal Alliance favors a nonnuclear Britain.

Parliamentary moderates reject the strategy of the left. They have fought to hedge Labour's unilateralist commitment in hopes that if they regain control of the government they would be able to continue Britain's nuclear role in some form, much as previous Labour governments had. Yet hedging on unilateralism proved a source of some embarrassment to the party in its 1983 election campaign. Its manifesto, or platform, reflected a compromise between the unilateralists and moderates. It committed the party to "rejection of any fresh nuclear bases or weapons on British soil or in British waters, and the removal of all existing nuclear bases or weapons," but it fudged the unilateralist demand that all bases be closed at once. The withering away of Britain's nuclear status would have to be more gradual: "All this cannot be done at once, and the way we do it must be designed to assist in the task to which we are also committed—securing nuclear disarmament agreements with other countries and maintaining cooperation with our allies." Its pledge on Britain's independent deterrent was even more decidedly ambiguous: "We will propose that Britain's Polaris force be included in the nuclear disarmament negotiations in which Britain must take part. We will, after consultation, carry through in the lifetime of the next parliament our non-nuclear defense policy."[74] Moderates stressed one sentence of the commitment, unilateralists the other, while opponents played on the

---

74. British Information Services, "The Labour Party Manifesto: General Election— 9 June 1983" (New York: BIS, 1983), p. 36.

inconsistency. Party leader Michael Foot was unable to clarify Labour's policy when questioned by reporters. By campaign's end the commitment to unilateralism was a shambles, and many Labour candidates were doing their best to avoid the issue. The issue finally had little bearing, however, on the outcome of the election, which Margaret Thatcher won handily; the split in the opposition's ranks ensured a substantial parliamentary majority in Britain's single-member districts, even though her share of the popular vote was slightly below that of 1979.

While the fight over unilateralism was dividing the Labour party and capturing most of the headlines, two other issues were being joined in the military services, on Tory back benches, within the Social Democratic–Liberal Alliance, and among members of Britain's strategic community. One was whether replacing Polaris with Trident was the most cost-effective means of preserving Britain's independent deterrent. The second was whether longstanding arrangements for controlling the firing of American nuclear weapons stationed on British soil were adequate for cruise missiles. The first issue was deeply divisive within the Royal Navy, which bore the brunt of the expenditure cuts that paid for Trident. Even after Navy Minister Keith Speed protested and was sacked for his troubles and after parliamentary debate over the implications of the Falklands war, the government held firm. Nor did the British Army of the Rhine come through unscathed, despite Prime Minister Thatcher's pledge to maintain conventional commitments to NATO. As Trident's fiscal impact grows in the late 1980s, further cuts will doubtless have to be made.[75]

The issue of nuclear release was an inviting target for members of Parliament troubled about the deployment of cruise missiles in Britain. It brought together concerns about national sovereignty, American reliability and prudence, and the rationality of nuclear deterrence. In March 1957, arrangements had been made for basing sixty American Thor ICBMs in East Anglia with provisions for dual-key release. Further clarification of operational control over American nuclear-armed bombers and missiles based in Britain had been worked out in discussions between President Dwight D. Eisenhower and Prime Minister Harold Macmillan in June 1958; this clarification had replaced the loose arrange-

75. On the incipient debate see Lawrence Freedman, "Britain: The First Ex-Nuclear Power," *International Security,* vol. 6 (Fall 1981), pp. 80–104.

ment that had been made by Prime Minister Clement Attlee with President Harry S Truman in 1951 and had been confirmed by his successor, Winston Churchill, in 1952.[76] It was the language of the 1952 agreement that the Thatcher government chose to stand behind: "The use of these bases in an emergency would be a matter for joint decision by Her Majesty's Government and the United States Government in the light of the circumstances at the time." When cruise missile basing in Britain was under negotiation, dual-key arrangements were an option: the United States was prepared to supply and maintain custody of the warheads if the Thatcher government were prepared to purchase the missiles and support equipment and to provide British manning for them. The Thatcher government was not prepared; it estimated the cost would be about £1,000 million.[77] In defending the arrangements, Defence Minister Michael Heseltine was unusually forthcoming about operating practices. The missiles could not be deployed from their bases, he told the House of Commons, "without the agreement of the British Prime Minister." He had earlier hinted at another safeguard: deploying the missile meant taking it "from Greenham Common to the places where it would be fired," he told an interviewer. "In order to do that, you have to involve British personnel."[78] Still, critics persisted, and David Watt, director of the Royal Institute of International Affairs, a prominent British research organization, spoke for many of them when he said:

European public opinion does *not* trust the US, and that is the root of the matter. If we really trusted the US we should not need cruise missiles and Pershings at all. . . . This fear that the Americans will fail to act when we want them to may seem different from the fear that they *will* act when we *don't* want them to, which is the main issue in the debate about control. But the two are in fact closely linked, for both are facets of the undoubted reality that in certain respects American and European interests are seen to be more divergent today than they were 10 years ago.

While conceding that "two keys will not make all that much difference in practice," he wondered why the arrangement could not be formalized,

76. John Baylis, *Anglo-American Defence Relations, 1939–1980: The Special Relationship* (St. Martin's Press, 1981), pp. 59, 65–66.
77. Francis Pym, "The Nuclear Element for British Defence Policy (Lecture)," *Journal of the Royal United Services Institute for Defence Studies*, vol. 126 (June 1981), pp. 3–9.
78. A report of the House of Commons debate is in "Two Stages in Deployment Chain," *The Times* (London), March 2, 1983, and R. W. Apple, Jr., "Control of Missiles Stirs Growing Debate in Britain," *New York Times*, February 16, 1983.

"thus reconciling large numbers of people to the deployment in the first place."[79]

Lack of sovereign control is one reason why opposition to cruise missiles extends far beyond those people of a unilateralist persuasion; physical proximity is another. A ditty about Polaris expressed British feelings clearly:

> Put the missile out to sea,
> Where the real-estate is free,
> And it's far away from me. . . .[80]

Some Tories also harbor doubts, originating in the experiences of 1914 and 1939 and reinforced by the 1956 Suez crisis and recently by the Falklands war and the Grenada invasion, that the United States will be there when it is needed and will stay out when it is not needed. Together, these perceptions help account for the continued unpopularity of cruise missiles, even compared with Trident, despite some decline in support for the antinuclear movement. They also suggest why the Thatcher government cannot afford to be as cavalier toward the opposition as it was about the demonstrations at Greenham Common, which one minister dismissed in the spring of 1982 as "a lot of froth generated by the old pinko fringe."[81] Even while Margaret Thatcher herself was being as combative as ever about the protesters, she was preparing to head off more serious opposition elsewhere. By January 1983 she was tiptoeing away from the American negotiating position. "One hopes to achieve the zero option," she told a parliamentary interlocutor, "but in the absence of that we must achieve balanced numbers."[82] Balanced numbers are not necessarily equal numbers.

The Netherlands and Belgium

As a moving force behind the antinuclear protests, the secularization of religion is nowhere more consequential than in the Netherlands, where church leaders and their flocks have turned to the politics of peace with

79. David Watt, "The Difference Two Keys Could Make," *The Times* (London), February 25, 1983.

80. Quoted in Michael Howard, "Surviving a Protest: A Reply to E. P. Thompson's Polemic," *Encounter*, vol. 55 (November 1980), p. 19.

81. R. W. Apple, Jr., "Britain's Nuclear Battle: The Political Lines Form," *New York Times*, January 11, 1983.

82. R. W. Apple, Jr., "The 'Zero Option': Mrs. Thatcher Softens Her Support," *New York Times*, January 20, 1983.

all the zeal of the newly converted. The organizational embodiment of the church's role is the Interchurch Peace Council (*Interkerelijk Vredes-beraad,* or IKV). Founded in 1966 by a coalition of Protestant and Catholic churches as a consciousness-raising effort on the issues of human rights, underdevelopment, and peace, the IKV staged what was to become an annual Peace Week in September in churches across the Netherlands. In 1977 it began a campaign for unilateral disarmament initiatives with the slogan, "Help rid the world of nuclear weapons—let it begin in the Netherlands." That slogan aptly captured the proselytizing spirit of the Dutch movement, which earned it the sobriquet, not always intended to be flattering, of "pastors of Europe." In 1980, after a year of discussion in its congregations, the Dutch Reformed church, the Netherlands' largest Protestant sect, endorsed unilateral disarmament in the Netherlands as an exemplary initiative.

The IKV campaign had repercussions on public opinion, party stands, and government policy at the time of the 1979 NATO decision and since. Substantial popular majorities, polls indicate, oppose basing cruise missiles on Dutch soil. Church sponsorship was especially effective in persuading members of the Christian Democratic party (CDA), then part of the governing coalition, to oppose Dutch participation in the NATO program in 1979. With the support of ten CDA dissidents, the parliament passed an opposition party motion 76–69 against the NATO two-track decision just one week before NATO ministers were scheduled to endorse it. Prior to the open break, the government had tried to placate its backbenchers by taking a stand in Brussels favoring a decision by NATO to produce the new missiles but deferring a decision to deploy for two years to await the result of negotiations with the Soviet Union. The Dutch also insisted that the alliance study nuclear roles and missions of member states and that it shift away from shorter-range forces to accommodate new long-range theater nuclear forces while reducing the overall number of warheads. Such a shift would have resulted in the substantial reduction if not elimination of dual-capable artillery and aircraft then based in the Netherlands. The Dutch won allied acceptance of the so-called shift study, but their proposal for a production-only decision was openly and sharply criticized in NATO. Faced with a party split if it endorsed the NATO decision and Liberal party withdrawal from the governing coalition if it did not, the government under Prime Minister Andreas van Agt, a CDA member, joined in endorsing the decision but attached a reservation about committing itself to accepting cruise missile deployments on its own territory: "In December 1981 the Netherlands will take a decision with its allies in accordance with the criterion of whether arms limitation negotiations have produced specific results."[83] This stand did not satisfy the opponents' call for teaching by example. As IKV spokesman Laurens Hogebrink noted:

This postponement policy can go on forever. . . . But what the Dutch peace movement wants is not a national "clean hands" policy, with the government agreeing with NATO but making an exception for itself. We want independent Dutch initiatives to stop the whole NATO program. Increasingly this requires a campaign beyond the Dutch borders.[84]

As the date for a Dutch decision neared, the government seemed to become less stable. An election in the spring of 1981 produced a marginal swing to the left, but it took three-and-a-half months of negotiations to form a government. Van Agt was again named prime minister, this time presiding over a center-left coalition that included the Labor party (PvdA) of Joop den Uyl. Although the PvdA had opposed cruise missile deployments from the outset, shortly after the elections den Uyl began to soften his stand. The PvdA's gradual shift away from outright opposition was given further impetus at meetings of the Scandilux group—the Dutch, Belgians, Danes, Luxembourgers, and Norwegians—in which the PvdA's isolation from other European socialist parties was increasingly brought home to it. Democrats '66, the third member of the coalition and the only one to post significant gains at the polls, took no firm stand on deployments. By December the government again deferred its decision.

A new election in September 1982 registered a further swing to the left, and prolonged negotiations to form a new government again ensued. Den Uyl continued to maneuver for flexibility within the PvdA on the missile issue. Because the Netherlands was not scheduled to receive the missiles until 1985, a final decision on deployment could await further developments on the negotiating front, but site preparations had to begin by early 1983. Den Uyl tried to pave the way for such "material measures of an administrative nature." Another potential member of the governing coalition, Democrats '66, this time a big loser in the election, insisted that nothing be done or omitted that could interfere with the talks in

83. "Van Agt Statement to Parliament on Dutch Euromissiles Stance," in FBIS, *Daily Report: WEU,* December 18, 1979, p. F1.

84. Quoted in press release by the International Fellowship of Reconciliation, November 18, 1981.

Geneva.[85] Outright rejection of deployments might have that effect; going ahead with site preparations, by implication, would not. The CDA took a similar stance, but PvdA rejected it. After trying and failing to form a government, van Agt abruptly resigned as CDA leader to be replaced by Ruud Lubbers. One barrier to coalition agreement on a missile policy, the personal distrust between van Agt and den Uyl, was thus removed. Upon forming a new government, Lubbers took a more forthright stance in parliament, a stance indicative of his increased leeway on the missile issue. Playing on popular support for NATO, though not for its missiles, he signaled the government's intention to proceed with site surveys by accepting the major premise of NATO's December decision: "If the North Atlantic Treaty Organization or individual NATO members give the impression of being hesitant about their preparedness to modernize [arms], the Soviet Union won't be tempted, or at least much less so, to negotiate seriously." He also announced his intention to press for a decision on the missiles by June 1984. IKV spokesman Hogebrink was quick to acknowledge the significance of the step: "In effect, Dutch policy is slowly adjusting to the reality of the NATO decision."[86] Nonetheless, public opposition to the missiles in the Netherlands remains strong, and the CDA delegation in parliament still includes at least six unreconcilables. Without an agreement in Geneva by 1985, Dutch acceptance of cruise missile basing remains in doubt.

The IKV campaign in the Netherlands had some impact in Belgium, where the Flemish-speaking majority often tunes in Dutch news broadcasts. Partly as a consequence, the Belgian government was forced to follow the Dutch example of a qualified endorsement of the NATO decision when the Flemish Socialist party (BSP) broke with its coalition partners over the missiles. Party differences over the missile issue often reflect the deeper social tensions in this country of divided loyalties. Linguistic, cultural, and class divisions fragment the political parties and cause government after government to fall. These divisions and

85. "Labor Party Maneuverings on Cruise Issue," in FBIS, *Daily Report: WEU*, September 27, 1982, p. F1; "Missile Issue Delays Cabinet Formation," in FBIS, *Daily Report: WEU*, October 1, 1982, pp. F1–2.

86. Michael Van Os, "Dutch Moving Toward Basing Cruise Missiles," *Wall Street Journal*, November 23, 1982; and Bradley Graham, "Economic Woes in Holland Set a New Realism," *Washington Post*, December 10, 1982. On the continued support for NATO membership, see Richard C. Eichenberg, "The Myth of Hollanditis," *International Security*, vol. 8 (Fall 1983), pp. 143–59.

resulting government weakness may prevent the parliament from mustering a majority in favor of the missiles, but at the same time it may keep missile opponents from rounding up the votes to block deployments. The lack of consensus may thus be permissive: in the absence of decisive parliamentary action, Belgian bureaucrats may proceed with implementation of NATO's December 1979 decision.

Even though democratization of foreign policy was not as advanced in Brussels as it was in The Hague, when the government of Wilfried Martens attempted to endorse the NATO decision without bringing the issue before parliament, the Flemish Socialists balked and the finesse failed. Francophone Socialists joined their Flemish compatriots in repudiating one of their own, Foreign Minister Henri Simonet, who had argued vigorously for the NATO decision. Although the Socialists insisted on a six-month moratorium on all NATO deployments to allow time for negotiations to get under way, Simonet refused to defend his party's views in cabinet and personally conveyed Belgian endorsement of the two-track decision to the NATO ministerial meeting. After a hastily assembled cabinet meeting, however, the Belgian government attached a proviso to its endorsement: "Application of this decision to Belgian territory would have to be confirmed by the Belgian government in May 1980 after analysis of what was hoped would be a positive reply from the Soviet Union to the signal sent by NATO, reflected by practical measures designed to restore a balanced situation." Simonet thereupon resigned.

By May yet another Martens government was still too shaky to confirm that decision (the further delay prompted one wag to note that the "waffle is a Belgian specialty"). An authoritative leak to *Le Soir* reported that the successive postponements were "worrying the people in charge of our diplomacy" and that "the Rue des Quatre Bras [the Foreign Ministry] takes the view that it is now necessary to put an end to any 'indecisiveness.' " At the instigation of Martens the cabinet was asked to approve a declaration that Belgium "agrees" to assume responsibility for its share of the NATO deployment at the "appropriate moment" and "indicates its agreement" to begin "work preparatory to such deployment."[87] The effort failed, but on September 19, Martens got his way. The cabinet issued a statement putting heavy emphasis on

87. "Le Soir Examines Belgian Decision on Euromissiles," in FBIS, *Daily Report: WEU*, August 7, 1980, pp. F1–2.

its role in arms control and the prospects for agreement. It continued, "Should the negotiations between the United States and the Soviet Union not produce any results, Belgium will, together with its allies, take all the measures agreed among the NATO partners." Left unsaid was the commitment to begin site preparations. That was slipped into a debate on the defense budget in the Chamber of Deputies on November 19 by Foreign Minister Charles Nothomb: "It goes without saying that the government must see to it that possible deployment of the missiles not be delayed through our fault. Since no decision has been made, the door remains open in both directions and nothing irreparable should be done." If the deputies knew what he was talking about, they did not challenge it. The reluctant Socialists remained in the government, as did the Liberals who had pressed for moving ahead. *Le Soir*'s analysis was to the point: "Lovers of clear and precise decisions will probably be disappointed but the majority has succeeded in avoiding a collapse."[88]

Whether, in the face of deep divisions in the country on this and other issues, a successor Belgian government will be able to muster a parliamentary majority for deploying the missiles there in 1985 seems doubtful unless it can redeem its pledge on arms control results. Yet, as long as no majority can be raised in parliament against the missiles, tacit government support may suffice for deployment to proceed without formal parliamentary approval.

Alliance Politics and Domestic Politics

Domestic politics sets the stakes, informs the stands, and shapes the perspectives for every participant in the alliance. When domestic politics in Europe and America are out of phase, as they have been since the late 1970s, they aggravate the underlying security dilemmas. Politicians expect "friends" abroad to understand their domestic plight, sympathize, and do what they can to help. When those abroad do not or cannot for reasons stemming from their own necessitous relations at home, the reaction is all too often one of pained surprise, of disappointment tinged with suspicion, not unlike that of unrequited friendship. It is a reaction aptly captured in the question, "How could *they* do that to me?" Richard

88. "Belgian Cabinet Links Missiles Decision with U.S.–USSR Talks," in FBIS, *Daily Report: WEU*, September 24, 1980, p. F1.

Neustadt observed this pattern of "muddled perceptions, stifled communications, disappointed expectations, paranoid reactions" in the Suez and Skybolt crises.[89] The pattern has been a recurrent feature of alliance relations from 1977 on—witness Schmidt's reaction to Carter's decision on enhanced-radiation warheads and Carter's letter to Schmidt on the eve of the chancellor's July 1980 visit to Moscow, and the high-level European dismay at the spate of Reagan administration utterances on nuclear war and Reagan's own reported reaction to European reluctance about imposing sanctions over Poland at the 1982 economic summit at Versailles.

Yet the differences over tactics do not quite obscure the common interest in a negotiated solution to the missile controversy that unites the European allies. It is an interest made all the more compelling by domestic politics in Europe.

With nuclear strategy as with other public endeavors, policy must be tolerable to those who have to put up with it, acceptable to those who have to support it, and manageable to those who have to administer it. When nuclear strategy engages public attention, none of these conditions is easily met. As long as it remained a matter for contending experts to resolve, nuclear strategy could be reduced to unpleasant technicalities debated in muffled tones and arcane language inaccessible to most laymen. It was also possible to command the public acquiescence and parliamentary support that made nuclear strategy bureaucratically manageable. Once the issue surfaced in public, however, as it did from time to time everywhere in NATO except France, it aroused intense moral anxieties that technically minded bureaucrats and strategists seemed unable to address, much less allay.

Although European publics may become more reconciled to the missiles' presence, the organized opposition movements will not. The prospect is for protests to continue if not intensify as the missiles move into Europe. With no arms control agreement in sight and heightened East-West tensions over the issue, the politics of the missiles may become all the more compelling. No longer will governments be able to exploit the argument that missile deployments improve prospects for negotiations. As 1984 wears on, pressures may build in Western Europe to slow down or halt deployments and to resume negotiating.

89. Richard E. Neustadt, *Alliance Politics* (Columbia University Press, 1970), p. 56.

CHAPTER FIVE

Negotiating a Way Out?

I only know that one must do what one can to cease being plague-stricken, and that's the only way in which we can hope for some peace or, failing that, a decent death. This, and only this, can bring relief to men and, if not save them, at least do them the least harm possible and even, sometimes, a little good. Albert Camus, *The Plague*

RENEGING on the December 1979 decision, as many Europeans are now inclined to do, would not lead NATO out of its political quandary. Renouncing deployments might allay, at least for a while, the fears of some Europeans that new missiles would make nuclear war more imminent, but it would subsequently deepen the fears of others that Europe could not count on the American deterrent. Coming after a prolonged Soviet campaign to reverse the decision, renunciation would also appear to give the USSR a *droit de regard* over NATO's own military plans, an appearance that is politically unattractive. Similarly, delaying the arrival of the missiles in Europe offers no escape; delay either opens the way to eventual renunciation or else prolongs the agony of politicians who have to preside over deployment. In either event, NATO's lack of resolve might not impress those who need convincing before deterrence or negotiations can succeed. Once halted, deployment might be hard to resume even if the USSR were to balk at agreement.

Simply proceeding with NATO's deployment without negotiating an arms control agreement at Geneva, as some American officials seem inclined to try, is no better. Deployment without agreed limits would likely exacerbate NATO's security dilemma. If the Soviet reaction is to build more SS-20s or, as seems more probable, to move nuclear warheads for short-range systems into Eastern Europe and build new IRBMs or cruise missiles of its own, NATO could not respond, and not only because of intensified domestic opposition in Europe. NATO deployments in excess of the 572 missiles now scheduled would contradict the alliance's own strategy, which is to commit the U.S. strategic deterrent

105

to Europe's defense. The 572 missiles by themselves are not enough in terms of either quantity or quality to satisfy the requirements of extended deterrence; U.S. strategic nuclear forces are still essential for that task. Increasing the missile force beyond 572 could heighten doubts in the minds of alliance members about U.S. determination to use its strategic forces. Yet failing to respond in kind to a Soviet counterdeployment might be mistaken as a sign of weakness.

An agreement in Geneva would take the steam out of opposition to the new deployments in Europe. While it would not put an end to all demonstrations, an agreement would slow the flow of recruits to the antinuclear movements and begin to dissipate latent support for them in the general population. Yet the allies' stake in arms control extends far beyond using Geneva as a safety valve. NATO's well-being would be enhanced by obtaining an agreement that precludes any successor to the SS-20 while permitting a modest NATO deployment. The need for constraints on Soviet deployments was intrinsic to the two-track approach as Helmut Schmidt, its architect, understood it. Without negotiated limits on Soviet forces, deployments would not ease NATO's security dilemma. Preventing further Soviet modernization is especially important: not only would that limit any additional threat, however marginal, to NATO's security, but it would also avoid the political repercussions in Europe of a deepening East-West crisis. The choice facing the alliance in the event of additional Soviet deployments and prolonged confrontation may make the decision of December 1979 seem trivial by comparison.

Yet it takes two sides to reach agreement. What are the Soviet interests in Geneva? One interest, at least in the short run, was to try to undo the December 1979 decision or, failing that, to maximize the political costs to the alliance of proceeding with implementation. In the view of many NATO officials, that was the only Soviet interest. Their conclusion was that no serious Soviet effort could be expected in Geneva until after the new NATO missiles began arriving in Europe.

But a contrary assessment is tenable. Once the American deployments appeared inevitable—and some months before they were actually under way—Soviet reluctance to sign any accord countenancing their presence may have given way to a desire to limit the deployments and to avoid having to react with new deployments of their own. For at least some in the Soviet hierarchy, this strategy would avoid the uncertainties that another round of arms competition in Europe would introduce into planning and resource allocation within their constrained economy. It would provide a breathing space to try to stimulate economic growth and keep Eastern Europe from further unraveling. It would preserve arms control as a centerpiece of détente in order to facilitate relations with Western Europe. It also held out some promise of minimizing the number of Pershing IIs in West Germany and precluding development of a MIRVed version, of some interest to Soviet military planners.[1] Others in the Soviet hierarchy may have objected, preferring a counter-deployment, with the pressure that would put on NATO, and viewing the accompanying superpower tensions as a means of tightening the Soviet political grip on Eastern Europe and aggravating American relations with Western Europe. As long as this harder line did not prevail, according to this assessment, Soviet interests in Geneva were complementary though not identical to NATO's. The implication of the assessment was that the USSR might have been more prepared to deal before the new NATO deployments took place than after. But without any clear indication from Washington of an American interest in accommodation, the prognosis was that the harder line would prevail in Moscow.

The Present Negotiating Deadlock

Despite shifts in nuance, the premise of the formal Soviet negotiating position has remained constant since the talks opened in October 1980. That premise was to deny the need for any new American missiles in Europe. Soviet negotiators began by arguing that a nuclear balance already existed in Europe, a conclusion they reached by counting U.S. forward-based systems—aircraft and Poseidon SLBMs dedicated to NATO—and adding to them British and French nuclear weapons. New NATO deployments would upset the balance, ran the Soviet line; the SS-20 program, by contrast, merely maintained the balance by modernizing its own obsolescent missiles. In March 1982, with enough SS-20s in place, Leonid Brezhnev announced "a moratorium on the deployment of medium-range nuclear armaments" in the European part of the USSR and "an end to the construction of launching positions" for such missiles.

1. Colonel General Nikolai Chervov, a disarmament specialist on the Soviet general staff, was explicit about such concerns in an interview with Theo Sommer, *Die Zeit*, March 18, 1983, as translated and reprinted in "Journalist on Soviet Counterarmament Stance," in Foreign Broadcast Information Service, *Daily Report: Western Europe*, March 18, 1983, pp. J2–5.

Continuation of the moratorium was made contingent on NATO's dropping any "practical preparations" for new American deployments.[2]

With the accession of Yuri Andropov the Soviet position underwent a further refinement that sharpened the political implications of the basic premise. In December 1982, Andropov announced a willingness "to agree that the Soviet Union should retain in Europe only as many missiles as are kept there by Britain and France." He later elaborated this to refer to either missiles or warheads.[3] This position posed an implicit challenge to NATO strategy by suggesting that British and French missiles along with U.S. aircraft were adequate to protect Europe. It also had the side effect of laying the blame for the stalemate at Geneva on London and Paris, especially in the eyes of antinuclear groups in Bonn and elsewhere.

In October 1983 Andropov pledged to reduce the number of Soviet SS-20 launchers within range of Europe to "about 140," which he said was "appreciably fewer" than the number of British and French launchers, on the condition that no U.S. missiles were deployed in Europe. The reference to launchers was noteworthy, since by Soviet calculations the 64 British Polaris missiles have six warheads apiece; thus in terms of warheads, the British and French forces count as 448 and 149, respectively. Andropov's proposed reduction to 140 launchers would thus allow approximate numerical equality in warheads. Significantly, however, the general secretary indicated his readiness to dismantle all SS-20s above the ceiling, the first time either superpower has been willing to destroy any of its modern weapons as a result of an arms control agreement, though the amount of dismantling might be reduced by any increase in British and French nuclear forces.[4]

Not only has the Soviet position basically been to preclude new missile deployments on the NATO side, but it has also been fundamentally consistent in another respect: all formal Soviet proposals would permit it to retain at least 140 missiles in place within striking range of

2. "Excerpts from Remarks by Brezhnev on Missiles," *New York Times,* March 17, 1982; and "Excerpts from Speech by Brezhnev on Nuclear Arms Talks," *New York Times,* May 19, 1982.

3. "Excerpts from Speech by Andropov on Medium-Range Nuclear Missiles," *New York Times,* December 22, 1982; and "Excerpts from Arms Speech with Andropov's Proposal," *New York Times,* May 4, 1983.

4. "Andropov Replies to Pravda Questions on INF," in FBIS, *Daily Report: Soviet Union,* October 27, 1983, p. AA2. The significance of the Soviet move is pointed out in Richard H. Ullman, "Out of the Euromissile Mire," *Foreign Policy,* no. 50 (Spring 1983), p. 41.

Europe. Because each SS-20 can carry up to three warheads, the USSR requires 225 to 400 warheads (making allowances for reliability and less-than-maximum force loadings on some missiles) for use against time-urgent targets in Europe—nuclear weapons storage sites, nuclear forces, NATO command-and-control facilities, early warning radars, and certain defensive installations such as surface-to-air missile sites.[5] Persuading Soviet military planners to accept reductions much below that level could prove difficult, especially because new NATO deployments add to those targeting requirements.

The zero option proposed by President Reagan was rejected because it demanded just such a major reduction on the part of the Soviet Union. The logic of the option lay in its appeal to Europe's disarmers: it held out the possibility of no new NATO deployments. The effect of the appeal was temporary, however; once the USSR rejected the zero option, disarmers could foresee only increases in deployment. At the same time, the zero option dismayed proponents of the deployments, who saw in it the unfortunate implication that new missiles would be unnecessary were it not for the SS-20s on the Soviet side.

In early 1983, under intense pressure from European governments to show negotiating flexibility, the Reagan administration abandoned the zero option and reverted to the position that NATO had endorsed in December 1979: "equality at the lowest possible level." By taking its stand on this principle, the administration could defer the awkward choice of specifying any numerical ceiling, but it initially adopted the principle in its most extreme form—equal ceilings on land-based inter-mediate-range nuclear force (INF) missiles globally, not just in Europe. In September President Reagan indicated that the United States would not exercise its right to match the Soviet global total by deploying an equal number in Europe alone, and administration officials said the United States had no plans to deploy land-based missiles outside Europe. The administration did not specify a numerical ceiling until November 1983 when it proposed equal worldwide limits of 140 launchers for each side. While that particular number was the same one Andropov had proposed the preceding month, he had applied it to missiles within range of Europe, not globally.[6]

5. For a suggestive set of calculations, see Dennis M. Gormley and Douglas M. Hart, "Euromissiles: A Plan to Satisfy the Russians—and NATO," *Christian Science Monitor*, March 25, 1983.

6. Bernard Gwertzman, "U.S. Offers Proposal on Nuclear Missiles to Soviet at Geneva," *New York Times*, November 15, 1983.

A European observer compared the negotiations in Geneva to "a provocatively slow striptease in which the two sides in turn make seductive gestures." But however seductive the gestures, neither side has gone very far in the formal talks.

Sketches from the Art of the Possible

Behind the scenes, however, the two heads of delegation were informally testing proposals that could serve as the basis for eventual agreement. On July 16, 1982, in the course of a walk in the woods of the Jura Mountains overlooking Geneva, Paul Nitze and Yuli Kvitsinsky outlined a deal that would have limited each side to a maximum of 75 intermediate-range missile TELs in Europe. It would also have frozen the Soviet SS-20 force east of Novosibirsk at existing levels—about 90 launchers. This proposal would have required the USSR to dismantle its older SS-4s and SS-5s, some 248 in all as of the end of 1982, and all but 75 SS-20 launchers, with at most 225 warheads, in a position to strike Europe. It would have allowed the United States to deploy 75 GLCM launchers, or 300 GLCMs, but no Pershing IIs. It said nothing about British and French nuclear forces. It also would have imposed limits on medium bombers—F-111s, Backfires, Blinders, and Badgers—at roughly the existing levels and a numerical freeze on shorter-range missile systems (500 to 1,000 kilometers). In addition, it would have permitted modernization of short-range weapons but not MIRVing, a provision that seemed designed to allow replacement of Pershing I by Pershing I-B, but, arguably, to prevent the USSR from improving its short-range forces in lieu of adding to its IRBM force. Finally, the proposal provided for a three-month moratorium on preparations for further deployments to permit a preliminary agreement to be turned into a treaty.[7]

The walk-in-the-woods understanding, characterized as a "joint exploratory package," in no way committed the two governments, however, and by September both had disowned their negotiators' efforts,

---

7. An authoritative account of the Nitze-Kvitsinsky understanding appears in John Newhouse, "Arms and Allies," *New Yorker* (February 28, 1983), p. 70. Eugene V. Rostow, former director of ACDA, confirms the main elements of Newhouse's account in an interview with Stephen Broening, "Arms Control—After the Shock," *The Sun* (Baltimore), February 22, 1983. Further detail is provided in John Barry, "Is There a Way Out of Zero-Zero?" *The Times* (London), June 1, 1983.

first the United States in the course of a September 28 meeting between Secretary of State George Shultz and his Soviet counterpart, Andrei Gromyko, followed two days later by Kvitsinsky when the Geneva talks reconvened. Although Shultz gave no reason for the American rejection, it was done at the insistence of senior civilians in the Pentagon who objected to trading away the Pershing II. The reason Kvitsinsky gave for Soviet rejection was the understanding's failure to take British and French systems into account, but at least two considerations are likely to have mattered more to his political masters in Moscow. The first was a military concern: the limit of 225 SS-20 warheads might have impinged on Soviet military targeting requirements. To add insult to injury, the understanding would have permitted the United States to have more warheads, 300 GLCMs, than the Soviet Union. The second consideration was political: the proposal conceded NATO's right to deploy some new missiles, and did so prematurely, before allied governments had paid the full political price at home in the coin of popular discontent, demonstrations, and parliamentary restiveness. It also exposed the Soviet position on British and French missiles as something of a sham, again before potential internal differences among NATO members could be fully exploited.

The rejection by both sides left the walk-in-the-woods understanding moribund but capable of being revived by either side at any time. At the eleventh hour the USSR may have tried to do just that. On November 13, 1983, just days before debate on the missiles was scheduled to begin in the West German parliament, Kvitsinsky requested another private meeting with Nitze. On "urgent instructions" from Moscow he said that if the United States was prepared to offer reductions of 572 missiles on both sides, he thought his government would find it acceptable. That would mean no cruise or Pershing II missiles for NATO and Soviet reductions of SS-20s to a level of 120 launchers in Europe. The Soviet ceiling was thus no longer tied to the number of British and French missiles, a key term of the walk-in-the-woods formula. Kvitsinsky made this explicit by suggesting that those missiles could be dealt with in another forum. Nitze sought instructions to allow him to explore the approach further but was turned down. In the meantime the allies were notified, and Chancellor Kohl hinted in a television broadcast that the USSR was no longer insisting on having British and French forces taken into account in any INF agreement. While this suggestion had the effect of undercutting his SPD opponents, who had been urging compromise on this Soviet demand, public disclosure of it may have prompted the Soviet government to disown the idea.[8]

The basic trade worked out during the walk in the woods remains the only way to break the deadlock on INF: no Pershing IIs in return for a ceiling on Soviet IRBMs below the number of SS-20s currently deployed within range of Europe, and a freeze on deployments in the Far East. But neither side has yet addressed the key issue of constraints on further modernization. Such limitations are critical if NATO is to avoid recurrence of a sequence of events similar to that of the SS-20 threat, the December 1979 decision, and the ensuing crisis. These limitations could take one of several forms: a ban on testing or deployment of new nuclear missiles, whether new models of already developed types or new types of missiles, for a limited duration, say seven years; a ban just on new types; or a limit of one new type for each side. Any of these would effectively trade American deployment of nuclear-armed sea-launched cruise missiles for equivalent limits on Soviet land-based or sea-based cruise missiles.

With these basic terms of trade as a starting point, it would be possible to proceed with a discussion of other issues to be resolved in the negotiations. Some of these issues are purely technical; others are political issues in technical guise. It is the latter that this chapter addresses: numerical ceilings, verification of such ceilings, medium-range missiles, reloads, INF missiles based out of range of Europe, aircraft, conventional cruise missiles, sea-launched cruise missiles, and the modalities of an INF agreement—in particular, its relationship to talks on strategic weapons, or START.

The Numbers Game in Europe

Arms control puts a premium on numerical ceilings, giving them symbolic importance out of all proportion to their consequences for military stability. Moreover, both enthusiasts and opponents of the NATO missile deployments have an unwarranted fascination with the question of the relative numbers on each side, regardless of their practical

8. Bernard Gwertzman, "U.S. Gives Its Version of Arms Dispute," *New York Times,* November 23, 1983, provides some of the details; Dusko Doder, "U.S., Not Moscow, Suggested Arms Stance Shifts, Soviets Say," *Washington Post,* November 22, 1983, gives the Soviet reaction.

significance in the military strategies of the two rivals. Numbers do matter, but not the same numbers for both sides, because each side has its own distinctive strategic rationale for its missile deployments.

To gauge from the history of Soviet deployments against Europe, Soviet military planners have long-standing targeting requirements against NATO that have held fairly constant for the past two decades. These requirements were partially satisfied by targeting some of the Soviet ICBM force on Europe, in addition to the SS-4s and SS-5s. Later, however, faced with the constraints imposed by SALT on their ICBM forces, the increasing vulnerability of those forces, and the obsolescence of the SS-4s and SS-5s, Soviet military planners chose to deploy about 225 SS-20s within range of Europe. The initial deployment plan probably called for fewer missiles, but the number may have been increased to take account of potential deployments of the GLCM and Pershing II by NATO as well as to have a reserve for bargaining purposes in Geneva. Moreover, though all these missiles could strike Europe, at least some had their primary targets elsewhere—the Persian Gulf, the Indian Ocean, and China, for instance. Because these missiles would also be covered in any ceiling on forces within range of Europe, Soviet planners may have an incentive to reassign their targets to forces farther east and to redeploy missiles there accordingly.

Unlike Soviet deployments, American deployments in Europe were not needed to satisfy specific targeting requirements; all critical targets were already adequately covered by existing U.S. and NATO forces. Of course, additional targeting requirements can always be generated or U.S. central systems can be reallocated to other targets, but target coverage is not the principal criterion for designing ceilings acceptable to NATO. Insofar as the ceiling number is dictated by NATO strategy, it should be high enough to leave some doubt about successful Soviet preemption yet low enough to avoid implications of decoupling. Those parameters may not be easy to satisfy. Primarily, however, the ceiling must satisfy political requirements. It must be high enough to accommodate the location of some missiles in all five basing countries for the purposes of risk-sharing yet low enough to satisfy popular demands for reduced force levels on both sides. Because GLCMs are configured in flights of 4 TELs or 16 missiles, a minimum of 160 warheads would meet the first criterion; any number sufficiently below 572 to permit reduced levels in all five basing countries would satisfy the second.

Another criterion NATO established for the ceiling number is the principle of equality in rights and limitations agreed to in its December 1979 decision. This is a political, not a military criterion: the decision expressly disavowed any need to match Soviet deployments on a one-for-one basis. Equality of rights, the right of sovereign states to deploy missiles for their own protection, is an easily understood principle. Any alternative would be inconsistent both with the sovereign status of the two negotiating parties under international law and with their real relationship as commensurate powers in the international system. Equality of limitations has a less compelling origin in the negotiating history of SALT: in reaction to the unequal ceilings of SALT I, the Senate passed the Jackson amendment stipulating equal limits in any future treaty. European sentiment may find the need for equal ceilings considerably less compelling because of decoupling concerns.

Equality of rights is readily satisfied by an agreement that provides for some deployments on both sides. Equality of limitations is somewhat more complicated because of differences in the capabilities, purposes, and operational arrangements of the two sides' missile forces. It also makes a difference whether the units to be equalized are launchers, missiles, or warheads. Launchers would presumably refer to TELs in the case of these mobile systems. Since each TEL carries four GLCMs, but only one SS-20 or Pershing II, an equal ceiling on TELs would give the United States some marginal numerical advantage. It would also give both sides an incentive to mount additional warheads on each missile. In order to meet its targeting requirements, the USSR would likely insist on a ceiling for Europe of 100 to 150 TELs. On the assumption that Pershing IIs were banned, this ceiling would exceed NATO's planned deployment of 116 GLCM TELs except at the lowest end of the range. An equal ceiling on missiles, by contrast, would give the USSR a marginal numerical advantage: its SS-20s are MIRVed and Pershing IIs and GLCMs are not.

Warheads, or more precisely warheads-on-launchers (excluding spares and reloads), are the units of account that most closely approximate a measure of military capability.[9] Equality in warheads-on-launchers,

___

9. Using warheads-on-launchers as units of account would also take advantage of precedents set in SALT, which limited both launchers and warheads. By comparison, a definition of missiles, or launch rails, would have to be negotiated, although the difficulties are unlikely to prove insuperable to the Talmudic legalists in the SALT community. If missiles or launchers are the units of account, however, other provisions such as a type rule and a ban on modernization would be needed to preclude fractionating and reconfiguring TELs.

however, would result in a higher ceiling than desirable to satisfy the desires of European publics because Soviet targeting requirements are 225 to 400 warheads. A ceiling of more than 572 warheads would also permit tacit compensation for British and French nuclear forces: if an agreement were within reach, European basing countries might consider relaxing the principle of equality in limitations either formally by agreeing to unequal ceilings on warheads-on-launchers or tacitly by making it understood that NATO would not exercise its right to build up to the ceiling.

The ceiling level and the unit of account, taken together, may affect the choice of procurement. A low ceiling reduces the incentive to procure two new systems because two small production orders would drive up unit costs as well as operating costs prohibitively. The GLCM is necessary to satisfy the West German insistence on nonsingularity and the NATO preference for spreading the risk; therefore, Pershing II is the likelier candidate for elimination. Limiting the numbers of launchers would further strengthen the case for the GLCM instead of Pershing II because the four GLCMs per TEL would quadruple the warhead total. If the unit of limitation were missiles, however, deployment of some Pershing IIs would be favored because they could be more readily MIRVed. A limit on warheads-on-launchers would marginally favor Pershing II over the GLCM at low levels because the more TELs per warhead, the greater the survivability.

The choice of particular ceilings primarily matters for the sake of appearances. What the ceiling levels should be and whether they should be equal for the two sides will have only a marginal effect on relative capabilities or on military stability in Europe. In the absence of radical cuts in central systems, the superpowers will retain thousands of warheads in their strategic arsenals to meet their targeting needs for European security. The alliance would benefit from an agreement that provides for a ceiling on Soviet IRBMs at or below their present level and for a modest U.S. deployment. The precise numbers are a secondary consideration. When it comes to appearances, NATO seeks equality at the lowest possible level. Yet it cannot have both equal limits and the lowest possible limits. If it wants to reach an agreement on ceilings, at some point the alliance will have to choose between the two. Opinions may then differ between those who prefer to reduce Soviet and NATO deployments below their planned levels and those who insist on equality even if that means relatively higher ceilings. So that such senatorial sentiments as those expressed in the Jackson amendment not become a point of trans-Atlantic tension, the choice may best be left to European governments, which are in a position to appreciate whether equal or lower ceilings will seem more palatable to their publics.

Mobility and Verification

Whatever the level, once numerical ceilings are in place, verifying the count of missiles becomes critical for sustaining political support for the agreement. It is by now an article of faith in arms control that any agreement be adequately verifiable. Like many an article of faith, however, the adequacy of verification is open to varying interpretations. Moreover, the SS-20, the GLCM, and the Pershing II are all mobile, inhibiting accurate assessment of their numbers in the absence of cooperative measures for verification.

The task of verifying an agreement is analogous to the task of threat assessment in the absence of any agreement, but with two key differences. First, an arms control agreement could provide, as SALT II did, that neither party "interfere with the national technical means of verification" of the other. Such a provision would facilitate the monitoring of compliance. Without an agreement, interference would, of course, be permissible, and monitoring would be up to each party to accomplish as best it could. Second, in the absence of an agreement imposing ceilings, both sides are free to increase their capabilities unilaterally or to respond as they see fit to increases by the other side; rights or obligations are not at issue. Once an agreement is in force, however, any unilateral buildup that threatens to breach the bounds of obligation takes on greater political significance because of what a breach implies about a state's intentions. Recognition of that fact helps hold both sides in check. To assert that an arms control agreement is adequately verifiable, then, is to say that no militarily significant breach is likely to go undetected for long and that lesser breaches are constrained by the prudential calculation that trivial military advantages are not worth the political risks.[10]

10. In his SALT II testimony, Defense Secretary Harold Brown said of "adequate verification":
No arms limitation agreement can ever be absolutely verifiable. The relevant test is not an abstract ideal, but the practical standard of whether we can determine

The adequacy of adequate verification tends to vary with political circumstance. How high a likelihood of a militarily significant breach is each side prepared to tolerate? How much leeway is each side prepared to give for militarily insignificant breaches? These political questions inevitably arise because in arms control, as in contract law, no agreement can ever be so ironclad that the parties cannot find some loopholes. Moreover, closing loopholes imposes costs of its own. Tight restrictions apply reciprocally, constraining one's own military preparations and operations as well as the other side's. Seeking measures that only restrict the other side tends to jeopardize agreement. These choices are all matters of political judgment that is only partly informed by technical know-how.

Verification is itself a political judgment in technical guise. It is often confused with monitoring, which contributes to verification by providing data through technical collection and other means. But just as raw intelligence data is not the same as net assessment, so monitoring is not the same as verification. Confidence in monitoring involves assigning a set of probabilities to the potential for national technical means to detect certain activities and to distinguish those proscribed from those permitted. Verification entails reaching conclusions, based in part on findings from monitoring, that an observed event should be taken up in the Standing Consultative Commission, the forum established by SALT to consider such questions, or in diplomatic channels to ascertain its meaning, whether it should be formally challenged, or whether it requires corrective or compensatory action. What to do when questionable enemy practices are detected as well as what practices to proscribe are political not technical issues.

Disagreements are likely between the United States and its European allies over how demanding a verification regime to negotiate for long-range theater nuclear forces. These disagreements could be exacerbated by America's characteristically legalistic and technocratic negotiating style. Legalism inclines Americans to apply the analogy of criminal law and prosecution to verification, as if the task were to draft provisions as

---

compliance adequately to safeguard our security—that is, whether we can identify attempted evasion if it occurs on a large enough scale to pose a significant risk, and whether we can do so in time to mount a sufficient response. Meeting this test is what I mean by the term "adequate verification."
The SALT II Treaty, Hearings before the Senate Committee on Foreign Relations, 96 Cong. 1 sess. (Government Printing Office, 1979), pt. 2, p. 241.

tightly as possible, apply strict construction to interpreting them, and catch and prosecute suspected violations. And the legalism is compounded by what Stanley Hoffmann has called the "engineering approach,"[11] a tendency to treat political questions as if they were susceptible to technological fixes, which leads some arms controllers to try to substitute detection devices for political judgment in distinguishing between the permissible and impermissible. The skepticism with which Europeans react to the American approach, however, may lead them to be overly dismissive of verification efforts. This frame of mind may be especially common among those Europeans who see arms control as a way to avoid new NATO deployments entirely. Yet in their eagerness for agreement they may jeopardize long-term political support for whatever arms control results may be achieved. Verification provisions are, after all, cooperative measures for threat assessment and response. In their absence there is a greater likelihood of wildly exaggerated threat assessments and pressure for unilateral corrective or compensatory action, which would upset the political environment if not undo the arms control regime.

In order to be adequately verifiable, an arms control regime must close off four possible routes for evading the numerical limits it imposes: deployment of more of an existing type of missile, deployment of new types, conversion of existing conventional or short-range missiles into the functional equivalents of land-based INF missiles, and deliberate concealment of additional missiles near but not on launchers until ready for use. The task is not to draft provisions proscribing each of these possibilities and then to devise means of verifying the provisions, but to regulate the activities of the two sides in ways that either permit monitoring at various stages or give neither side much incentive to evade.

Deployment of new types of missiles illustrates some of the important issues of verifying an accord on long-range theater nuclear missiles. A new missile has to pass through five stages: research, development, testing, production, and deployment. For evasion to succeed, all five stages would have to be concealed. While research, development, and to some extent production are difficult to monitor, testing and deployment are not. SALT II took advantage of this fact to design provisions constraining activities in these two stages in ways that facilitated

11. See, *Gulliver's Troubles, or the Setting of American Foreign Policy* (McGraw-Hill for the Council on Foreign Relations, 1968), pp. 146–47.

monitoring by a variety of means: cameras to photograph test and deployment areas, infrared sensors to detect heat from rocket engines, radar to track test flights, and radio receivers to pick up telemetry signals. Together, these sensors give the United States an ability to gauge the size, launchweight, throwweight, maximum range, and payload (MIRVs, MARVs, MRVs, and other characteristics) of a missile over the course of its test program. The redundancy of sensors and the frequency of monitoring also provide a fairly comprehensive picture of Soviet procurement practices from design through deployment, although blanks in the picture remain. As Defense Secretary Harold Brown has testified:

We know that the Soviets have four design bureaus for the development of their ICBMs. We monitor the nature of the projects and the technologies pursued at these bureaus. We know which bureau is working on each of the new or significantly modified ICBMs known to be under development. We have a reasonably good idea of when they will begin flight-testing of these missiles. . . . We monitor the Soviet ICBM deployment areas on a regular basis, observing construction activity, movement of people and materials, and training exercises. We have a good understanding of the organizational and support structure for deployed ICBM units.[12]

There is a tension between the desire for tightly drawn provisions to facilitate verification and the desire for more permissive restraints to allow military programs to proceed unhampered. The SALT II provisions for verification, for instance, are unusually complex because both sides wanted to permit modernization of existing types of missiles within certain limits as well as to allow deployment of one and only one wholly new type of ICBM. While these provisions effectively prevent either side from conducting an entire test program—normally twenty to thirty test launches—for more than one new type, they do not preclude tests of improved versions of existing types—up to a maximum of twelve tests in all. In practice, neither side is likely to risk deploying a wholly new missile system on the basis of fewer than twelve tests. Negotiators can draw upon the experience of SALT II to modify limitations on INF missile tests. That experience suggests, for instance, that a ban on new types of long-range theater nuclear missiles would be easier to monitor than an agreement permitting some modernization. With a ban, only a limited number of tests need be permitted to ensure missile reliability. Without a comparable ban to cover missiles of intercontinental range,

---

12. *The SALT II Treaty*, Senate Hearings, pt. 2, pp. 241–42.

however, the USSR could still upgrade its capability against Europe by modernizing its strategic forces.

Some adjustment in the SALT approach to testing may be necessary to accommodate land-based INF missiles. SALT provisions on ballistic missiles, for instance, take advantage of the inherent conservatism of military organizations: because the armed services are reluctant to deploy weapons that have not been tested to maximum capability, tests usually yield data that are valid indicators of peak performance. Not so for cruise missile range: unlike a ballistic missile, a cruise missile may be given increased range without significantly altering any of its other flight characteristics simply by adding or changing fuel. Cruise missiles therefore need not be tested to maximum range. Although the size of the missile sets ultimate limits on fuel capacity and range, range estimates based on volume alone may only be an approximation. The room for doubt may have little military consequence, but it could prove politically nettlesome in the alliance if an INF agreement sought to limit cruise missile range. Nevertheless, the SALT provisions, cautiously applied, could be the basis for INF provisions on testing.

By comparison, to ensure verifiable ceilings on INF will require going beyond the precedents set in SALT II. This is especially so in trying to prevent deployment of additional missiles in excess of ceilings. By drawing attention to numbers, ceilings call for a precision in accounting far more demanding than that needed for military assessments. SALT II satisfied that need by means of a "type" rule and a "counting" rule. The type rule stipulates that once a launcher or silo of a certain type has been used to launch a MIRVed missile, then all launchers of that type count as if they too contain MIRVed missiles. The counting rule says that a missile counts as MIRVed once it has had a flight test with MIRVs, and it is assumed to have the maximum number of warheads with which it was ever flight tested. Paradoxically, these rules, while necessary to meet the strict standards of verifiability demanded by treaty skeptics, occasionally result in more permissive limits—and greater levels of military threat—than might otherwise be the case. For example, the silos housing single-warhead SS-11s at Derazhnya and Pervomaysk are hard to distinguish from others at those sites containing SS-19s, which have been tested with as many as six warheads. Even though U.S. intelligence estimated that two-thirds of the 180 silos contained SS-11s, not SS-19s, and even though some SS-19s actually carry fewer than six warheads, the type rule required that all 180 silos count as if they held SS-19s, and the counting rule required that all SS-19s count as if they had six warheads. This situation thus allows the USSR eventually to deploy more than twice as many warheads at those sites than it was thought to have during SALT II negotiations.[13] Nonetheless, similar rules of accounting will be useful for INF ceilings on warheads on launchers: an SS-20 TEL would count three, a GLCM TEL, four, and a Pershing II TEL, one.

The fixed location and visibility to satellites of ICBM silos and construction sites for ballistic missile submarines made the task of monitoring launcher numbers relatively easy in SALT II. The mobility of INF launchers, however, makes it essential to obtain agreement on cooperative measures in addition to rules of accounting to make numerical ceilings on INF more verifiable. In framing these cooperative measures the purpose should be to facilitate detection of militarily significant breaches of numerical ceilings, not to validate or falsify counts with a precision significantly more demanding than that required for typical military assessments. Cooperative measures that interfere with operational flexibility are likely to be unacceptable not only because of Soviet objections but also because of their reciprocal effects on NATO's standard operating procedures.

In counting mobile launchers, it is useful to distinguish among types. Freely roaming mobiles can run and hide over a wide enough area and can relocate quickly enough to reduce their vulnerability to attack but do not necessarily have unlimited off-road mobility. Runway mobiles, like the MX in its multiple-protective-shelter basing mode, can move along a constrained path, a road or set of tracks, but cannot range far afield. Tethered mobiles can roam freely but over a restricted area or patrol zone in the vicinity of a fixed operating base, which itself cannot be relocated rapidly or temporarily. Soviet SS-20s are loosely tethered; U.S. GLCMs and Pershing IIs are more tightly tethered because they are based in more densely settled locations and their operating practices confine them more to base. All are capable of roaming freely but not for a protracted period. All can be temporarily relocated far afield from their operating bases. Rapid relocation in a crisis, however, would strain airlift capabilities beyond existing capacity. As an aid to verification of

13. Strobe Talbott, *Endgame: The Inside Story of SALT II* (Harper and Row, 1979), pp. 111–12; and Paul C. Warnke's remarks in Alan F. Neidle, ed., *Nuclear Negotiations: Reassessing Arms Control Goals in U.S.-Soviet Relations* (Austin: Lyndon B. Johnson School of Public Affairs, University of Texas, 1982), p. 76.

INF launcher numbers, it will be necessary to "fence in" all existing patrol zones and declare areas beyond those perimeters off limits to any INF missiles or launchers. The dimensions of each perimeter would depend on operating practices, but for illustrative purposes, it could be a circle perhaps fifty miles in diameter with its center on the operating base. Bases would be identified in the agreement. Bases and launchers could be relocated only with prior notification through the Standing Consultative Commission.

To increase confidence in the counts of launchers at or near each operating base may require displaying all launchers on their operating bases outside their garages or caserns two or three times a year so that they may be monitored by reconnaissance satellites. Launchers detected in the area outside the base perimeter would constitute a violation. Because the missiles would be more vulnerable on display, such "parades" would not be held at all bases at the same time. It may be possible to arrange them first at one geographic cluster of bases, then another, allowing enough distance between clusters and too short an interval between parades to permit relocation of launchers. Because parades do interfere with Soviet as well as NATO operating practices, their intrusiveness may make them difficult to negotiate, but that difficulty may be worth the added monitoring confidence. A still more intrusive cooperative measure would be on-site inspection by sensors located at production facilities to count the missiles as they rolled out of assembly areas. Such a mechanism would have little value if additional missiles or modernization were banned. On-site inspection in the form of visits by qualified observers to predesignated deployment or production areas, either on a regular basis or upon request, would add little to confidence about numbers of INF launchers. Indeed, visits may be harmful because they are more liable than overhead reconnaissance to generate confirmation of compliance when in fact evasion is taking place.

The mobility of land-based INF launchers thus raises difficulties for verifying ceilings but not insuperable ones. So long as effective verifiability is understood to mean a reasonable assurance that militarily significant evasion cannot succeed, the probability of deploying an appreciable number of additional INF missiles and of testing and deploying wholly new types or substantial modifications of existing types is acceptably low. Other possible evasion routes will be addressed in subsequent sections of this chapter.

Reloads

Launchers of SS-20s, GLCMs, and Pershing IIs are all capable of being reloaded within a matter of hours after initial firing. While some analysts talk of rapid reloading, they exaggerate the speed with which refire missiles can be mounted on used TELs and retargeted during a nuclear war. In addition, because the launch of a missile reveals the location of the launcher, operational plans probably call for the launchers to be relocated immediately after firing, which would add considerably to the time it would take to reload.

Reloads represent an additional threat to both sides but a very marginal one compared to the capabilities for initial use. The other side's missile forces are a primary target for both sides' time-urgent forces. Regardless of which side goes first, few TELs are likely to survive the initial nuclear exchange. Even if some do and even if the TELs of the side that strikes first escape relatively unscathed, their marginal utility will have declined sharply: an initial nuclear exchange in Europe will leave few valuable targets in place.

The low regard for reloads is apparent in the case of Pershing II. The fact that reloads would accompany Pershing II launchers to West Germany received only passing mention in NATO deliberations; no study seems to have been made on the need for them. Indeed, the main motives for deploying them had more to do with organizational routine and cost-accounting practices than with any assessment of military worth. Because Pershing II was to be a one-for-one replacement for Pershing I and Pershing I had reloads, standard operating procedure dictated that Pershing II would also. And in the eyes of Pentagon accountants trying to amortize program costs, the more missiles produced, the lower the unit cost of each. When word leaked in West Germany that reloads and spare missiles (264 by one count) were scheduled for deployment there, Bonn sought and won assurances that no more than 108 missiles and 108 warheads would be deployed.[14] The

14. Uwe Zimmer, "Das falsche Spiel mit den Raketen," *Stern Magazin,* no. 42 (October 14, 1982), pp. 275–77; Defense Minister Manfred Wörner, interview on Hamburg Norddeutscher Rundfunk Network, November 9, 1982, as reprinted in "Woerner Interview on Missile Deployment Issue," in FBIS, *Daily Report: WEU,* November 12, 1982, p. J4; and Richard Burt, "The Pershing II Missile: A Defense," *Washington Post,* April 10, 1983. Spares and reloads may still be stored in the United States.

putative military value of reloads is important to keep in perspective in assessing the importance of seeking constraints on them through negotiations.

Ceilings on reloads would not be verifiable with present surveillance technology because they are small enough and portable enough to be readily concealed. Any operational plan for their use in the event of war would require concealed locations away from operating bases in order to make survivability possible. Even a cooperative measure forbidding deployment of reloads off-base would add little to monitoring confidence; reloads could be concealed on bases and might be hard to distinguish from spares used for training and replacement. A ban on exercises of reloading could be unenforceable because such exercises bear considerable resemblance to removal and replacement practices in routine maintenance. Finally, on-site inspection on a challenge basis would not suffice to provide high-confidence monitoring, and insistence on such a provision would almost certainly be interpreted as an effort to block agreement.

The reload issue is likely to be exploited by those opposed to any agreement, because constraints on reloads are likely to be undevisable and unnegotiable or unverifiable. The preoccupation with numbers will also tempt those who see the NATO deployment as inadequate to exaggerate the magnitude of the reload threat. Yet it is warheads-on-launchers, not reloads, that pose the principal threat. Insistence on constraining a marginal threat could jeopardize agreement constraining the main threat. Whether to do so is a judgment best left to European governments mindful of the need to keep their eyes upon the doughnut and not upon the hole.

Medium- and Short-Range Missiles

INF is arbitrarily defined to include all systems capable of delivering nuclear weapons at distances of 1,000 kilometers or more. Both U.S. and Soviet arsenals, however, also include nuclear-capable missiles with ranges of less than 1,000 kilometers. On the Soviet side are the SS-12, with a range of 900 kilometers, and a recent follow-on, the SS-22; the SCUD-B, with a range of 300 kilometers, and its modernized replacement, the SS-23, with a range of 500 kilometers; and the FROG-7, with a range of 70 kilometers, and its successor, the SS-21, with a range of

120 kilometers. The United States has 108 Pershing Is with a range of 720 kilometers that are being replaced by Pershing IIs. West Germany has another 72, with their warheads in U.S. custody. All reportedly can deliver conventional and chemical as well as nuclear payloads.[15] Other U.S. nuclear weapons with even shorter ranges will be discussed in chapter 6.

Soviet shorter-range missiles pose some threat of breakout, the circumvention of limitations on LRTNF, in the event of crisis. Deployed in forward locations in Eastern Europe, they would be in a position to perform some of the missions of SS-20s against many Continental targets. NATO's shorter-range systems cannot achieve the equivalent against the USSR; only Pershing I, moved to forward locations, could reach the Soviet frontier, but it could not reach far enough beyond it to threaten strategic targets. NATO makes much of this geographic asymmetry. Perhaps too much. Even though the alliance's medium-range missiles cannot do to the USSR what equivalent Soviet missiles could conceivably do to Western Europe, they can wreak havoc in Eastern Europe. This is a source of anxiety in the Warsaw Pact that should not be altogether comforting to a Soviet hierarchy already uneasy about the loyalty of its allies. And while Soviet sources acknowledge the presence of short-range nuclear-capable weapons in Eastern Europe, they deny that medium-range weapons have been stationed outside Soviet territory. Nuclear warheads for even the short-range weapons are probably not generally deployed forward, either.[16] The difficulty of ascertaining the location of the warheads may be attributable to Soviet concealment, but another possibility is that the USSR may be reluctant to store them where they are not wanted or are less than secure.[17]

15. The data are drawn from International Institute for Strategic Studies, *The Military Balance, 1983–1984* (London: IISS, 1983), pp. 6, 14, 118–19. No solid estimates of the quantities on the Soviet side are publicly available. IISS puts the numbers in Europe at 80 SS-12s, 440 SCUDs (As and Bs), 440 FROG-7s, and 62 SS-21s; there are said to be 100 SS-22s and 10 SS-23s overall. Another 24 FROG-7s and 18 SCUD-Bs are said to be in the GDR (p. 21).

16. In a text subsequently cleared by Soviet officials, Col. Gen. Nikolai Chervov recently acknowledged, "Everywhere outside the Soviet Union where Soviet Army divisions are stationed, appropriate missile units have tactical nuclear weapons with a range up to 100 kilometers." William Drozdiak, "Soviet Admits Missiles Already in Bloc States," *Washington Post,* October 18, 1983.

17. Recent Soviet suggestions that it intended to move nuclear weapons forward in response to the new NATO deployments aroused considerable concern in Eastern Europe.

Nonetheless, any arms control agreement would have to take into account the marginal threat of breakout through redeployment. This agreement need not take the form of numerical ceilings—the number and variety of shorter-range systems and the difficulty of verifying their numbers would lend false concreteness to any ceilings. Cooperative measures prohibiting exercises in forward-deployed postures are also impracticable. These systems are part of both sides' conventional capabilities, and as such they have military value mainly within range of the battlefront. Any differences between nuclear and nonnuclear modes of exercising these systems may not be readily observable. A nuclear-free zone along the lines proposed by the Palme Commission is another possibility,[18] but the current difficulty in ascertaining the location of Soviet nuclear warheads may be a measure of the difficulty of monitoring such a provision. The marginal threat of breakout might also be contained by a noncircumvention provision on the model of SALT II coupled with an agreement that any additional deployment or modernization of medium-range missiles would constitute circumvention.

Achieving a freeze on Soviet shorter-range missiles to limit the threat of breakout might exact an equivalent price from the United States. If the price were a reciprocal freeze on U.S. shorter-range nuclear-capable missiles, the agreement could preclude any modernization of Pershing I. The Pershing I-B arguably could pose a breakout threat to the USSR because it is distinguishable from Pershing II only by observable differences in its TEL. For the army, which set Pershing modernization in motion in order to improve its ability to strike Warsaw Pact field headquarters and other C^3, trading away the Pershing II may seem less than tragic if it were left with the Pershing I-B; it might have reservations about being deprived of both.[19]

18. The Palme Commission, officially the Independent Commission on Disarmament and Security Issues, proposed a nuclear-free zone for short-range or battlefield systems in central Europe. While it did not specify the boundaries of the zone, it cited a strip 150 kilometers wide on each side of the intra-German and FRG-Czech borders for illustrative purposes. It would ban nuclear munitions, storage sites, and prepositioned sites for atomic demolition munitions from that zone. It would also prohibit exercises simulating nuclear operations. While not specifying verification provisions, the report noted that they "would have to include a number of on-site inspections in the zone on a challenge basis," a point that the Soviet member of the commission, Giorgi Arbatov, subscribed to in accepting the text. See Barry M. Blechman and Mark R. Moore, "A Nuclear-Weapon-Free Zone in Europe," *Scientific American*, vol. 248 (April 1983), pp. 37–43.

19. Army testimony in 1982 supports this view: "Since the beginning of Engineering Development, the Office of the Secretary of Defense has required the development of

Geographic Scope

Thus far, the discussion has focused on limiting land-based LRTNF missiles in Europe.[20] Yet the NATO position is that any limitations on LRTNF missiles must apply worldwide. The USSR, at least in its public posture, initially maintained that the negotiations must be confined to Europe, though in the Nitze-Kvitsinsky dialogues the Soviet side did show some willingness to entertain a broader conception of the geographic scope of the negotiations. In October 1983 the Soviet side formally modified its position. In line with an Andropov interview in *Pravda*, it said it would unilaterally halt deployment of additional SS-20s in the eastern USSR upon entry into force of an agreement covering Europe and contingent on no change in the "strategic situation" in Asia.[21]

The principal motive for American pursuit of global limits comes from Japan and other Asian allies, who have cautioned against constraining Soviet missile deployments against Europe at their expense and allowing SS-20s to be redeployed from west to east. China has also voiced its displeasure at such a prospect.[22]

a Pershing missile which has the I-A's range for two reasons: as a 'fallback' system, should future arms control negotiations result in an agreement not to field the extended-range Pershing II; and, to have available a shorter range system that could be acquired by the Germans if they decide to modernize their Pershing system." *Department of Defense Appropriations for 1983*, Hearings before the Subcommittee on the Department of Defense of the House Committee on Appropriations, 97 Cong. 2 sess. (GPO, 1982), pt. 4, p. 444.

20. With SS-20 range at 4,400 kilometers, the dividing line is roughly 80 degrees longitude. Soviet bases to the east of that line, at Novosibirsk and eastward, are out of range of all but peripheral areas of Europe. Some areas of Europe—in Turkey and Finnmark—would remain in range no matter where the line was drawn; so would Alaska. These anomalies would have to be lived with, just as in the SALT agreements, which did not include shorter-range weapons capable of reaching Alaska from the eastern USSR, or vice versa.

21. The Soviet delegation made the shift by simply transmitting the Tass text of the interview. U.S. Department of State, "INF: Progress Report to Ministers," December 8, 1983, p. 33 (mimeo).

22. The Japanese were especially vocal in stating their concerns both in Washington and in European capitals at the time the United States backed away from the zero option. See Henry Scott Stokes, "Japan Sharply Protests Soviet Proposal on Shifting Missiles to Asia," *New York Times*, January 26, 1983; Don Oberdorfer, "Japan Voices Concern on Missiles Pact," *Washington Post*, February 1, 1983; and *La Repubblica* interview with Italy's foreign minister, Emilio Colombo, in "Foreign Minister Denies Japan Included in NATO," FBIS, *Daily Report: WEU*, June 10, 1983, pp. L2–3. The Chinese made their reservations known to Egon Bahr; see "Interview with SPD's Bahr on China Talks," in FBIS, *Daily Report: WEU*, September 8, 1982, p. J3.

A second motive, and the principal stated rationale for global limits, is the threat of breakout—that the USSR, if otherwise unconstrained, could deploy as many missiles as it wanted in the eastern USSR only to relocate them within range of Europe in the event of a crisis. Cooperative measures fencing in patrol zones would restrict noncrisis redeployment, but some risk would remain that in a crisis and in the absence of some combination of numerical limits and patrol zones for Soviet deployments at Novosibirsk and farther east, relocation could greatly increase the numbers of SS-20s aimed at Europe. Conceivably, too, the United States would remain free to deploy additional missiles at home for relocation to Europe under similar circumstances. The breakout threat should not be exaggerated, however; the USSR already has enough missiles within range of Europe to meet its targeting requirements, so relocation would be needed only if deep cuts were negotiated in that missile force. Moreover, rapid relocation in a crisis would demand diversion of most airlift capacity from other tasks, to the point of virtually exhausting present capabilities.[23] Yet the ability to relocate rapidly some INF missiles could aggravate crisis instability possibilities already present.

A third motive for global ceilings, but one with strong resonance in some European circles, especially in Bonn, is to avoid any decoupling connotation of codifying a Eurostrategic balance by ceilings that apply only to Europe without any limits on the same systems outside that theater.

To advance the NATO position, the United States has formally proposed equal ceilings at the lowest possible level on land-based INF missiles regardless of their location. Were it to seek a worldwide ceiling below the level of the planned NATO deployment, the United States would in effect be cutting the Soviet SS-20 deployment in half. In order to maintain SS-20s in the Far East, it would have to reduce SS-20s in Europe to a number below the number NATO maintains in Europe. Such a ceiling stands no chance of acceptance in Moscow. Alternatively, were the United States to seek a much higher global ceiling, one requiring at most a modest reduction in current Soviet deployments, the ceiling number would seem awkwardly high for public presentation in Europe. Were NATO to indicate its intention not to avail itself of the right to

23. Even though the USSR has begun building a new airplane, the Antonov 400, reportedly capable of transporting SS-20s, the plane will probably have other more pressing airlift missions in wartime. See *Jane's All the World's Aircraft, 1983–84* (London: Jane's Publishing Co. Ltd., 1983), p. 59.

build up to the ceiling, however, this formula might serve as a tacit form of compensation to the USSR for British and French forces.

Even if applying a single ceiling to both Europe and the Far East turns out to be nonnegotiable, there are still plausible security reasons for placing some limits on Soviet Far Eastern deployments. One form of limit might be to ban rapid relocation, but it might prove hard to negotiate and even harder to monitor. Another might be separate ceilings for deployments beyond the range of Europe. These ceilings could be relatively permissive—indeed they would have to be in order to avoid putting the United States in the awkward position of having to withstand European pressures for an agreement on behalf of Japan and China. Yet they must not worsen the threat to Japan and the rest of Asia. The path Nitze explored with Kvitsinsky during their walk in the woods again provides a useful way out: an agreement to freeze existing deployments in the far eastern USSR that would not allow the Soviets to redeploy eastward the SS-20s in excess of the European ceiling. That the United States could confine the threat to the Far East and would not fix Europe's problem at Asian expense should be acceptable. That the ceilings would not apply only to Europe should be welcomed there as blurring any connotation of a Eurostrategic balance.

Aircraft

Whatever formula is used on geographic scope for missiles, it need not and should not set a precedent for ceilings on aircraft. Because they are not just mobile but are readily relocatable in a way that INF missiles are not, aircraft require ceilings that would apply worldwide.

The United States and the Soviet Union have a variety of aircraft that could deliver nuclear weapons against targets throughout Eastern and Western Europe. The U.S. arsenal has 172 F-111 and 176 F-4 fighter-bombers on air bases in Europe; 68 A-6 and A-7 fighter-bombers on U.S. carriers permanently on assignment in European waters; and 63 FB-111 fighter-bombers based in the United States that the USSR considers designated for NATO use. The Soviets have 100 Backfire, 310 Badger, and 125 Blinder bombers and 550 Fencer fighter-bombers.[24] While all

24. IISS, *The Military Balance, 1983–1984*, pp. 4–5, 14–15, 120–21; and author's interview.

are classified dual-capable, not every plane in each category may be wired for nuclear delivery or carry crews trained for nuclear roles. Other classes of aircraft—Soviet Floggers, Fitters, and Fishbeds and U.S. F-4s, for instance—also have the potential to carry nuclear bombs. Both sides also have aircraft outside the theater that have the potential to perform nuclear missions if redeployed to Europe—U.S. carrier aircraft and Soviet fighter-bombers based in the Far East, for instance. American allies in Western Europe—and by some accounts, Soviet allies in Eastern Europe—have comparable aircraft at their disposal. Indeed, the Soviets have sought to have any INF agreement cover French Mirage IVs.

Even a glance at the variety of aircraft indicates that negotiating a ceiling will be a complex endeavor. Differing estimates of ranges, capabilities, and roles and missions, and consequently differing assessments of the force balance, make the terms of trade hard to calculate. A notorious example is the Backfire bomber. While estimates of Backfire's range vary, it has been the U.S. view that these aircraft can reach targets in the continental United States and with mid-air refueling fly two-way missions there. The United States succeeded in SALT II in getting a commitment from the USSR in the form of a note handed over by President Brezhnev on June 16, 1979, that the Soviets did "not intend to give this airplane the capability of operating at intercontinental distances" by increasing its radius or equipping it for in-flight refueling and that it would not increase its production rate, then thirty planes a year. Regardless of its intercontinental potential, the Backfire is capable of nuclear attacks against the periphery as well as the heart of Western Europe and is deployed both on land and at sea with units responsible for that mission.

For aircraft of any given type it is also hard to distinguish in practice between those in nuclear and those in nonnuclear roles for purposes of verifying any ceiling. Externally observable design features might be added to facilitate that task, but they would not necessarily be functionally related. Differentiation on the basis of training practices would be hard to monitor. One way out would be a type rule stipulating that any aircraft type in which crews have been trained for nuclear delivery is by definition nuclear-capable and will be included in the ceilings. This method, however, could have perverse effects on NATO's conventional capability because most nuclear-capable planes still have the primary mission of conventional bombing. An additional rule on types of aircraft would also have to be applied if nuclear bombloads were to be limited, as in General Secretary Andropov's May 3 proposal. This rule might be difficult to frame, however, in view of the claim by both sides that many planes in the category of nuclear-capable aircraft are not presently equipped and manned for nuclear roles.

In the negotiations the two sides have stressed differences over the balance of aircraft in Europe and which aircraft, if any, are to be included in any agreement. Neither side has been wholly consistent in its approach, in part because any consistency can be shown to be somewhat foolish. Soviet negotiators have wavered between making substantive arms control proposals on aircraft and scoring political debating points on "forward-based systems," which in Soviet parlance refers to all U.S. emplacements and aircraft in Europe. As such, the phrase has the connotation, unacceptable to the United States and its allies, that only American aircraft, not Soviet, are at issue. It has the further political implication that the American presence in Europe is an alien intrusion, unnecessary if not antithetical to Europe's own defense needs.

Substantively, the Soviets had initially proposed limiting each side to 300 medium-range delivery vehicles, including British and French missiles, which would impose severe constraints on American land-based and carrier-based aircraft. Yet in his October 1983 interview, Andropov opened the way to a resolution of the issue, indicating Soviet readiness to "establish for the USSR and NATO equal total levels of medium-range [nuclear-carrying] aircraft in a mutually acceptable quantitative range which could be substantially different from the range proposed by us previously."[25] Agreement could be reached, he said, on a specific ceiling and the composition of aircraft to be included under that ceiling.

Although prepared to engage Soviet negotiators on the aircraft issue, the United States initially took the position that the principal threat to military stability in Europe comes from missiles and that inclusion of aircraft would only complicate the already difficult task of obtaining an agreement to limit that threat. Yet the U.S. position made much of the Backfire threat to Europe. While it continued to introduce Backfire into discussions of heavy bombers—in START rather than in INF negotiations—the United States counted Backfire in its tally of intermediate nuclear forces as well. Then in September 1983 the United States proposed equal limits on certain unspecified types of land-based aircraft.

How might the aircraft issue be resolved? One possibility is to set

25. "Andropov Replies to Pravda Questions on INF," p. AA2.

aircraft aside during the current stage of INF negotiations but state in a protocol to the agreement that they would be dealt with in a subsequent stage of talks. That, however, is almost certainly insufficient to satisfy the longstanding Soviet position that there be limits on U.S. aircraft threatening the USSR from bases in Europe. Another possibility is to ignore aircraft in the limitations, except for a noncircumvention proviso applying specifically to medium bombers and fighter-bombers and banning any increase or modernization of those forces. A third possibility is a ceiling.

Any ceiling would have to apply worldwide because aircraft are readily relocated. One possible ceiling would limit all nuclear-capable aircraft with a range over, say, 1,000 kilometers. The number would have to be permissive enough to satisfy arguments about the incommensurability of the two sides' forces. From NATO's standpoint, short-range U.S. aircraft based in Western Europe could not strike the USSR, but short-range Soviet aircraft using bases in Eastern Europe could attack NATO. From the Soviet standpoint, improvements or increases in allied capabilities would allow the West to circumvent any ceiling. Yet too high a ceiling would raise objections that it did little to constrain the threat.

Perhaps the best solution is an interim one along the lines explored by Nitze and Kvitsinsky: to single out roughly comparable aircraft on both sides and limit them. The most obvious quid pro quo is limits on Backfire, Blinder, and Badger on the Soviet side in return for limits on F-111s and/or FB-111s on the American. But this would require both sides to modify their negotiating positions. To date, American negotiators have insisted on excluding FB-111s and including Fencers, while their Soviet interlocutors wanted to exclude Fencers and include F-4s. Moreover, the Reagan administration continues to regard Backfire as an intercontinental system to be limited in START, not in INF talks. Whether NATO military chiefs will be willing to accept reciprocal restraints on F-111s and FB-111s is a measure of how seriously they take the Backfire threat and how much they are prepared to pay for limits that go beyond the minimal constraints on production now in place.

A deal on aircraft might also provide modest leverage for resolving other issues as part of an overall package for agreement. It would satisfy the Soviet need to claim success in its long quest for limits on American aircraft in Europe and could arguably serve as a precedent for future negotiations while not burdening an interim agreement on INF with the intricacies of aircraft limitations. A partial deal would also reflect the current state of the military balance of nuclear-capable aircraft in Europe, which is generally a steady one with no significant trends and, apart from Backfire, no prospect of dramatic developments on either side.

Yet, from its own strategic perspective, NATO may want to consider eliminating dual-capable aircraft altogether by converting them to purely conventional roles and missions. The rationale for doing so is not based primarily on arms control considerations but on the consequences of dual capability for NATO's own strategy, which will be addressed in chapter 6. Somewhat perversely, putting the issue of dual-capable aircraft on the table in arms control negotiations may deflect NATO from considering conversion of dual-capable aircraft into purely conventional aircraft.

Conventional Cruise Missiles

Whether they carry nuclear or conventional warheads, ground-launched cruise missiles are to all outward appearances identical.[26] Thus another way, at least in theory, of circumventing ceilings on land-based LRTNF missiles is to deploy land-based conventionally armed cruise missiles (CCMs), which have the potential to be converted into their nuclear-armed look-alikes by altering their payloads.

If the objective were only to frame a verifiable arms control agreement, the remedy for CCMs would be to ban them or else to include them in LRTNF ceilings by defining any land-based cruise missile as nuclear-capable regardless of how it was in fact armed. Yet verification is not the only objective; indeed, it is not an objective in and of itself but only a means to another end, NATO's security through a reduced likelihood of nuclear war. And in the view of some, deploying CCMs would do more for this objective than banning them. Doubtless, CCMs are being oversold. Yet the salient fact remains that many Europeans, not only in army circles but also among experts in the antinuclear movement, regard them as the technological fix that will make high-confidence conventional defense of Europe possible. Any arms control proposal that forecloses

---

26. A comparable problem might arise if conventionally armed versions of Pershing II were deployed.

their deployment could face serious opposition on both sides of the Atlantic.

Is a workable set of constraints on the breakout threat posed by CCMs conceivable? Yes, provided that the threat posed is understood to be a modest one. The incremental advantage of converting CCMs to nuclear use in a war in Europe would be marginal because the nuclear arsenals of both sides are more than ample to blanket European targets under prevailing conditions. Three provisions in any LRTNF agreement should suffice to reduce the breakout threat even further. One would require platforms for CCMs to be readily distinguishable from TELs carrying nuclear-armed GLCMs. These externally observable design features would not strictly speaking be functionally related. A second provision would prohibit CCM carriers from being exercised in a nuclear capacity. A third would bar the carriers from being collocated with nuclear GLCMs. The first provision is essential; the other two might prove beneficial.

Sea-Launched Cruise Missiles

In some ways, sea-launched cruise missiles pose problems analogous to those posed by CCMs. Some SLCMs are already deployed; others are now in testing. America's nuclear-armed version is outwardly indistinguishable from some of its conventionally armed ones. Both versions have their enthusiasts in the armed forces. Finally, conventionally armed SLCMs could, at least theoretically, be converted into nuclear weapons by replacing their warheads, thereby posing a threat of breakout in wartime.

There the similarities to CCMs end. The CCM problem is a minor one in military terms; the SLCM problem is not. Because of the numbers each side could deploy, to allow procurement of nuclear land-attack SLCMs to proceed unconstrained while limiting land-based LRTNF missiles would be to leave a loophole of some military significance that critics of any agreement would be quick to seize upon in their opposition. Yet limitations on SLCMs are hard to devise. The platforms are not designed to provide a clear basis for distinguishability, and once the missiles are deployed aboard ships or submarines, counting them becomes difficult. Finally, the military utility of nuclear SLCMs is open to more serious reservations than is that of their conventional cousins.

The navy currently has three cruise missile programs under way. Starting in 1984, two variants of the Tomahawk are scheduled for deployment: the TLAM-N, a land-attack missile armed with a 200-kiloton nuclear warhead and presently judged capable of a range of 1,500 nautical miles, and the TLAM-C, identical to the TLAM-N in appearance and in mission but armed with a 1,000-pound conventional warhead and capable of a range of 600 nautical miles. Already deployed aboard surface ships, submarines, and naval aircraft, the conventionally armed Harpoon is intended for antiship roles and has a maximum range of 60 nautical miles.[27]

Although the TLAM-N is designed to be fired from existing torpedo tubes, it will be put in vertical launch systems, special containers for storing and launching the missiles that are to be fitted into the ballast tubes of most navy attack submarines so that the missiles will not take up space needed for conventional weapons loads. They will also be placed on Spruance-class destroyers, nuclear-powered cruisers, and two battleships that the navy is taking out of mothballs. The surface ships will be retrofitted initially with armored box launchers, which can accommodate only Tomahawks, and later with vertical launch systems capable of accommodating all three types of SLCM in numbers large enough for barrage attacks. The new Aegis cruisers and Arleigh Burke–class destroyers will be fitted with vertical launch systems.[28]

With Navy Secretary John Lehman, an SLCM enthusiast, at the throttle, procurement was expected to proceed at full speed, but some technical trouble has occurred. Lehman's rationale for the TLAM-N has also raised forceful criticism, both from below decks and from outside the navy. Trying not to encourage renewed European interest in a sea-based alternative to the GLCM and Pershing II, Lehman initially justified the TLAM-N in terms of a strategy of horizontal escalation—countering a threat to one region by threatening a response elsewhere. In response to criticism, he subsequently downplayed this strategy in favor of more traditional rationales: extending the American nuclear

27. Michael MccGwire, "The Tomahawk and General Purpose Naval Forces," in Richard K. Betts, ed., Cruise Missiles: Technology, Strategy, Politics (Brookings Institution, 1981), pp. 233–34.

28. Edward H. Kolcum, "Vertical Launching System Scheduled for Sea Tests," Aviation Week and Space Technology, vol. 114 (March 2, 1981), pp. 49–50; Department of Defense Authorization for Appropriations for Fiscal Year 1983, Hearings before the Senate Committee on Armed Services, 97 Cong. 2 sess. (GPO, 1982), pt. 6: Sea Power and Force Projection, p. 3807.

umbrella to Japan and elsewhere and taking advantage of American naval superiority to show the flag in far-flung theaters of war. In private, those uniformed officers who are attracted to the TLAM-N have another less exalted purpose in mind for it: service autonomy. It would give the navy a capability to attack Backfire bombers assigned to Soviet naval aviation without having to rely on the air force to perform this role for them.

The navy's public rationale for TLAM-N remains questionable. While American policy in recent years has put the emphasis on equipping allies to defend themselves, treaty commitments as well as ties of history and common interest still oblige the United States to do more. Despite obligations that do not preclude nuclear deterrence, the ability to meet a conventional challenge with a nuclear response in the Persian Gulf or in Northeast Asia is open to doubt. Just how nuclear SLCMs would prove useful in the Persian Gulf, for instance, has never been clear. Any demonstrative use against Soviet forces would invite counterdemonstrations against the American fleet as well as ports, bases, and other American facilities in the region. The exchange could easily escalate. The net result would not obviously be to America's advantage. A threat to attack Soviet territory would assume an added risk of retaliation against the United States itself. If such a threat appears less than wholly credible in the European context, it is far less so elsewhere. While the presence of ships armed with TLAM-Ns may provide visible reassurance to some, it may be a source of anxiety to others in a region menaced more by internal unrest than by external aggression. Ship visits and basing TLAM-Ns in foreign ports would hardly allay that anxiety. Even in Northeast Asia, keeping a nuclear-armed fleet on station will be difficult without access to neighboring ports. Most countries in the region are likely to prove no more hospitable than Japan, where rumors of possible port calls by American nuclear-carrying ships are enough to mobilize demonstrations.

The Soviet navy has long been equipped with cruise missiles, some nuclear but most not, all but one in antiship or antisubmarine roles, and none with a range over 600 kilometers. In a sharp break with past practice, the USSR is now developing a sea-launched cruise missile, the SS-NX-21, with an estimated range of 3,000 kilometers. The SS-NX-21 is unique in one other respect, too: like the Tomahawk and unlike the typically large Soviet missiles of the past, it can be launched from torpedo tubes. This capability could permit the Soviets to put SLCMs on ships or submarines performing multiple roles and missions, again in contrast to the past when most SLCMs were on vessels dedicated to antiship roles. The missile's long range would permit it to be fired from well off American shores. If it proves accurate, and this is not yet clear, it could be used to circumvent any potential American ballistic missile defense to strike C^3 in the United States.[29]

The enthusiasm for nuclear land-attack SLCMs does not adequately take into account the Soviet response—to arm its navy with comparable weapons. Once that occurs, and evidence suggests that Soviet programs are not lagging very far behind American ones, the net advantage to the United States is far from obvious. American allies in Europe and elsewhere and the United States itself are at least as vulnerable to SLCM attack as the USSR. Soviet fleets would not have to sail very far to get at targets in Europe, thus easing command-and-control difficulties, while an American fleet would have to challenge Soviet naval strongpoints in order to attack most Soviet land targets. The United States has more effective means than the SLCM to threaten Soviet naval installations, a particular concern for the U.S. Navy. Yet no interagency net assessment seems ever to have been undertaken of the strategic environment once the Soviet Union is armed with nuclear land-attack SLCMs.

Any LRTNF arms control regime that imposed ceilings on land-based cruise and ballistic missiles without constraining nuclear land-attack SLCMs could have the perverse effect of redirecting the nuclear arms competition to sea, a direction with eventually undesirable consequences for European if not American security. Yet meaningful limitations on nuclear land-attack SLCMs are hard to design.

A ban on all SLCMs is impracticable; both sides have already deployed conventional variants and have sound security grounds for continuing to do so. A ban on all nuclear-armed SLCMs would require the Soviet navy to dismantle the antiship versions it already has, but the ban would run into monitoring difficulties because of the indistinguishability of nuclear from conventional types. There are no externally observable differences between them, at least in the case of Tomahawk; if some way were found to design features differentiating them expressly for the purpose of monitoring, their effectiveness would remain in doubt. SLCMs pose more of a verification difficulty than their land-based look-

29. Joel Wit, "Soviet Cruise Missiles," *Survival*, vol. 25 (November–December 1983), pp. 249–60.

alikes, the GLCMs. It is easier to change warheads on SLCMs and to exercise them in nuclear form once they are on board ships or submarines out of view of national technical means of verification. Nuclear arming could be precluded at the point of testing, but both sides' programs have already passed that point. On-site inspection, in the form of sensors aboard ships or attached to each SLCM, might be able to distinguish between nuclear and conventional variants, but even if such sensors were developed, getting either the Soviet or the American navy to accept them would be an arduous negotiating task, and a time-consuming one.

One possible solution may be to ban nuclear-armed SLCMs with ranges in excess of 600 kilometers. Such a ban would minimize interference with existing deployments but would prohibit both sides from deploying new SLCMs they have already tested. It would also require limitations on modernizing existing short-range types so that the new versions would not violate the range limits. Furthermore, such limitations might not be inviolate; SLCMs tested at ranges under 600 kilometers might be capable of flying greater distances, though perhaps not more than one order of magnitude greater.

A ban on nuclear SLCMs under present technological conditions may be harder to verify than alternative forms of numerical constraints, however. Monitoring a count of nuclear SLCMs aboard any ship is very difficult because they are small enough to be stowed away without being detected. Yet the number of SLCMs could be indirectly limited in a militarily meaningful way by imposing ceilings on their platforms—ships and submarines—and on the number of nuclear SLCMs each may carry. These limits would be analogous to those imposed on ALCM carriers in SALT II. Carriers of nuclear SLCMs could be made distinguishable from other ships or submarines by functionally related observable differences in the form of uniquely configured facilities for storing and launching the missiles. But although cannisters to hold Tomahawk are longer than those that accommodate other SLCMs and are thus easily recognizable, the cannisters for the TLAM-N are the same as those for the conventionally armed TLAM-C and would have to be made distinguishable. In addition, limits could be placed on the number of torpedo tubes aboard submarines carrying nuclear SLCMs.

An alternative limit, but one that would interfere with both sides' programs, would be to set upper limits on the size of torpedo tubes and lower limits on the size of nuclear SLCMs to prohibit them from being fired from such tubes. Such limits would facilitate counting somewhat by forcing nuclear SLCMs to be stored and launched from unique and thus more countable containers. Monitoring might be further aided by type rules covering the classes of vessels carrying nuclear SLCMs or by severe numerical limits on such ships. Distinguishing these SLCM carriers from other ships has been made more feasible by the special procedures both superpowers have adopted for handling nuclear weapons, at least some of which are observable.

This combination of cooperative measures and counting rules would effectively raise the chances of detection for any party trying to evade an agreement by putting nuclear SLCMs aboard ships that are barred from carrying them. Although the provisions would not entirely prevent either side from slipping additional nuclear SLCMs onto designated nuclear SLCM carriers, the military advantage of additional SLCM reloads would be marginal. If their numbers were sufficiently limited, such ships would themselves be prime targets in a war and would be unlikely to launch more than a salvo or two before they were destroyed or disabled.

The prospect of limitations could lead to a thorough consideration of the military utility of nuclear SLCMs in comparison with conventional SLCMs. Limitations would give the navy some incentive to economize on the number or types of ships carrying nuclear SLCMs in order to leave most of the fleet free to load up with conventional cruise missiles. A similar incentive could affect Soviet navy calculations. There is at least some evidence that U.S. admirals are having second thoughts about nuclear SLCMs: when Pentagon civilians considered putting up to eighty TLAM-Ns on each of the eight Polaris submarines scheduled for replacement by Trident, the navy balked. It went ahead with plans to use the eight in antisubmarine warfare roles for the remainder of their useful lives.[30] Potential constraints might also prompt reconsideration of the roles and missions for nuclear SLCMs. For instance, armed with these weapons, ships become dual-capable. Even though the navy does not plan to commit TLAM-Ns to the Strategic Integrated Operational Plan or to NATO's general strike plan but to keep them in a strategic

---

30. The motives for doing so were undoubtedly mixed: some may have included the conversion as a competitor for scarce resources, perhaps jeopardizing full procurement of Trident itself. "Submarine Cruise Missile Plan Mulled," *Aviation Week and Space Technology*, vol. 112 (June 16, 1980), pp. 119–20.

reserve role, dual capability would confront fleet commanders with an awkward choice in wartime between carrying out their conventional war responsibilities and preparing for nuclear missions.[31]

The superpowers are fast approaching the end of a strategic environment free of nuclear land-attack SLCMs. The initial operating date for the American versions was estimated to be 1984, although technical problems have caused that date to be put back already and could put it back even more. Rather than rushing headlong to stuff nuclear SLCMs into every available ship, the United States should use this delay to undertake a net assessment of the effects of SLCM deployment on the superpower balance and to consider ways of constraining the SLCM threat by arms control. Negotiating limits on SLCM will take time, however, and might delay the conclusion of an agreement on land-based INF. With this in mind, the United States might well consider proposing a temporary moratorium on TLAM-N deployments. Such a proposal might give it some negotiating leverage on other issues in INF, since it has a short if temporary lead in the race to deploy sophisticated versions of these weapons. A moratorium could also turn the production delay to the ultimate advantage of the nation's security if it prompted a more thorough review of the costs and benefits of an arms race in which the development and deployment of nuclear SLCMs went ahead unconstrained on both sides.

British and French Nuclear Forces

The United States is not, of course, the only member of NATO to have nuclear weapons in Europe; Great Britain and France also possess them. The Soviet Union has insisted that these weapons be taken into account in any agreement on INF, something that the United States has refused to do. The significance of this Soviet demand can only be appreciated by examining British and French nuclear forces and their negotiating history in the contexts of both SALT and INF negotiations.

The composition, targeting doctrine, and declaratory policy of British and French nuclear forces differ from those of the United States. So do

---

31. *Strategic Force Modernization Programs,* Hearings before the Subcommittee on Strategic and Theater Nuclear Forces of the Senate Committee on Armed Services, 97 Cong. 1 sess. (GPO, 1981), p. 203.

the respective national interests and calculations of the circumstances in which these weapons might be used. And although one implication of the Soviet position is that these forces are an adequate substitute for American nuclear missiles in Europe, British and French forces cannot plausibly take the place of the American nuclear deterrent in guaranteeing the security of all of NATO. At best, they can complement the American deterrent, especially against threats to their own territory. Complementarity works both ways, however; it is the American deterrent and the American presence in Europe that lend added credibility to British and French nuclear forces in carrying out their deterrent roles by presenting the possibility that nuclear use would not be limited to Britain and France alone.

Some of the French, not all of them Gaullists, have long preached that no nation could be counted on to risk its own destruction to protect anyone but itself. As Defense Minister Charles Hernu noted, "France is developing its own deterrent strategy because when the time comes to make decisive choices a great country is alone."[32] Yet great countries can make decisive choices to cooperate as well as to dissociate at such times.

In its own force posture and declaratory policy, France acknowledges at least some residual capacity for extending deterrence to West Germany. And even though its nuclear forces are not as formidable as those of the United States, geographic proximity may lend credibility to a French guarantee in a way that it cannot to the American. This is true only for West Germany, however, not for the rest of NATO Europe. French declaratory policy on extended deterrence has always been somewhat ambiguous. Part of the ambiguity is deliberate and part circumstantial. Deliberately, no French government has ever specified the vital interests for which it would be prepared to invoke a nuclear threat. In particular, no French government has ever excluded West Germany from those vital interests. What gives this silence meaning and extended deterrence some credibility are the circumstances in which France might have to consider using nuclear weapons. Were it to come under conventional attack by the Warsaw Pact, that attack would probably follow from the expansion of a war in West Germany. Because West Germany is no more than 275 miles wide and is 130 miles at its

---

32. Charles Hernu, "Une Défense, des Choix, des Moyens," *Le Figaro*, January 30–31, 1982.

narrowest, France, acting solely to preserve its own territorial integrity and survival, would have to consider using its nuclear deterrent before Germany was overrun. Extended deterrence is at least to this extent unavoidable.

Beyond this zone of ambiguity, those in a position to speak authoritatively on behalf of France in recent years have on occasion openly embraced an expanded area of vital interest. In the mid-1970s, General Guy Mery, armed forces chief of staff, sparked considerable controversy by referring publicly to *sanctuarisation élargie*—enlarged sanctuary— by which he implied extending France's deterrent to its European neighbors, in particular West Germany.[33] The government retreated under heavy fire, particularly from right-wing Gaullists who denounced the idea as being beyond France's capabilities and hence lacking credibility, the same view they have held about the American deterrent. Yet the Giscardists eventually settled on a declaratory policy of Meryism without Mery. Announcing tests of France's enhanced-radiation weapon, President Valéry Giscard d'Estaing told a June 26, 1980, press conference, "In our reflections about the employment of this weapon, we will take account of the following assumption: France is directly concerned with the security of neighboring European states."[34] Defense Minister Yvon Bourges later traced this line of policy to a 1972 white paper, which stated that

though deterrence is reserved for the protection of our vital interests, the limits of the latter are necessarily somewhat hazy. . . . France lives in a network of interests which go beyond her borders. She is not isolated. Therefore, Western Europe as a whole cannot fail to benefit indirectly from French strategy.[35]

The policy of extended deterrence continues under Giscard d'Estaing's Socialist successor. In his first formal statement on defense, Prime Minister Pierre Mauroy made the point somewhat more unequivocally when he stated that "an attack against France does not begin when an

33. "The Purpose of Pluton," Address by the French Prime Minister M. Chirac, February 10, 1975, *Survival*, vol. 17 (September–October 1975), pp. 241–43; and "French Defense Policy," comments by General Guy Mery, March 15, 1976, *Survival*, vol. 18 (September–October 1976), pp. 226–28.

34. "La Conférence de Presse," *Le Monde*, June 28, 1980.

35. Michel Debré, *French White Paper on National Defense*, vol. 1: *1972* (New York: Service de Presse et d'Information, 1972), p. 13. See also "Yvon Bourges Interviewed on Defense Capabilities," in FBIS, *Daily Report: WEU*, May 9, 1980, p. K7.

enemy enters her territory."[36] Even Jacques Chirac, keeper of the flame of Gaullist nationalism, has called for a "strategic nuclear guarantee" for Western Europe involving French nuclear forces along with the British and American.[37] For those French generations that have fought Germany, extending a nuclear guarantee to West Germany has political meaning that transcends military technicalities. But because doctrine is only intermittently a subject of public discussion in France, public support for it is largely untested, and French officials are hesitant to put it to a test.

Today, more than ever before, the dominant view of France's strategic doctrine, widely shared among French officials in and out of uniform, contemplates first use of nuclear weapons. In a conventional war against the Warsaw Pact, they would be prepared initially to use tactical nuclear weapons to warn of impending strikes by their strategic nuclear forces and to demonstrate their resolve, then attack the Soviet Union itself. They insist on distinguishing their strategy from the flexible response of NATO, which they continue to disparage as too flexible to ensure a response, but they remain skeptical of controlling escalation once the nuclear threshold is crossed. They see a continuing role for land-based IRBMs to underline the risk of any attack on France and to shift the assumption of that risk to the attacker, who would have to eliminate those IRBMs, presumably by using nuclear weapons first. Were an attacker to try, France would have SLBMs in reserve.

Current French nuclear weapons programs, begun under Giscard d'Estaing and expanded under President François Mitterrand, seem consistent with this strategic doctrine. Modernization of France's strategic forces will reduce somewhat their vulnerability to enemy attack while nearly doubling the number of warheads they can deliver against Soviet targets. A new missile, the M-4, with up to six warheads not independently targetable, will replace the sixteen single-warhead M-20 missiles aboard France's five nuclear submarines. A sixth nuclear submarine is under construction, and a seventh, the first of a new generation, is scheduled to be launched in 1994. The latter will carry a

36. Speech before the Institute of Advanced National Defense Studies, September 14, 1981, quoted in François de Rose, "Updating Deterrence in Europe: Inflexible Response?" *Survival*, vol. 24 (January–February 1982), p. 22.

37. "Politicians Plan Group to Counter Socialists," *International Herald-Tribune*, July 6, 1982.

new MIRVed missile, the M-5, as yet of undecided specification though undoubtedly of longer range. France's IRBM force, consisting of eighteen S-3s with a range of 3,500 kilometers, is based in vulnerable fixed sites in the Albion Plateau of Haute-Provence in southern France. A new mobile IRBM, the SX, is being designed to replace them and the aging Mirage IV force by 1992. In the meantime, the thirty-three Mirage IVs will be armed with air-to-surface cruise missiles to enhance their penetrativity and to prolong their usefulness at least until the new IRBM is deployed. Command, control, and communications facilities will also be hardened. France's strategic forces will then have the combination of range and relative inaccuracy that is appropriate for attacking Moscow and other cities and soft targets in the USSR yet that poses no serious threat to the Soviet land-based ICBM force except if used in conjunction with U.S. nuclear forces. Improved survivability will enhance their deterrent capacity.

Modernization of French tactical nuclear forces is not incompatible with their role in signaling escalation as well as in extending deterrence. A new tactical nuclear missile, Hades, with nearly triple Pluton's range of 120 kilometers, could reach Warsaw Pact territory from either side of the Franco-German border, thereby conveying seriousness of purpose without jeopardizing West German territory. Enhanced-radiation weapons, tested but not yet deployed, could, French officials argue, be used against Warsaw Pact forces in West Germany more readily than other tactical nuclear weapons because they reduce collateral damage somewhat. Although these weapons are designed to stop tank attacks in densely settled areas, that is not the purpose that the French claim to have in mind for them. As Defense Minister Bourges said shortly before the weapons tests were announced,

They show that our wish is to warn, to reprimand, to say: Stop, our vital interests are threatened; we cannot accept this aggression and we are ready to raise the battle to the strategic nuclear threshold. . . . In the hypothesis that you have to use these arms on a friendly territory which has been invaded, the advantage is that you may perhaps avoid killing your friends at the same time as the enemy's army.[38]

Bourges' Socialist successor, Charles Hernu, less concerned about arousing Gaullist ire, could afford to be more explicit about the implications of enhanced-radiation weapons. Acquiring the weapon, he told

38. "Yvon Bourges Interviewed on Defense Capabilities," p. K6.

an interviewer in September 1982, would mean that France "was prepared to enter a war not only as soon as our territory was threatened (since, in that case, we have the deterrent force), but as soon as enemy tanks entered Germany. France would, therefore, be prepared to take part in a 'forward battle.' "[39] The implication of Hernu's remark, that France was contemplating early first use of nuclear weapons, is less than wholly credible, however, and especially so if not backed by the American nuclear guarantee.

Great Britain's strategic nuclear deterrent resembles France's insofar as the decision to use it does not require American assent, but there the resemblance ends. Britain's declaratory policy, strategic doctrine, and force posture all differ from France's. So, too, does the breadth of domestic support for remaining a nuclear power: the issue of an independent deterrent is not above politics as it is in France.

France's rejection of NATO's doctrine of flexible response precludes it from openly committing its nuclear deterrent to the alliance or from formal reintegration with NATO. By contrast, the British deterrent is formally tied to NATO. The ties may be mere formality. Planned coordination of targeting could in practice prove purely coincidental; even the terms of the Nassau agreement dedicating Polaris submarines to NATO permit them to be used independently when Great Britain's "supreme national interests are at stake"—presumably the only circumstances in which their use would be considered. Yet government after government has reiterated the commitment of Britain's deterrent to NATO.

The British reconcile independence with dedication of their deterrent to NATO by stressing the need for a "second center" of decision, a rationale originated by General André Beaufré to justify France's deterrent. As stated in the 1980 British white paper justifying the decision to acquire Trident,

A Soviet leadership . . . might believe that it could impose its will on Europe by military force without becoming involved in strategic nuclear war with the United States. Modernised U.S. nuclear forces in Europe help guard against any such misconception; but an independent capability fully under European control provides a key element of insurance. A nuclear decision would of course be no less agonising for the United Kingdom than for the United States. But it would be the decision of a separate and independent power, and a power whose survival

39. *Le Figaro Magazine*, September 4–10, 1982, pp. 54–55.

in freedom would be directly and immediately threatened by aggression in Europe.[40]

The second-center argument seems intended more to deflect British domestic criticism than to devise a sound strategic doctrine. Unlike France, the United Kingdom's insular position sets it apart from the Continent. Although discouraging hegemonic drives on the Continent has been a fundamental purpose of British foreign policy for the past three centuries, the prospect of Soviet nuclear retaliation might seem a more imminent threat to Britain's survival. Consequently, it is not apparent why the Warsaw Pact, in contemplating a conventional attack on central Europe, would consider British use of nuclear weapons more likely than American use of them.

Alternatively, the second-center rationale may imply that British first use would somehow act as a powder train to set off American nuclear forces or that British strategic forces would deter Soviet retaliation against the British Isles in the event that Britain used its battlefield nuclear forces on the Continent, alone or in concert with its allies. The British white paper on Trident addresses the second possibility:

British nuclear forces include both strategic and lower-level components. If we had only the latter they could not serve the key "second-centre" deterrent purpose, since the threat of their use would not be credible. An aggressor faced with an armoury comprising only non-strategic nuclear weapons would know that he could if necessary use strategic nuclear weapons to overbear it without risking strategic retaliation upon himself. . . .[41]

Yet the second-center rationale assumes that whether as catalyst or as sanctuary the United Kingdom might act before and independently of the United States. Why the British would risk nuclear first use alone in either case—and in circumstances in which the United States was reluctant to join—is not at all clear. British unilateral first use of nuclear weapons, especially of its "lower-level components," hardly seems credible under these conditions. Even if first use by NATO were to involve the lower-level components of British nuclear forces on the Continent, London could hardly view that step with detachment, despite its independent strategic deterrent.

What the British independent deterrent can do more credibly than the American guarantee is to deter a Soviet attack on Great Britain, period.

40. "The Future United Kingdom Strategic Nuclear Deterrent Force," Defence Open Government Document 80/23 (Ministry of Defence, 1980), pp. 3–4.
41. Ibid., p. 4.

How much the added insurance is worth and whether the country can afford it are likely to remain matters of heated parliamentary debate in London.[42]

Britain's lower-level nuclear components include one regiment equipped with twelve Lance missiles and three regiments armed with dual-capable artillery whose nuclear warheads are controlled under two-key arrangements with the United States. The components also include gravity bombs for medium-range dual-capable aircraft—Buccaneers, Jaguars, and Tornadoes. Britain's strategic nuclear forces presently consist of four nuclear submarines, each with sixteen missiles. Each missile is now being equipped to carry up to three warheads, although it has three additional racks to hold advanced penetration aids, leading Soviet negotiators to treat it as if it had six independently targetable warheads. The Chevaline program will give the new reentry vehicle a capacity to maneuver in space, though not to target the warheads over a wide enough area to qualify as being MIRVed. With the retirement of Britain's fifty-seven Vulcan bombers armed with gravity bombs, what remains is consonant with a minimum deterrent capable of surviving a Soviet first strike and of retaliating against Soviet cities or soft targets, especially Moscow. But Great Britain cannot credibly extend deterrence to its Continental allies without American backing: it has too few submarines on patrol to make possible withholding warheads in a limited attack, and those warheads are too inaccurate to threaten targets other than Soviet cities. Indeed, current British targeting doctrine, to the extent it contemplates a decapitation attack on Moscow, would be somewhat incompatible with the extended deterrence provided by American strategic forces.

Acquisition of Trident D-5 missiles will add to Britain's ability to deter an attack on itself, but it will not make Britain's independent deterrent any more credible for extending a nuclear umbrella to its Continental allies. The D-5 has twice the range of the Polaris A-3 missile, allowing a nuclear submarine to patrol a much greater area. Increased range not only improves its survivability but may also make withholding more feasible. Each D-5 can carry up to fourteen independently targetable warheads, although the British presently intend to put no more than eight MIRVs on each missile. MIRVing the sixteen missiles on each submarine would increase the number of targets they could strike by an

42. A lucid and authoritative discussion of the debate over British nuclear posture and policy is found in Lawrence Freedman, *Britain and Nuclear Weapons* (London: Macmillan Press for the Royal Institute of International Affairs, 1980).

order of magnitude, and the accuracy of the D-5s enables them to attack hard targets, including Soviet ICBM silos. They could not, however, strike in sufficient numbers to give Britain a first-strike capability against the entire Soviet land-based missile force unless they were used as part of the American Single Integrated Operational Plan. In addition to increasing the credibility of minimum deterrence, therefore, the D-5 might enable Great Britain to withhold an attack on cities and strike a variety of other targets. The British white paper on Trident hints at this prospect in justifying acquisition of the earlier generation of Trident missile, the C-4:

Successive United Kingdom governments have always declined to make public their nuclear targetting policy and plans, or to define precisely what minimum level of destructive capability they judged necessary for deterrence. The Government however thinks it right now to make clear that their concept of deterrence is concerned essentially with posing a potential threat to key aspects of Soviet state power. *There might with changing conditions be more than one way of doing this, and some flexibility in contingency planning is appropriate* [emphasis added].[43]

British and French nuclear forces are a critical element in the Soviet negotiating position in INF. The position is that British and French nuclear forces must be "taken into account," a phrase that has at least two meanings. For the moment, it seems to mean that the existence of these forces requires no new American LRTNF missiles to be deployed in Europe. At some later date, however, the USSR may shift to demand formal numerical compensation for these forces, other limits, or the right to add to its forces once Britain and France MIRV theirs. This implication is also present in the Soviet insistence on "equality and equal security." The Soviet position thus has the effect of directing pressure toward the two nuclear powers from other NATO allies who are anxious to get an accord. If the superpowers were nearing an agreement in START, especially one involving substantial reductions, pressure would grow for Britain and France to join the negotiations or to accept some limitations.

France, for its part, has shown no interest in negotiating over its own nuclear forces; it considers them to have an altogether different function from those to be limited in INF talks. It has also opposed any American compensation. Foreign Minister Mauroy has taken care to reduce France's political exposure somewhat by leaving open the possibility of

43. "The Future United Kingdom Strategic Nuclear Deterrent Force," p. 6.

negotiating eventually. "Our means could not initially be affected by negotiations," he told the West European Union Assembly on November 29, 1982, presumably allowing for the unlikely event that the superpowers agree on sharp reductions.[44] The British government has been only slightly more forthcoming in public, although there is some sentiment for joining the negotiations among those who have always looked upon British nuclear forces as a means of being invited to the top table—the Labour party made a small point of this in its 1983 election manifesto. But Britain's second white paper on Trident refuses to countenance negotiations on its forces on two grounds: first, they are strategic forces, and second, as such they "account for no more than a very small fraction of the total size of the strategic nuclear forces" of the superpowers. But it does not quite bar the door: "If these circumstances were to change significantly, e.g., if Soviet military capabilities and the threat they pose to the United Kingdom were to be reduced substantially, we would of course be prepared to review our position in relation to arms control. But this point would appear to be a long way off."[45] These positions do little to ease pressures in Europe, and in Britain itself, for including British and French systems in the INF negotiations. Moreover, the reason France and Britain give for not including their SLBMs—that they are national strategic nuclear forces—runs counter to recent rationales for their forces—that they provide a second center of decision and extend deterrence to West Germany.

In both SALT I and II Soviet negotiators argued that British and French systems be taken into account.[46] They also sought a nontransfer provision prohibiting the United States from passing on missile technology to its allies. The United States successfully resisted these demands. The USSR has taken a similar position in INF, but it has been slow to tie proposed ceiling levels to the specific numbers in allied forces. The

44. "Premier Mauroy Cited on European Defense," in FBIS, *Daily Report: WEU*, December 6, 1982, p. K1.

45. "The United Kingdom Trident Programme," Defence Open Government Document 82/1, Cmnd. 8517 (Ministry of Defence, 1982), p. 6.

46. In SALT I, too, the Soviet delegation twice made the unilateral statement that if, during the period that the agreement was in effect, "U.S. allies in NATO should increase the number of their modern submarines," not SLBMs, "the Soviet Union will have the right to a corresponding increase in the number of its submarines." Both times the United States rejected the claim. See Roger D. Labrie, ed., *SALT Handbook: Key Documents and Issues, 1972–1979* (Washington, D.C.: American Enterprise Institute for Public Policy Research, 1979), p. 31.

walk-in-the-woods formula also notably omitted any mention of compensation to the Soviets for those forces, as did Kvitsinsky's November 13, 1983, proposal. These are not the moves of negotiators who deem an issue fundamental to their security and the sine qua non of any settlement.

That the Soviet position is intended primarily for political effect and not to achieve a particular negotiating result is evident. The USSR seeks limitations only on American missiles and has not attempted to draw Britain and France into negotiations, which is the only way to achieve limitations on their weapons systems. A Tass commentator made the Soviet position unusually explicit in January 1983 when he told a French broadcast audience that

the Soviet side has not tried—nor is it trying—to discuss French and British nuclear weapons at the Soviet-American talks. The Soviet Union does not propose limiting or reducing the nuclear forces of France or Great Britain. If the USSR and the United States come to an agreement in Geneva on the reduction of nuclear weapons in Europe, not a single provision of such an agreement would impose obligations on France or Great Britain. At the same time, the USSR cannot omit from the sum total of nuclear weapons those possessed by Great Britain and France, because these are not neutral countries, but allies of America in the Atlantic pact: They are nuclear powers whose missiles are capable of reaching Soviet territory.[47]

While many on both sides of the Atlantic are ready to concede the Soviet point and grant formal compensation for British and French missiles, there is not much merit for this view on security grounds. Andropov's December 1982 proposal to reduce Soviet missiles in Europe to equal those of the British and French implies that British and French forces, along with some American aircraft and other nuclear forces committed to NATO, are all Europe needs to counter Soviet forces and that any supplement to the American deterrent is unnecessary. Andropov's subsequent refinement, to count warheads or missiles, amounts to the same thing; by counting British SLBMs as if they carried six warheads, the Soviets come up with a combined total of 482 warheads on British and French missiles. The numbers would have a different meaning once both countries MIRV their SLBMs, although the Soviet count, by crediting the British Polaris with six warheads per missile,

47. Leonid Ponomarev, "Only on the Basis of Equality and Equal Security," Radio Moscow, broadcast in French to Europe, January 22, 1983, translated and reprinted in "Tass Observer Explains Soviet Weapons Proposals," FBIS, *Daily Report: Soviet Union*, January 24, 1983, p. AA6. On February 23, 1981, Brezhnev spoke of drawing other nuclear powers into talks "in due time."

makes it easier to adjust to a Trident missile carrying eight. The one-for-one formula is consistent with previous Soviet proposals that speak only of taking British and French systems into account. While the other formulas are less explicit in numerical terms, all are designed to deny deployment of new American missiles. In this light, any formal inclusion of British and French nuclear forces as part of the U.S. ceiling, especially on a one-for-one basis, could not avoid creating an impression of decoupling.

Second, when Soviet bean counters tally up what they need to counter the strategic weapons arrayed against them, the number they add in for Britain and France bears no particular relationship to the 162 or 140 or 120 missiles they propose as a ceiling for SS-20s. All but 18 of the French and British missiles are SLBMs on just 9 submarines. These submarines cannot be attacked by SS-20s unless they are in port. Even if all other British and French nuclear forces as well as command-and-control and other nuclear facilities were targeted by SS-20s, and there are indications that Soviet planners intend that ICBMs be used for this purpose, the number of SS-20s required would be far less than 162 or 140 or 120—or 486 or 420 or 360, if warheads rather than launchers were the unit of account. It makes no difference whether the missiles on the other side are MRVed, as the British SLBMs presently are, or MIRVed, as both British and French SLBMs will eventually be.

Moreover, as the British white paper makes clear, it is only in the context of negotiating ceilings on missiles in Europe that the numbers of British and French weapons stand out. These numbers disappear in the rounding once the strategic arsenals of the two superpowers are considered. Only if the superpowers were to negotiate substantial reductions in their nuclear arsenals while Britain and France added substantially to theirs would the Soviet demand to take those systems into account have some military validity.

At this point, however, the demand for formal compensation serves Moscow's political purpose more than its military strategy. NATO is unlikely to countenance satisfying it. Apart from the demands of formal compensation, however, NATO has no need to retain a number of INF missiles equal to the number of Soviet INF missiles within striking range of Europe. If European governments were prepared to accept a ceiling that, de facto or de jure, left the USSR with a few more warheads-on-launchers in Europe than the United States has, so long as the difference bore no relationship to the number of British and French warheads or launchers, the United States should have no trouble agreeing to it. There is some precedent for this approach in SALT I.[48]

Modalities: INF Negotiations and START

That SALT II would be ratified and SALT III would follow promptly was a political premise of INF negotiations from their inception. The December 1979 decisions spoke of conducting negotiations on INF "within the framework of SALT III." The "III" was quietly jettisoned soon thereafter, and the term "SALT" fell into disuse a little later, but the principle of linkage between intercontinental and intermediate-range systems remains.

In the largest sense this principle is less a commitment to formal linkage than an acknowledgment of political and military reality: negotiations to limit INF cannot be conducted wholly apart from negotiations to limit intercontinental systems. Militarily, numerical ceilings on INF are meaningless in the absence of ceilings on nuclear weapons of intercontinental range because numerically they constitute a small proportion of the superpowers' nuclear inventories. From the perspective of both Soviet and European military planners, moreover, nuclear weapons based in Europe are just as strategic as ICBMs in their ability to put homelands at risk. To the Soviet Union a missile is a missile, to paraphrase Robert McNamara's comment during the Cuban missile crisis, whether it is based in North Dakota or at Greenham Common. And from the perspective of European politics, at least the appearance of linkage between the two sets of talks is essential to underscore coupling. In addition, informal linkage in bargaining is unavoidable; any

48. The interim agreement permitted the USSR "no more than 950 ballistic missile launchers on submarines and no more than 62 modern ballistic missile submarines." In proposing that, the United States counted the 740 SLBMs then on submarines in operation or under construction and was prepared to allow the USSR to trade in ICBMs for additional SLBMs beyond that baseline up to the higher ceiling. But the baseline figures assumed inclusion of some 30 G- and H-class diesel submarines, by definition not modern, which contained about 100 SLBMs. The Soviet negotiators accepted the baseline figure but rejected the inclusion of the G- and H-class submarines and their missiles. The ensuing bargaining resulted in exclusion of the 60 older SLBMs aboard the G-class submarines. Among alternative rationales offered for this compromise by the Soviet Union but not accepted by the United States was compensation for British and French SLBMs. See Raymond L. Garthoff, *Detente and Confrontation: American-Soviet Relations from Nixon to Reagan* (Brookings Institution, forthcoming).

move at one table by either side is examined for its implications at the other. This fact of negotiating life takes on institutional embodiment in Washington, where the so-called backstopping groups, bureaucrats who draft the cables of instructions to the negotiators in Geneva, have the same composition for both INF and START. The inevitability of bargaining linkage, even if it does not take similar institutional form in the USSR, will make Soviet negotiators reluctant to conclude an agreement in one forum without at least seeing the outlines of agreement in the other take shape.

Some have proposed merging the two sets of talks in Geneva. Formal merger would facilitate bargaining linkages between INF and START, a desired result among its proponents, many of them Europeans, who doubt that the West has the leverage to conclude an acceptable agreement in INF alone or who do not want cruise and Pershing II missiles even as bargaining chips. Merging the talks would also diminish the visibility of British and French systems, whose numbers stand out only in the INF context. Merger might also ease the Soviets' way back to negotiating on LRTNF.[49]

Merger, however, would possibly make concluding an INF agreement hostage to results in START. And because the prospects of a START agreement are not much better than those for INF, merger would redirect European pressure from one forum to the other, a consequence the Reagan administration recognizes and resists. Merger would also inevitably lead to demands for more detailed consultation with the allies on START, which would impinge on the autonomy of the American services, a jealously guarded prerogative: "getting the allies into our knickers" is the way they sometimes put it. It is difficult enough for the navy and the air force to cooperate in preparing the Single Integrated Operational Plan and worse yet to have civilians intimately involved, however indirectly, through the procurement and arms control processes; but the situation might become almost intolerable if some of these civilians were foreigners, even if they are allies. Merger would encounter some service resistance.

An alternative to formal merger would be to adopt a common ceiling covering both LRTNF and intercontinental weapons. One way to

49. The Soviet press has hinted at this possibility by publishing an interview with Finland's prime minister, Kalevi Sorsa, in which he proposed merging the talks. See "USSR Leans Toward Strategic-Missile Talks Merger," in FBIS, *Daily Report: WEU,* November 15, 1983, p. P1.

construct such a ceiling would be simply to aggregate the ceilings on nuclear delivery vehicles or warheads negotiated separately in INF and START upon completion of both agreements. This combined aggregate might have some beneficial effect on perceptions: it would attempt to demonstrate coupling and would allow the British and French numbers to pale in significance. Other variants of the common ceiling resemble informal merger of the two talks in disguised form. One that has gained considerable currency on both sides of the Atlantic would allow ceilings reached in an interim INF agreement to become subceilings within an equal combined aggregate to be negotiated eventually in START. If the agreement were to allow both sides to trade in intercontinental systems for LRTNF or vice versa, it might facilitate Soviet acceptance of some new NATO deployments that would come at the expense of American central systems.

Such a common ceiling would also permit a lower level of American LRTNF to be deployed without decoupling consequences. The common ceiling could aggravate relations in the alliance, however, if a U.S. choice to retain fewer LRTNF were seen as a move to protect itself at the expense of Europe. The common ceiling might also aggravate relations in the alliance if the USSR chose to trade in many of its SS-20s for central systems; such a move, though unlikely, could inspire American unilateralists to claim that the United States was sacrificing itself for Europe. A low enough INF ceiling in relation to the overall aggregate would minimize these possibilities. It remains to be seen, however, whether such an approach would be acceptable to the USSR.

Arms Control and Stable Deterrence in Europe

Those who contemplate fighting a nuclear war and those who demand nuclear disarmament tend to have one thing in common: they think in prenuclear terms and insist that what counts is mostly the numbers of weapons on each side, even though they differ on whether those numbers should go up or down. In so doing, they ignore or try to wish away nuclear interdependence. In disarmament circles, current talk focuses on freezing deployments and reducing them. While disarmers yearn for a world in which nuclear weapons would somehow disappear altogether and with them all risk of nuclear war, that yearning is unlikely to be satisfied in the foreseeable future, if ever. It will have to await techniques of monitoring far more comprehensive than any currently available and provisions for verification far more intrusive than any now politically acceptable. In the meantime, military stability remains the measure of arms control. Steps can be taken to reduce the likelihood that nuclear arsenals will be used, steps that can preserve a modicum of military stability, however precarious. And the preservation of military stability may facilitate further steps toward political stability.

A stabilizing outcome is possible at Geneva. Such an outcome would not eliminate instability, but it could keep the current situation from worsening. Whatever the results at Geneva, however, their effects on strategic stability will be marginal because mutual deterrence depends on the state of the conventional balance in Europe and on the ultimate ability and will of the United States to use nuclear weapons in Europe's behalf. Neither the conditions nor the perceptions of them will be appreciably altered by new nuclear deployments against European targets on either side or by negotiated limits on those deployments. Crisis stability, and consequently arms race stability, could be enhanced though not assured by reaching an accord at Geneva that holds Pershing II deployments to a minimum well below the levels currently planned and reduces the number of SS-20s targeted on Europe. Although no arms control agreement is currently conceivable that would eliminate all incentive for one side or the other to use nuclear weapons first should nuclear escalation appear imminent, limiting Pershing II would move in the right direction. So too would unilateral acts by NATO taken in its own security interests, above all efforts to protect whatever INF missiles it deploys against the ravages of a first strike. Another helpful unilateral step would be a drastic reduction in NATO's short-range nuclear forces, a step addressed in chapter 6.

CHAPTER SIX

Battlefield Nuclear Weapons
and Stable Deterrence

*I don't know what effect these men will have on the enemy, but, by God,
they frighten me.*   Sometimes attributed to the Duke of Wellington

RECENTLY, European publics have paid the most attention to long-range theater nuclear forces because of the deployment of the GLCM and Pershing II. Yet four other aspects of NATO's nuclear posture pose a more immediate problem for stable deterrence in Europe. First, the disproportionate number of short-range systems in its nuclear arsenal adds little to NATO's deterrent. Second, the physical location and the difficulty of dispersing those weapons make them vulnerable to preemptive attack by either conventional or nuclear forces. Third, the difficulties that NATO is likely to encounter in deciding whether to use the weapons cast doubt on whether they would ever be usable. Fourth, the commingling of nuclear and conventional capabilities may actually detract from rather than supplement NATO's ability to conduct conventional defense.

While proposals are often entertained to consider these weapons in arms control negotiations along with those of longer range, the issues they raise for NATO nuclear doctrine are so pressing that they are better addressed by the alliance unilaterally outside the negotiating context. For that reason these issues deserve separate treatment here.

The Short-Range Emphasis in NATO's Present Nuclear Posture

Short-range nuclear forces designed for use on or near the battlefield make up the largest part of NATO's nuclear inventory. Most are owned

156

and operated by the United States and are attached to American forces in Europe. Others are dual-key systems, U.S.-owned but operated under various provisions for joint control by allied forces. Still others are owned and operated by various European forces.

Of the roughly 6,000 American nuclear warheads currently at NATO's disposal in Europe, 1,670 are artillery shells that can strike targets less than 10 miles away. Another 700 warheads are designed for air defense, detonating with a blast sufficient to knock a wing of enemy aircraft out of the sky. A further 370 are atomic demolition munitions (ADMs), which can be installed in a few hours at previously dug sites—tunnels, mountain passes, and other topographically opportune locations—to retard the advance of tanks and other vehicles.[1]

Although these weapons are referred to as deterrents, in a strict sense they are not. Short-range or battlefield nuclear weapons could be used against enemy forces in battle or to prevent their massing prior to an attack. They cannot, however, threaten to impose such prohibitively high costs on the enemy, that they can prevent either a conventional or a nuclear attack. Nor could they deny the enemy gains without destroying what they are supposed to defend. Indeed, by virtue of their location and vulnerability, they, like the American fleet at Pearl Harbor in December 1941, are more an invitation for than a deterrent to enemy attack. Without exception, American exercises have shown that whenever NATO might try to use nuclear weapons, it would prompt a preemptive strike.[2]

Location and Relocation

Nuclear weapons require special storage and handling facilities to protect them from accidents and terrorism. The trained manpower and extraordinary expense involved in maintaining these facilities has led the United States to economize on their number: most U.S. short-range warheads in central Europe are concentrated at just twenty-odd storage sites, all of them recognizable and doubtless known to the Warsaw Pact.

1. Richard Halloran, "Report to Congress Provides Figures for Nuclear Arsenal," *New York Times,* November 15, 1983.
2. *Department of Defense Authorization for Appropriations for Fiscal Year 1979,* Hearings before the Senate Committee on Armed Services, 95 Cong. 2 sess. (Government Printing Office, 1978), pt. 9: *Research and Development,* pp. 6559–61.

Protection of these weapons in peacetime, needless to say, comes at the expense of their vulnerability to attack in war.

Dispersing the weapons, however, poses other problems. It is sometimes claimed that dispersal would reduce the weapons' vulnerability to attack and would strengthen the enemy's conviction about NATO's will to use them. But host governments are reluctant to consider either relocation or peacetime exercises involving dispersal because the movement of nuclear weapons could arouse popular opposition in the immediate vicinity. Moreover, to affect Soviet perceptions of U.S. will, dispersal would also require putting the weapons into the hands of commanders in the field—those who would have some incentive to use them—thus raising the prospect of unauthorized employment and the risk of enemy preemption. Such a prospect is unappealing to publics fearful of nuclear war, and it is unacceptable to leaders who would like to believe that they retain control of the ultimate decision.

To leave the weapons where they are does not avoid the problem. Nuclear artillery shells, for example, are stored only a few hours' march from the intra-German frontier. To redeploy them to forward positions during a crisis might signal a hardening of NATO's will but at the risk that they might be preempted, overrun, or used prematurely. To hold them back would mean that if they were used at all, they would be used on West German territory. Authority to use them in that case might be hard to obtain. Measures to reduce the collateral damage of the weapons would not diminish the difficulty because the collateral damage caused by a Soviet response or preemptive strike is unlikely to be low.

ADMs sharpen the dilemma of peacetime location and crisis relocation. These munitions are designed to be emplaced along access routes at or near the frontier to plug gaps in NATO defenses and to retard Warsaw Pact advances into NATO territory. Because of the time required to dig these weapons into tunnels, mountain passes, and other suitable locations, ADMs must be put into place well before use. But peacetime dispersal, in addition to risking accidental or unauthorized use or even seizure by terrorists, would make ADM sites more visible to enemy surveillance. In the event of war, ADMs could be overrun and captured or at least preempted, not necessarily by nuclear means. Prechambering—digging holes to accommodate ADMs at preselected sites without actually relocating them in forward positions—might enhance their security in peacetime, but it would not avoid the dilemma of whether to deploy them in a crisis. Forward deployment of ADMs during a crisis would have a more purely defensive character than redeploying other nuclear systems and should not prompt nuclear preemption by the other side. But redeployment would be visible to enemy reconnaissance and would leave ADMs in exposed positions that could be overrun. Fearing their loss, theater commanders would propose using them. Political leaders might well hesitate to grant authority, finding the first use of nuclear weapons on their own territory an uninspiring signal for all to see, not the least for those living in the vicinity. For this very reason, prechambering has never found favor with European governments.

Hobson's Choice in Nuclear Decisionmaking

The decision to employ nuclear weapons of shorter ranges could prove as difficult for Europeans to make as the decision to use longer-range weapons would be for the United States. As a West German white paper on defense put the issue in 1975–76, "The first use of tactical nuclear weapons must come as late as possible (i.e., time) but as early as necessary (i.e., space)."[3] The procedures for making the decision and the extraordinary circumstances in which the choice would arise do not bode well for timely action. A request for authority to use nuclear weapons on or near the battlefield could be transmitted from corps commanders through Supreme Headquarters, Allied Powers Europe (SHAPE) to the North Atlantic Council and the National Command Authority. The council consists of representatives of all NATO member states except France; the National Command Authority is the president of the United States or his lawful successor. If both approve, orders would then be dispatched back through channels to corps and divisions, and ultimately to the commanders of nuclear delivery units. Even assuming no interruption in communications, the process would take twenty-four hours, according to a U.S. Army estimate. While set procedures for consultations are subject to "time and circumstances

---

3. Bundesminister der Verteidigung, *Weissbuch 1975/76* (Bonn: Presse- und Informationsamt, 1976), p. 21.

permitting,'' any hint of short-circuiting the formal channels could disrupt allied unity.[4]

Although the channels of communication are well established, the rules governing the use of nuclear weapons are much less so. NATO agreed on political guidelines for nuclear use at Athens in 1962 and on procedures for consultation in 1969. Guidelines on the initial selective use of nuclear weapons, including battlefield weapons, ADMs, and theater weapons, were adopted in the early 1970s, but ten years of negotiation within NATO have brought no agreement on rules governing follow-on use.[5] Bilateral agreements between the United States and host countries define some release procedures for U.S. nuclear warheads deployed in Europe under programs of cooperation.

Release procedures within the NATO Military Committee have never been spelled out in public. Indeed, prudence counsels silence. If it were clear to Warsaw Pact countries that any member of NATO could veto the use of nuclear weapons, the possibility of executing deterrent threats might seem too remote to have much credibility. On the other hand, if it were clear to domestic publics that no veto existed, alliance unity might break up on the shoals of national sovereignty. Thus, even the ability of host countries to prevent nuclear launches from their territory is left ambiguous, although they do have physical means to halt launches whether or not two-key arrangements exist.

Apart from the murky procedures, the strains of the moment of decision can readily be foreseen. Once a conventional war is under way in central Europe, the issue of nuclear use is unlikely to be settled in the cool, calculated manner envisioned by some strategists. Regardless of declaratory policy, once nuclear war seems imminent, the advantages of first use will be obvious to everyone. But some whose homeland would become a nuclear battlefield, as well as others on the periphery, will wish to avert nuclear war if at all possible. Organizational as well as

4. U.S. Department of the Army, *Operations: FM 100-5* (Dept. of the Army, 1976), p. 10-9. See also James G. Lowenstein, *U.S. Security Issues in Europe: Burden Sharing and Offset, MBFR and Nuclear Weapons,* Committee Print, prepared for the Subcommittee on U.S. Security Agreements and Commitments Abroad of the Senate Committee on Foreign Relations, 93 Cong. 1 sess. (GPO, 1973); and North Atlantic Assembly's Special Committee on Nuclear Weapons in Europe, *Second Interim Report on Nuclear Weapons in Europe,* Committee Print, Senate Committee on Foreign Relations, 98 Cong. 1 sess. (GPO, 1983), p. 8, note 8.
5. North Atlantic Treaty Organization, *Facts and Figures,* 10th ed. (Brussels: NATO Information Service, 1981), pp. 152–54.

national differences will create confusion about enemy intentions, and a cloud of intelligence reports may only thicken the fog of war. While a few may pound the table, demanding that NATO use nuclear weapons before the Warsaw Pact does, others may shrink from the decision, and still others may improvise.[6] Paralysis or fatalism rather than flexibility and resourcefulness may be the result. Command and control may also prove precarious: in some cases there are no physical impediments to keep division commanders from deciding on their own to use the nuclear artillery at their disposal.

If military organizations go by the book, political leaders might well wonder how limited a nuclear war could be. Short-range or battlefield nuclear weapons are not prescribed for in the nuclear operation plan of the supreme allied commander, Europe (SACEUR). Instead, corps commanders are to propose prepackaged options, resembling those rehearsed in peacetime exercises. "A package," according to the U.S. Army manual on tactical nuclear operations, "is a group of nuclear weapons of specific yields for use in a specific area and within a limited time to support a specific tactical goal." In actuality, it would consist of 100 to 200 warheads programmed for an objective that is neither specific nor limited: "Each package," says the manual, "must contain nuclear weapons sufficient to alter the tactical situation decisively and to accomplish the mission ."[7]

A decision to use short-range nuclear weapons will sorely test NATO's targeting and intelligence capabilities. The prime targets for the weapons, Warsaw Pact tank and troop concentrations and short-range nuclear forces, will be hard to locate and still harder to pin down. Enemy ground forces already engaged in battle are not suitable targets; short-range nuclear weapons do not discriminate easily between enemy and friendly forces. (Indeed, the enemy might take advantage of this fact by timing attacks to take advantage of prevailing winds and by adopting "hugging" tactics, remaining in close proximity to NATO forces.) Intelligence about potential targets beyond the forward edge of battle is likely to come through separate channels, from aerial or satellite reconnaissance or from special teams on the ground behind enemy lines. Real-time or instantaneous transmission, processing, and coordination of intelligence

6. On this point, see Fred Charles Iklé, "NATO's 'First Nuclear Use': A Deepening Trap?" *Strategic Review,* vol. 8 (Winter 1980), p. 20.

7. U.S. Department of the Army, *Operations: FM 100-5* (Dept. of the Army, 1982), p. 7-12.

will therefore be unattainable under wartime conditions. To transmit intelligence through channels, evaluate it, and bring it to the attention of relevant commanders could take an hour or more; in the meantime, the targets could have moved out of range. A tank column, for example, can attain speeds of ten to fifteen miles per hour against minimal resistance; short-range nuclear artillery, if self-propelled, can move even faster. If nuclear release were yet to be authorized, even more time would elapse between spotting enemy forces and reacting to their presence. In such urgent circumstances, intelligence would be unable to compensate for the measured pace of deliberation and decision.

Theater commanders may wonder whether they could ever receive timely authorization to use short-range nuclear weapons. Thirty years of experience in war games shows how difficult it is to get the participants to decide on first use. When allies have been among the players, authority to use nuclear weapons has seldom been granted, no matter how hypothetical the situation. In a crisis, even a decision to move nuclear forces out of garrisons might be difficult to obtain because of the increased risk of preemption. Simple logistics might dictate the ultimate decision; clogged roads could prevent subsequent redeployment of the weapons and allow them to be overrun.

Commingling of Nuclear and Conventional Forces

The commingling of nuclear and conventional capabilities not only adds little to nuclear deterrence and defense, but also detracts from NATO's conventional capabilities. Many short-range as well as medium-range systems are dual capable: M-109, M-110, and M-114 howitzers can fire either nuclear or conventional shells; F-4 and F-16 fighter aircraft and A-6, A-7, and F-111 fighter-bombers can carry either nuclear or conventional ordnance; so can Lance and Nike-Hercules missiles. Hunter-killer submarines, when armed with SLCMs, will also be dual-capable.

Although the delivery vehicles for all nuclear-capable systems are under the control of NATO field commanders, the nuclear warheads are not. Except for those assigned to aircraft, to surface-to-surface missiles on quick reaction alert, and to SLCMs, the warheads for use by allies remain at special storage sites under U.S. custody. Some of those for use by American forces are in the hands of battalion commanders; others

are in separate units supervised by corps, division, or brigade commanders, depending on the geographic proximity of the unit to the storage
site. Regimental or firing-unit commanders take possession of the
warheads once they are dispersed from storage, but authority to use
them is supposed to remain at the corps or division level.

Possession of dual-capable weapons without the authority to use them
in nuclear form puts field commanders in a predicament. Anticipating
escalation, they might be tempted to withhold or withdraw dual-capable
forces from conventional battle in order to ready them for nuclear
missions. The temptation would be greatest when the conflict is most
intense and its outcome most uncertain—precisely when the maximum
conventional effort is most urgently needed. At that point, for instance,
the commander of attack submarines with nuclear SLCMs on board
might be uncertain whether to hide or seek. Dual-capable aircraft present
similar difficulties. Dual-capable artillery along with their nuclear rounds
require forces to protect them that might be more effectively employed
elsewhere. To compound the predicament, if field commanders were to
withdraw dual-capable systems from battle, the Warsaw Pact might
interpret the redeployment to mean that nuclear war is imminent and
preempt when NATO is most vulnerable and least able to respond in
kind. And if allied commanders withhold or withdraw these forces and
have their requests for nuclear authorization refused, enemy preemption
might still occur. Worst of all, the Warsaw Pact might mistake preparations for conventional use of dual-capable systems—for instance, at
airfields where nuclear weapons are stored—as indicating a decision to
use nuclear weapons and preempt with nuclear forces before conventional battle could be joined. Paradoxically, then, the commingling of
conventional and nuclear capabilities that is intended to strengthen
NATO in fact leaves it muscle-bound or paralyzed.[8]

By the same token, integrating conventional and nuclear capabilities
in the tactics, planning, and training of NATO ground forces, while
essential to prepare troops for nuclear battle, may have the consequence

---

8. Soviet artillery, by comparison, has avoided the commingling of nuclear and
conventional capabilities, according to Douglas M. Hart and Dennis M. Gormley, "The
Evolution of Soviet Interest in Atomic Artillery," *Journal of the Royal United Services
Institute for Defence Studies,* vol. 128 (June 1983), pp. 27–28, 32. France is taking steps
in this direction as it replaces its short-range Pluton with the Hades, which has three
times Pluton's range. Jacques Isnard, "Les Explications de M. Charles Hernu," *Le
Monde,* June 18, 1983.

of leaving them less prepared to wage conventional war. Drill does more than prepare troops for expected contingencies; it also leaves them less prepared for other eventualities. Forces that have practiced dispersing for a nuclear attack are less adept at massing for a conventional response. Forces trained to expect nuclear use in the event of an enemy breakthrough may be unprepared to regroup if that expectation is not fulfilled. Such forces may be unable to meet conventional attack without resorting to nuclear weapons for tactical ends.

Toward a More Stable Short-Range Posture

The dilemmas of nuclear location, relocation, and dual capability suggest that if, as the saying goes, armies are designed by geniuses to be run by idiots, the reverse is true for short-range nuclear forces in Europe. The hard choices that would be posed by introducing short-range nuclear weapons into a war in central Europe make clear why exponents of nuclear war-fighting strategies seek to obscure any firebreak, physical or psychological, between nuclear and conventional weapons and would predelegate authority for first use of nuclear weapons to commanders in the field. It is equally clear why heads of government wishing to maintain political control have ample reason to resist such efforts.

The political difficulty of getting the allies to agree on using nuclear weapons and the vulnerability of NATO's nuclear arsenal to Soviet preemption make it virtually impossible for NATO to use its short-range nuclear forces first in a calculated response to a Soviet conventional attack. In practice, if not in theory, NATO has already adopted a no-first-use policy with respect to those weapons. A formal declaration of no first use of nuclear weapons would reconcile policy and practice. It would also provide a rationale for reducing drastically, if not eliminating, short-range nuclear forces—at a minimum, ADMs and artillery and air defense rounds—and for reassigning dual-capable systems to purely conventional roles and missions. Whether or not the United States formally adopts no first use as declaratory policy, the analysis suggests taking these steps because short-range and dual-capable systems are ill suited either for first use or for retaliation and because commingling compromises NATO's conventional strength. Regardless of the outcome of the no-first-use debate, NATO's nuclear posture stands in need of correction.

NATO has begun to move in this direction, albeit hesitantly. As part of its December 1979 decision the alliance withdrew 1,000 obsolescent short-range warheads from its arsenal and agreed to replace another 572 such warheads with LRTNF warheads on a one-for-one basis. In December 1983 the alliance decided to remove another 1,400 short-range warheads from Europe.

Removing short-range nuclear weapons from Western Europe has not been made contingent on reciprocal moves by the USSR or on arms control, nor should it be. The difficulty of verifying any agreement on short-range forces—or indeed of discovering the physical location of Soviet short-range nuclear warheads—would prolong any negotiation and jeopardize concrete results. Moreover, the political advantages of unilateral action by NATO outweigh the value of any negotiated quid pro quo from the Warsaw Pact. A reduction in NATO's short-range nuclear arsenal could mitigate public unease in Europe even while the deployment of a modest number of long-range theater nuclear weapons goes forward. Unilateral reduction would also increase the political price the Warsaw Pact would pay if it would upgrade or expand its own short-range nuclear forces. Drawing down NATO's short-range nuclear forces and ending commingling are in NATO's own political and security interests; otherwise these measures would not be worth instituting. They should not be delayed on the pretext of negotiating arms control with the USSR.

Technological fixes or modernization will no longer suffice to make short-range nuclear forces more usable. Those who advocate the deployment of enhanced-radiation warheads, for instance, tend to overlook the possibility that reduction in blast effects and collateral damage may be more than offset by unknown radiation effects and by innocent casualties. In any event, the usability of battlefield nuclear weapons is an issue that transcends the technicalities of weapon design. Strategists may theorize, but political leaders and generals are unlikely to forget that nuclear weapons are different from conventional weapons and carry with them a risk of escalation beyond the endurable.

CHAPTER SEVEN

Present Prospects

Fanaticism consists in redoubling your efforts when you have forgotten your aim.
George Santayana

THE ARRIVAL of new American missiles on European shores has predictably provoked a sharp Soviet reaction, one likely to take both military and political forms. Those who dismiss this reaction as an attempt to frighten European publics or as mere bluff understate its significance. The NATO deployments have set in motion long-delayed Soviet weapons programs, programs that will soon become irreversible. These actions suggest that a fundamental reassessment of American intent may be under way in the USSR that will not be affected by just a softening in American rhetoric.

Authoritative Soviet spokesmen have been unusually explicit in threatening counterdeployments, and Soviet test programs have given every indication of producing the wherewithal to carry out those threats.[1] In announcing a moratorium on further SS-20 deployments in Europe in March 1982, President Brezhnev made clear it would no longer "be in force" once NATO began "practical preparations" for its missile deployment. Whether his warning was already being carried out by the end of 1983, and some American analysts suspect it was, as long as the production line remains open, additional SS-20 deployments are a possibility. But even though the marginal cost of producing more may be cheap in comparison to designing and building a wholly new type of missile, operating additional SS-20 bases is not, and the military benefit is probably well past the point of diminishing returns. Rolling more SS-20s off the assembly line would satisfy a political motive, however. It

1. Theo Sommer arrays these threats in *Die Zeit,* March 18, 1983, as translated and reprinted in "Journalist on Soviet Counterarmament Stance," Foreign Broadcast Information Service, *Daily Report: Western Europe,* March 18, 1983, pp. J1–6.

represents a relatively inexpensive way to deepen NATO's quandary. For NATO to respond with additional deployments of its own would call into question the alliance strategy of coupling American central systems to Europe's defense; to ignore the additional Soviet buildup might raise doubts in some quarters about NATO's will.

Besides the SS-20, at least four new Soviet missiles are undergoing testing, two of which could add, albeit marginally, to the threat to Europe. The SS-X-25, otherwise designated the PL-5, is a more modern, solid-fuel, probably mobile follow-on to the SS-13 capable of intercontinental range but with the potential to be used for certain theater missions as well. The development of such an SS-13 follow-on would be consistent with projections of past programs: in the 1960s Soviet design bureaus built an SS-15, a two-stage adaptation of the SS-13 for theater use, that was never put into full-scale production. If the SS-X-25 is mobile—and solid fueling gives it that potential—it would be better able to survive attack and thereby add to Soviet retaliatory power.

Another of the test vehicles, the SSN-X-21, is a cruise missile thought capable of a 3,000-kilometer range that can be deployed either on land or at sea. Used in a nuclear land-attack role against Europe, the SSN-X-21 would complicate NATO defenses. Placed on board ships or submarines operating not only near Europe but also off America's coasts, it would offer a symbolically appropriate counter to forward deployments of American GLCMs and SLCMs. Although keeping ships or submarines permanently on station so far forward would be contrary to Soviet operating practices and would stretch supply lines, occasional forays into American waters would obtain the desired political effect without permanent redeployment. Such a step would carry out President Brezhnev's threat to take "retaliatory steps" for American missile deployments in Europe that would place the United States in an "analogous position." President Andropov seemed to confirm this in a statement issued two days after the start of missile deployments in West Germany: "Since by deploying its missiles in Europe the United States increases the nuclear threat to the Soviet Union, the corresponding Soviet systems will be deployed with due account for this circumstance in ocean areas and in seas."[2]

2. "Text of Andropov's Statement on Missile Dispute," *New York Times*, November 25, 1983. Forward patrolling of Soviet Delta-class submarines has already occurred, perhaps a sign of things to come. See Robert C. Toth, "Advanced Soviet A-Subs Move to North Atlantic, Navy Secretary Asserts," *Los Angeles Times*, February 15, 1984.

Brezhnev's threat initially prompted speculation on a third possible Soviet response, an attempt to install land-based missiles in the Western Hemisphere, perhaps in Cuba or Nicaragua. That possibility raised fears in the minds of some Europeans, not the least of them West German Foreign Minister Hans-Dietrich Genscher, of a rerun of the Cuban missile crisis, but one in which the United States might trade away cruise and Pershing II missiles in return for a Soviet pledge not to put missiles in the Americas. More plausibly, the Soviet leadership might have been tempted to make an explicit threat to introduce missiles into this hemisphere without actually doing so in hopes of triggering an overreaction by the Reagan administration in the form of a blockade or other military action. That would bring home to American as well as European audiences what is at stake in NATO's deployments. It would also arouse the fear of nuclear holocaust that inspires much of the antimissile sentiment in Europe.[3]

An additional reaction to the new U.S. deployments, one that has been officially announced by the Warsaw Pact, is forward deployment of new Soviet dual-capable short-range missiles and, possibly, their associated nuclear warheads in Eastern Europe, especially in East Germany, where they would be in a position to reach targets in Western Europe. While these weapon systems would have a capability comparable to that of the SS-20 against some classes of targets, their main impact would be political. That political dimension was aptly captured in Andropov's remark to Kohl about the two Germanys facing each other through "palisades of missiles." Such a prospect is bound to

---

3. If so, the threat did not have that effect immediately. The Reagan administration ordered naval maneuvers in the Caribbean in 1983 to demonstrate and practice a blockade, ostensibly against the flow of weapons from Cuba to El Salvador; it made no reference to Soviet missiles. But shortly after the maneuvers had ended, President Reagan hinted that he would no longer feel bound by any restraint on invading Cuba. Contending that the USSR and Cuba had repeatedly violated what he termed an "agreement" made at the time of the Cuban missile crisis not to introduce "offensive weapons" into the hemisphere—the euphemism then employed by Kennedy to refer to nuclear weapons—President Reagan went on to say, "As far as I'm concerned, that agreement has been abrogated many times by the Soviet Union and Cuba in the bringing in of what can only be considered offensive weapons, not defensive, there." The threat of Soviet emplacements is alluded to by Colonel General Nikolai Chervov in a conversation with Theo Sommer in "Journalist on Soviet Counterarmament Stance," p. J5. Genscher's concern is reflected in Walter Pincus, "Brezhnev Threat Brings Echoes of 1962's Cuban Missile Crisis," *Washington Post*, March 18, 1982. President Reagan's comments are quoted in Francis X. Clines, "President Accuses Soviet on '62 Pact," *New York Times*, September 15, 1983.

interfere with intra-German relations, a source of some sensitivity on both sides of the border.[4] It will also arouse anxiety in Eastern Europe, where exposure to a prolonged propaganda campaign to convince NATO publics that basing missiles on their soil will make their countries targets may have had the unintended effect of persuading Eastern Europeans of the same possibility.[5]

There are other ways for the Soviets to drive home the political point at less risk to themselves. One is to press East Germany to hinder border crossings and other contact with the West, which will be hard to do because it would make life more disagreeable in both Germanys. Another is to walk out of INF and delay the resumption of START, as they have done. The suspension of both negotiations seeks to highlight the connection that the Soviets perceive between America's central systems and its "forward-based systems" in Europe; from the vantage point of Moscow they both constitute a strategic threat. Eventually, however, European reaction might bring the Russians back to the negotiating table, much as it did in 1980, when Soviet refusal to negotiate following the December 1979 decision proved unpopular. At that point, the double suspension would permit resumption of negotiations in a merged form, bringing allied pressure to bear on the United States for a comprehensive settlement. At the same time, the Soviets might also try to fan European fears that the United States was preparing to trade away European interests in LRTNF for a more favorable deal on central systems.

4. As if to insulate German relations from the heightening tensions, leaders on both sides of the border moved toward accommodation. Franz Josef Strauss arranged for a loan to East Germany in 1983, a move that will not harm his bid to become West Germany's foreign minister. West German economic assistance has been reciprocated by East German relaxation of controls over cross-border transportation and exchange. But East German leader Erich Honecker continued to warn of the consequences of the missile deployments for intra-German relations: "What has been achieved and that for which we strive could not only be tested but also brought into question." "East Germany Warns Kohl about U.S. Nuclear Weapons," *Washington Post*, October 10, 1983.

5. Czech and East German party dailies have even resorted to publishing letters to the editor expressing concern about potential nuclear deployments there. The Warsaw Pact refrained from characterizing the new missiles as nuclear-capable—it referred only to "missile complexes of operational tactical designation"—in order to head off adverse reaction. Small protest demonstrations have taken place in both countries, and there as well as elsewhere in Eastern Europe small indigenous peace movements have sprung up that enjoy neither official sponsorship nor sanction. Disagreements have also surfaced at Warsaw Pact meetings, and Romania's president, Nicolae Ceausescu, publicly distanced his country from the Pact's deployments by urging a halt to preparations for them.

Whatever the ultimate Soviet reaction, and only part of it is now apparent, one consequence is clear: it will only increase the political price most European governments have had to pay at home for the new NATO deployment. Keeping that price to a minimum and thereby preserving alliance unity should have a priority in American policy that it has not always had in the recent past.

The object of the December 1979 decision was to reassure America's allies in Europe by limiting or offsetting the Soviet missile threat there, not to match the Soviet Union warhead for warhead or to turn implementation of the decision into a litmus test of allied loyalty. The means NATO chose was a combination of modest deployment and an attempt to achieve negotiated limits on both sides' arsenals. Deployment alone was never the desideratum for most architects of NATO's decision; negotiated limits on Soviet forces and future modernization, which NATO was in no position to match strategically or politically, were considered the best outcome obtainable. Failure in the negotiations was always considered a real possibility, but most were prepared to do whatever possible to have them succeed. At a minimum that effort would make it easier for European publics to accept the missiles in the event of failure to sign an agreement. At times during the ensuing years some governments seem to have lost sight of this object. Now modernization is once again getting ahead of arms control.

The Reagan administration has clung to the belief that no agreement would be possible until the NATO missiles began moving into Europe and that once they did, Soviet negotiators would become more pliable. The evidence for this claim was never persuasive. For Soviet leaders to become more pliable would be to validate the Reagan strategy of negotiating from strength, something they are loath to do. It is at least as plausible that Soviet leaders have long written off some NATO deployments as a foregone conclusion, based on their assessment of political currents in Europe. Authoritative spokesmen consistently warned of a hardening of the Soviet position once the missiles were fielded.

While the rhetorical excesses on both sides must be discounted as mere posturing, their effect may have been much more pernicious than either government would acknowledge. They seem to have inspired each side to magnify the worst in the other side's actions, resulting in a gross misreading of each other's intentions. In Washington the Soviet SS-20 deployment is understood not as modernization of obsolescent missiles and a hedge against additional targeting requirements but as an attempt at neutralizing Europe through blackmail. In Moscow the American missile deployments in Europe are seen not as an attempt to shore up the credibility of NATO's doctrine of first use but as part of a comprehensive effort to acquire the capability for a disarming first strike. Yet neither side's interpretation is sustainable. Sober realists in Moscow are unlikely to calculate that the SS-20 threat could lead to the neutralization of Europe and the breakup of NATO, no matter how many right-wing Westerners say so—and by their insistence, inadvertently encourage this result. Similarly, prudent minds in Washington recognize that, much as some ideologues may want to try, a disarming first strike against forces as sizable and diverse as the Soviet Union's is simply unattainable under present technological conditions. The misperceptions may be grotesque, as in the Soviet response and the American reaction to the intrusion of KAL 007 into Soviet airspace, but they are nevertheless driving both superpowers toward exaggerated threat assessments and overreactions in military programs.

The heightening conflict threatens to loosen NATO's bonds of solidarity. More and more Europeans are holding the United States and the Soviet Union equally responsible for menacing Europe's existence by their unbridled rivalry. Americans naturally resent Europeans' equating an ally with an enemy. The longer the superpower tensions mount, the more people on both sides of the Atlantic will be calling the alliance into question. The continuing confrontation is threatening to narrow the base of support for the alliance as moderate left-of-center parties, such as Britain's Labour party and West Germany's SPD, try to dissociate themselves from the direction NATO seems to be taking.

To avoid further jeopardizing the alliance, it is in America's interest to try to break the spiraling confrontation. The walk in the woods of Geneva showed the way: forgoing Pershing II deployments in return for dismantling some SS-20s in Europe and a halt to deployments in the Far East. One step more has yet to be taken by either side: a proposal to limit modernization of nuclear forces in Europe.

Yet a resumption of negotiations in Geneva, regardless of the forum, and meaningful progress toward agreement will take a dramatic gesture by the West, a clear and authoritative signal to reassure the Soviet Union and anxious allied publics that negotiations are not simply a fig leaf for deployments and that NATO is prepared to address Soviet concerns. First, to signal its willingness to forgo deployment of Pershing II, and thereby disown any first-strike intent, the United States could announce a one-year halt in deployments of the missile while proceeding with cruise missile deployments at a more deliberate pace. Second, the United States could unambiguously put the Pershing IIs—all of them—on the negotiating table by announcing its willingness to reconsider the walk-in-the-woods formula. Third, without further delay NATO could begin the withdrawal of 1,400 short-range warheads already announced and make clear its intention to disengage the rest of its nuclear posture somewhat by redeploying the remaining warheads from the front and eliminating dual-capable systems. Fourth, the United States could announce a moratorium on deployment of nuclear land-attack SLCMs with ranges in excess of 600 kilometers, conditional on Soviet reciprocity.

The United States and its allies can no longer afford to wait for the Soviet Union to return to the negotiating table. Expecting the Soviet Union to become more amenable to the present American negotiating position assumes that it has a greater stake in resolving differences over the missiles or in reassuring restive publics than does NATO and that a breakthrough will have an easier time emerging from Moscow's policy process than from Washington's. Neither assumption seems tenable.

Even with the best will on both sides, reaching agreement in Geneva remains an arduous task. Yet refusing to try only increases the price to allied governments of putting missiles on their territory. Under public pressure, European governments have a considerable stake in breaking the negotiating deadlock, whether by serving as go-betweens or by framing specific proposals of their own and pressing them on American negotiators. They have refrained from doing so for nearly two years. Moreover, for the United States to stand in the way of European or Soviet initiatives to settle the controversy, should they be forthcoming, would be a sure sign of fanaticism. Nothing would do more to ensure reconsideration of the value of the alliance in Europe than firm evidence of American intractability in Geneva.

Both sides are rapidly passing a point of no return. As Tass declared after the West German parliament voted to proceed with deployments, "The Rubicon has been crossed."[6] New weapons now being installed and tested threaten to upset the precarious military stability that has

6. John F. Burns, "Moscow Reiterates It Will Respond by Deploying Its Missiles,"*New York Times,* November 24, 1983.

prevailed between the superpowers for two decades. Some of these steps are already irreversible; others can be slowed or halted in the next two or three years. If nothing is done to reverse the present direction, the problem of how to prevent nuclear weapons from being used— inadvertently, accidentally, or deliberately—will become all the more unmanageable. And the arms control measures of today—trying to preclude the most destabilizing developments while holding down the numbers of weapons in a verifiable way—will no longer be able to contain the instability. At that point leaders on both sides will look back on the past decade with incomprehension and ask why nothing was done to keep the nuclear predicament from becoming more awful.

Index